THE FUTURE OF LIBERAL THEOLOGY

Two hundred years after the publication of Schleiermacher's epoch-making Speeches, *The Future of Liberal Theology* presents a comprehensive and critical re-assessment of the past, present and future of the liberal tradition in Christian theology.

In dialogue with the different forms of liberalism emerging from the Enlightenment, each of which is carefully defined, distinguished international theologians draw on a range of perspectives which represent the diversity of liberal theology. Discussing the criticisms of liberalism offered in the twentieth century, and engaging with contemporary theological debate which is often deeply hostile to liberalism, the conclusions offered for liberal theology range from the deeply pessimistic to the thoroughly optimistic. Students, clergy, and theological educators more broadly will value this critical reflection on the current state of theology and suggestions for its future course, together with the serious engagement with issues in theological education, which this book presents.

The Future of Liberal Theology

Edited by
MARK D. CHAPMAN
Ripon College, UK

Routledge
Taylor & Francis Group
LONDON AND NEW YORK

First published 2002 by Ashgate Publishing

Reissued 2018 by Routledge
2 Park Square, Milton Park, Abingdon, Oxon OX14 4RN
711 Third Avenue, New York, NY 10017, USA

Routledge is an imprint of the Taylor & Francis Group, an informa business

A Library of Congress record exists under LC control number: 2002100377

ISBN 13: 978-1-138-72819-6 (hbk)
ISBN 13: 978-1-138-72815-8 (pbk)
ISBN 13: 978-1-315-19058-7 (ebk)

Contents

Part Three: Addressing the Critics

Conclusion: An Outsider's View

Notes on Contributors

Paul Badham is Professor of Theology and Religious Studies at the University of Wales, Lampeter. His most recent work is *The Contemporary Challenge of Modernist Theology* (University of Wales Press, 1998).

Rita Nakashima Brock is Research Associate at the Center for Values in Public Life, Harvard Divinity School, and from 1997-2001 was Director of the Fellowship Program at the Radcliffe Institute for Advanced Study, Harvard University. She is author of *Journeys By Heart: A Christology of Erotic Power* (Crossroad Continuum Press, 1988), and (with Rebecca Ann Parker) of *Proverbs of Ashes: Violence, Religion, and a Witness for Life* (Beacon Press, 2001).

Steve Bruce is Professor of Sociology and Head of the Department of Sociology at the University of Aberdeen. From 1978 to 1991 he taught at The Queen's University of Belfast. His most recent works include: *Religion in the Modern World: from Cathedrals to Cults* (Oxford University Press, 1998), *Conservative Protestant Politics* (Oxford University Press, 1998), *Choice and Religion: a critique of rational choice theory* (Oxford University Press, 1999), and *Fundamentalism* (Polity Press, 2001)

Mark D. Chapman is Vice-Principal of Ripon College, Cuddesdon, Oxford and a member of the Theology Faculty at Oxford University. His books include *Ernst Troeltsch and Liberal Theology* (Oxford University Press, 2001) and *The Coming Crisis* (Sheffield Academic Press, 2001).

Steve Else teaches Philosophy and Religious Studies at King's College School, Wimbledon. He is writing a book on Martin Heidegger's and Richard Rorty's interpretations of Friedrich Nietzsche.

Timothy Gorringe is Professor of Theological Studies at the University of Exeter. He is the author of many books, most recently *Karl Barth: Against Hegemony* (Oxford University Press, 1999) and *The Education of Desire* (SCM Press, 2001).

Elaine Graham is Samuel Ferguson Professor of Social and Pastoral Theology at the University of Manchester. She is the author of *Making the Difference* (Mowbray, 1995) and *Transforming Practice* (Mowbray, 1996). Her next book, *Representations of the Post/Human* (Manchester

University Press, forthcoming), considers the relationship between science, religion and popular culture in a digital and biotechnological age.

Friedrich Wilhelm Graf is Professor of Systematic Theology and Ethics at the Evangelical Faculty at Munich University, Germany. He is a prolific author on the history of modern theology, and winner of the Leibniz Prize.

Peter C. Hodgson is Charles G. Finney Professor of Theology in the Divinity School of Vanderbilt University, Nashville, Tennessee. His most recent books are *Theology in the Fiction of George Eliot: The Mystery Beneath the Real* (SCM and Fortress, 2001) and *Christian Faith: A Brief Introduction* (Westminster/John Knox Press, 2001).

Gavin Hyman is Lecturer in Religious Studies at the University of Lancaster. He is author of *The Predicament of Postmodern Theology: Radical Orthodoxy or Nihilist Textualism?* (Westminster/John Knox Press, 2001).

Clive Marsh is Secretary to the Faith and Order Committee of the Methodist Church in Great Britain, having taught Christian theology from 1989-2000. He is author (with Steve Moyise) of *Jesus and the Gospels* (Cassell, 1999) and co-editor (with Gaye Ortiz) of *Explorations in Theology and Film* (Blackwell, 1997) and (with Jane Craske) of *Methodism and the Future* (Cassell, 1999).

Paul D. Murray is Lecturer in Systematic Theology, Ushaw College, Durham and was previously Senior Lecturer in Theology at Newman College of Higher Education, Birmingham. He co-wrote *God, Humanity and the Cosmos: A Textbook in Science and Religion* (ed. Christopher Southgate, T & T Clark, 1999).

David A. Pailin was Professor of Philosophy of Religion at the University of Manchester where he taught from 1966 until his retirement in 2001. His books include *God and the Processes of Reality* (Routledge, 1989), *The Anthropological Character of Theology* (Cambridge University Press, 1990), and *A Gentle Touch: From a theology of handicap to a theology of human being* (SPCK, 1992).

Keith Ward is Regius Professor of Divinity at Oxford University. The author of numerous books, his most recent work is *Religion and Community* (Oxford University Press, 2000).

Preface

Some of the chapters collected in this book were first presented at a Conference, 'The Future of Christian Theology – The Contribution of Liberal Traditions – A Critical Appraisal', which was held at the University of York in March 1999 to celebrate the two-hundredth anniversary of the first publication of Schleiermacher's *Speeches*. Other chapters have been specially commissioned for this volume in response to the conference papers. The principal aim of the conference was to survey the prospects for the future of the liberal tradition in theology: what soon became apparent, however, was that to talk of *the* liberal tradition in theology was rather misleading. In the relative informality of Vanbrugh College a genuine discussion took place: definitions, redefinitions and new definitions grew in the context of an often vigorous but always friendly debate. These definitions are the focus of Part One.

The buildings of Vanbrugh College themselves provided something of a parable for those of us who are interested in the survival of liberal theology. The visionary modernism of Harold Wilson's educational policy appeared decidedly shabby and deteriorating after thirty years or so. What these chapters show is that theological liberalism is in an equally parlous state. Some forms have deteriorated or sunk virtually without trace; others, however, have survived despite hostility from both inside and outside theology. Similarly, the vision of liberal education has just about been kept alive by dedicated academics and teachers, despite the best efforts of the educational policy of successive governments to starve universities of funds and morale. The future of liberal theology is bound up with the future of liberal education: the three chapters in Part Two pay particular attention to these relationships between liberal theology and liberal education. The final Part brings liberal theology into dialogue with other traditions: some chapters are more hopeful than others, but all provide a challenge for liberal theologians working in an increasingly hostile atmosphere. And it is my hope that this challenge will be taken up for the sake of God's world. Read against Steve Bruce's frightening conclusion, this task proves ever more urgent.

Mark D. Chapman
June 2001

Acknowledgements

I would like to acknowledge a special debt to Clive Marsh for his help in putting this volume together and for masterminding the York Conference. Thanks are also due to David Law of the University of Manchester for gathering the papers for the conference, as well as Elizabeth Stuart, Martyn Percy and Brent Sockness for their insightful responses to the conference, all of which have fed into the chapters that follow. The Conference received financial support from the College of Ripon and York St John (which has since that time sadly cut back on its support for theological research), The Modern Churchpeople's Union and the Humanities Research Board (now the Arts and Humanities Research Board) of the British Academy. Thanks are also due to the following publishers for permission to reprint material from copyright publications: Westminster John Knox Press for sections in Chapter 7 which are reproduced in a modified form from *God's Wisdom*, © 1999 Peter C. Hodgson; and for sections in Chapter 12 which are included in a modified form in *The Predicament of Postmodern Theology: Radical Orthodoxy or Nihilist Textualism*, © 2001 Gavin Hyman.

Part One

Types of Liberal Theology

Chapter 1

Introduction

The Past, Present and Future of Liberal Theology

Mark D. Chapman

This is a book about the future of liberal theology. But if there is to be a future, it is one that is built on a past. And if the first publication of Schleiermacher's *Speeches* in 1799 marks (at least symbolically) the beginning of liberal theology, then that tradition is now over two hundred years old: older indeed than many of its apparently more orthodox alternatives (including, for instance, Fundamentalism, Anglo-Catholicism, and Radical Orthodoxy). Unlike their opponents, however, most liberals have little desire to recreate a golden age, be that in the first, fifth or the thirteenth century. Theological liberalism, like liberalism in other areas of thought, is suspicious of golden ages. It is only too aware that every age has its problems, its authoritarianism and its tendencies towards absoluteness and the uncritical acceptance of the status quo. As a movement which emerged in the concrete political and economic circumstances of late eighteenth- and early nineteenth-century Europe, liberalism rests on some degree of acceptance of the guiding principles of enlightenment thought, particularly its criticism of the supernaturally-justified authorities of scripture, dogma and tradition. And if liberalism is to survive and not to become yet another form of authoritarianism which simply idolises the modern at the expense of the tradition (which has always been a tendency), then it will be a theological position which is based on methodological criticism, and will thus be a theology which can never be satisfied with itself, at least this side of the Parousia.

A straightforward definition of 'liberal theology', however, is virtually impossible. As John Habgood commented in a perceptive account of what he understood by 'the Liberal Position': 'Liberalism is a slippery concept. I doubt whether "the liberal position" ... exists as such, or whether there is any one set of ideas or attitudes on which those who value the word "liberal" would agree.'[1] The difficulty of using the term 'liberal' is undeniable: it can cover a wide range of different and sometimes quite incompatible methodologies. There are, for instance, many liberals who would not agree with the preliminary account offered above. After all, some theological liberals are very far from critical, many latching onto the latest voguish philosophy, however silly that might be. There are some who refuse to grapple with the tradition at anything other than a superficial level. While such thinkers might provide useful apologetics for a brief period, they seldom if ever leave anything of lasting value.[2] This is not a book about that kind of liberalism or for those kinds of liberals – even the most unsympathetic reader will detect few breaches of orthodoxy in the following chapters, and those in search of controversy will look in vain through the pages that follow. Instead, what is offered is a book which subjects the liberal tradition to critical scrutiny. The reason for this is simple: if liberal theology is by nature critical, then it needs to be critical of itself. The contributors to this volume would probably not all want to label themselves as liberal, but all are aware of the massive contribution that the liberal tradition has made to Christian theology. And all offer in one way or another a challenge for the future. If, as I will suggest in this introduction, Christianity itself is a methodologically critical religion, then its method should always be more or less liberal. Consequently it is vital for theology that liberalism lives on into the future; but whether it will or not is altogether another question.

[1] John Habgood, 'Reflections on the Liberal Position', in *Making Sense*, London: SPCK, 1993, p. 197.

[2] Here one might include such well-meaning thinkers as R. J. Campbell, whose 'religion of science' offered in *New Theology* (London: Chapman & Hall, 1907) was little more than a shallow monism. A more recent example is the notorious Bishop Jack Spong, formerly Bishop of Newark. His call for a New Reformation would, I suspect, be accepted by very few liberals, past, present and probably future. Most liberals do not find things quite so straightforward. See, for instance, thesis 2: 'Since God can no longer be conceived in theistic terms, it becomes nonsensical to seek to understand Jesus as the incarnation of the theistic deity. So the Christology of the ages is bankrupt.' See his theses at http://www.dioceseofnewark.org/jsspong/reform.html.

The chapters collected in this volume all take as their foundation the great shift in thinking marked by the Enlightenment: in Part One several different strands of liberalism which stem from the Enlightenment are analysed, regarding it on the whole as a positive contribution towards the development of critical thought as well as the decisive break with the authoritarianism of the past. Although it might be berated by many, the Enlightenment brought with it a new understanding of freedom, democracy and hope. That said, there are decidedly different approaches to liberalism in the pages that follow. These range from the bold and racy triumphalism of Paul Badham's efforts to revive what to many must have seemed the lifeless corpse of a very experiential form of English Modernism, through Friedrich Wilhelm Graf's sophisticated and challenging political critique of much of the so-called 'liberal' tradition deriving from Germany (many theological liberals simply were not that liberal), to Keith Ward's moderate and orthodox plea for tolerance, dialogue and openness in theology. Alongside this stands Steve Else's discussion of pluralism and David Pailin's lively challenge to theologians to engage with people where they are against the increasingly specialised and irrelevant discourse of much professional theology.

Part Two offers three connected chapters which outline the possibilities and difficulties for theology which emerge from the liberal educational tradition. In a wide-ranging survey Peter Hodgson calls for a revisionary postmodern liberal theology based on a transformative pedagogy which pays attention to the massive changes presented by the contemporary world. Elaine Graham's response reveals just how counter-cultural the pursuit of learning for learning's sake really is, a fact that will be immediately obvious to anybody involved in English higher education at the turn of the new millennium with its commodification of learning. Clive Marsh in turn offers a critical and challenging discussion of experiential learning.

Part Three carries the discussion forward by bringing 'liberal theology' into explicit dialogue with some of the alternative strands of recent theology. After a pithy and provocative chapter on Karl Barth and liberalism by Timothy Gorringe, which suggests that Barth was far more liberal than many have been willing to concede, Rita Nakashima Brock raises a number of far-reaching challenges to any liberal. Her acute awareness of the élitism and cultural specificity of the Enlightenment tradition, and her uncovering of the violent undercurrents of much so-called liberal theology, has to be addressed if liberal theology is to have any future. Similarly, in their accounts of three conflicting responses to liberalism, Gavin Hyman and Paul D. Murray ensure that liberalism will have to address its critics carefully if it is to remain credible. There might even be something to be learnt from the competing strands of contemporary theological debate. Finally, and perhaps most importantly, there is an outside view from the sceptical sociologist, Steve Bruce: liberal religion may simply not have enough of an understanding of itself or its appeal to attract any converts. That makes the future of liberalism extremely precarious. And, as will be shown in the remainder of this introductory chapter, things do not look too rosy for liberalism from within theology either.

Liberalism and its cultured and not so cultured despisers

Not surprisingly, what one thinks about theological liberalism will depend on one's attitude to the criticism of authority and tradition demonstrated in the Enlightenment more generally. The fate of liberalism cannot solely rest with developments in theology: it is tied up far more with broader movements in society and politics. And it is for that reason that even if ever there was a time when liberalism was in the ascendant, it is quite clear that this is not any longer the case. Indeed, in recent years 'liberalism', like much else associated with the Enlightenment (for example, individualism and even the language of human rights), has frequently become a term of abuse among more conservatively-minded theologians and philosophers. This can be clearly seen in much recent theological and philosophical writing: for instance, in his ground-breaking work of moral philosophy, *After Virtue*, Alasdair MacIntyre speaks eloquently about the inevitable 'failure' of what he calls the 'Enlightenment project'. In the Enlightenment, he suggests, with its invention of the 'individual', morality was dislocated from inherited modes of thought, as reality became increasingly fragmented as it collapsed into distinctive and competing spheres. According to his thesis, the inter-relatedness of all aspects of reality—and of all people within an objective moral system—was destroyed as everything was uprooted from its traditional and divinely-sanctioned context.[3] The Enlightenment was thus about competing egos uprooted from traditional patterns of community.

[3] *After Virtue*, London: Duckworth, 1981, pp. 58-9.

This thesis has proved popular amongst some theologians. In several of his books, the prolific Colin Gunton of King's College, London, for instance, has analysed the isolation of the individual from his or her embeddedness in a social context in a manner reminiscent of MacIntyre. In response to such dislocation Gunton (and here there are parallels in many other best-selling theologians)[4] pleads for a revitalisation of a tradition of 'being-in-relation' which, in his opinion, had been lost during the long dominion of Augustinianism (used here as a synonym for the isolation of the individual) in the West. In turn, the Enlightenment, with its emphasis on the isolated individual's reason at the expense of any sense of the whole, marks the culmination of this breakdown of being-in-relationship. Indeed it becomes a means of replacing God 'with a plurality of finite wills each aspiring to divinity'.[5] Consequently, Gunton sees the Enlightenment as chiefly responsible for the increasing individualism of modern life where 'the human mind fills the space left empty by the displaced deity'. This, he claims, can be discerned most clearly in what he understands to be Kant's fragmentation of morals, science and art.[6] In response, Gunton proposes what he considers a Trinitarian theology of relationality: 'of both God and man it must be said that that they have their being in their personal relatedness: their free relation-in-otherness'.[7]

From a different perspective, the Enlightenment and the liberalism it spawned have been attacked by those who see in it the idolisation of human reason. In his 1990 Bampton Lectures, for instance, the best-selling (and erstwhile liberal)[8] Alister McGrath could write that 'it remains doubtful whether two competing traditions, such as Christianity and Enlightenment rationalism, each with its associated rationalities, can really be said to "understand" each other, still less to objectively "evaluate" or "justify" each other'.[9] On this view, Christian reason is a

[4] For example, John Zizioulas, *Being as Communion. Studies in Personhood and the Church*, London: Darton, Longman and Todd, 1985; Jürgen Moltmann, *The Trinity and the Kingdom of God*, London: SCM, 1981.

[5] *The One, The Three and the Many*, Cambridge: Cambridge University Press, 1993, p. 65. Cf. *The Promise of Trinitarian Theology*, Edinburgh: T. & T. Clark, 1993.

[6] *The One, The Three and the Many*, p. 114f.

[7] Ibid., p. 229.

[8] *The Renewal of Anglicanism*, London: SPCK, 1993.

[9] Alister E. McGrath, *The Genesis of Doctrine*, Oxford: Blackwell, 1990, p. 199.

species of reason *distinct* from that of the Enlightenment; as a consequence it is only from within the *Christian* system of reason, that is from within the church's tradition, that it is fully possible to understand the Christian logic. Thus Christianity (like Enlightenment reason) is simply one rationality alongside many others, and it is quite impossible for the one to communicate with the other. Consequently, Enlightenment reason is reduced to a species of logic of no greater relevance than other forms of logic (like presumably astrology, phrenology or other delights from Glastonbury). Not surprisingly, for conservative theologians, the fragmentation of the intellectual world into competing traditions of reasoning, which has become a feature of some varieties of postmodernism, is of great interest. As John Milbank suggests, postmodernism is the 'end of a single system of truth based on universal reason, which tells us what reality is like'.[10]

Again, McGrath provides an interesting example: as if stating an uncontested fact, he notes in a recent encyclopaedia article on the Enlightenment, that 'the credibility of the Enlightenment world-view, especially its emphasis upon the total adequacy of human reason, has been severely challenged through the recognition of the non-universal character of human rationality and the special mediation of traditions of discourse and reasoning'.[11] Elsewhere, this attack on the Enlightenment becomes somewhat less veiled. Thus he asserts in a book on *The Renewal of Anglicanism*, that 'there is a tidal wave of dissent rising against the Enlightenment', and its theological concomitant of liberalism, which, he boldly claims, 'is now increasingly dismissed as an irrelevance by both conservative and mainline writers. ... Its critics charge it with playing to a secular gallery, and giving encouragement to an increasingly self-confident anti-Christian tendency in western culture.'[12] And in an even less guarded statement, he suggests that in reality the Enlightenment was responsible for most of the evils of the modern world, including the Stalinist purges and the Nazi extermination camps. And he goes on to ask: 'Who wanted anything to do with an intellectually dubious movement, which had given rise to the Nazi holocaust and the Stalinist purges?'[13] This is certainly not a moderate

[10] 'Postmodern Critical Augustinianism', in *Modern Theology* 7 (1991), pp. 225-37, here p. 225.

[11] In *The Blackwell Encyclopaedia of Modern Christian Thought* (ed. Alister E. McGrath), Oxford: Blackwell, 1993, p. 156.

[12] McGrath, *The Renewal of Anglicanism*, p. 110.

[13] Ibid., p. 17.

charge and to some it might seem quite tasteless and inaccurate,[14] especially when it is juxtaposed against a quotation from the somewhat less bellicose Leslie Houlden who, in that manifesto of 1970s English liberalism, *The Myth of God Incarnate*, suggested that as Christians we 'must accept our lot, bequeathed to us by the Enlightenment, and make the most of it'.[15] Patently, many theologians begged to disagree.

Equally hostile criticisms of the Enlightenment come from the so-called 'post-liberals', most importantly George Lindbeck,[16] who sees theological language as a distinctive and incommensurate 'form of life' different from other (secular) forms of life. 'The task', he claims, 'of descriptive (dogmatic or systematic) theology is to give a normative explication of the meaning a religion has for its adherents'.[17] Lindbeck sets this view of doctrine against what he calls the 'experiential-expressivist' model of Schleiermacher and later liberals, who, he claims, regard 'doctrines as noninformative and nondiscursive symbols of inner feelings, attitudes, or existential orientations'.[18] Countering the whole Enlightenment emphasis on the primacy of the senses, Lindbeck sees the believer not so much as the one who experiences the feeling of salvation, but rather as the one who is most schooled in the language and the cultural symbols of the community. Indeed, before one can have the experience, first one must live within the community of faith. Thus he claims: 'First come the objectivities of the religion, its language, doctrines, liturgies, and modes of actions, and it is through these that passions are shaped into various kinds of what we call religious experience.'[19]

In turn, theological language can be established by anthropological and sociological methods; these, however, can never be a substitute for an immersion within the life of the community.[20] For Lindbeck, as for McGrath, there is no over-arching system of truth which unites all the

[14] The role of liberal theology in the 1930s has been recently discussed at length by Matthias Wolfes, *Protestantische Theologie und moderne Welt. Studien zur Geschichte der liberalen Theologie nach 1918*, Berlin, New York: Walter de Gruyter, 1999. Blanket assertions about the methodology of the Nazi theologians are impossible to make.

[15] *The Myth of God Incarnate* (ed. John Hick), London: SCM, 1977, p.125. Cited in McGrath, *The Renewal of Anglicanism*, p.16.

[16] George Lindbeck, *The Nature of Doctrine*, London: SPCK, 1984, pp. 38-44.

[17] Ibid., p. 113.

[18] Ibid., p. 16.

[19] Ibid., p. 39

[20] Ibid., p. 74.

partial systems (including the Christian); instead truth is relative to the system ('intrasystematic'). Consequently, Lindbeck offers a functionalist understanding of Church doctrines, as 'communally authoritative teachings regarding beliefs and practices that are considered essential to the identity or welfare of the group in question'. Theology is fundamentally about working out the rules of a particular subculture or 'form of life', which 'regulate truth claims by including some and ruling out others'.[21] However amenable *The Nature of Doctrine* might be to anthropology and sociology, however, it is not difficult to locate the subtext of the book in a thinly veiled attack on modernity and its theological counterpart, a somewhat caricatured and misrepresented liberal theology. His less than eirenic thrust is clear in his piece of rhetoric (which resembles McGrath's) that 'Christian fellow travellers of both Nazism and Stalinism generally used liberal methodology to justify their positions'.[22] Against such an identification of Christian truth with secular ideology, true religion, according to Lindbeck, is concerned less with propositional truth than with the purity of its own authoritative system, to which all truth is relative, over and against a hostile world.[23] Christianity in such a system has thereby isolated itself from the rest of world. Consequently a system like liberalism—and this is true of any form of liberalism—which methodologically seeks to learn theologically from the world, as well as to criticise it, is ruled out of court.

The most important and far-reaching theological attack on the Enlightenment of recent years, however, comes from the self-designated 'radical orthodox'[24] theologians. For this school of thought led by John Milbank, which makes use of the latest French critical theory to attack Enlightenment Reason (and much else besides), any attempt to render an account of Christianity in anything other than theological terms is to side with those who seek to reduce Christianity to the ideology of violence which is dominant in the contemporary world. The movement has developed a new mythological history to explain the demise of Christendom and its replacement with a secular parody of Christianity,

[21] Ibid., p. 19.

[22] Ibid., p. 126.

[23] See also Lindbeck, 'The Church', in Geoffrey Wainwright (ed.), *Keeping the Faith*, London: SPCK, 1989, p. 196, and 'The Sectarian Future of the Church' in J. P. Whelan (ed.), *The God Experience*, Westminster, Maryland: Newman, 1971, pp. 226-43.

[24] Cf. John Milbank, Catherine Pickstock and Graham Ward (eds), *Radical Orthodoxy. A New Theology*, London: Routledge, 1999.

of which liberalism is but one aspect. Against such a parody, Christians need to rediscover a 'Christian counter-history'[25] defined over and against all other history. 'For several centuries now', write the authors of the introduction to *Radical Orthodoxy*, 'secularism has been defining and constructing the world. It is a world in which the theological is either discredited or turned into a harmless leisure-time activity of private commitment.'[26] Liberal theology is accused of shoring up 'universal accounts of immanent human value (humanism)' and defending 'supposedly objective reason'. Radical orthodoxy in distinction, by turning to the great critics of the Enlightenment (including Christopher Smart, Hamann, Jacobi, Kierkegaard, Péguy, and Chesterton – some of whom are equally intolerant), seeks a participative understanding of theology, treating all so-called independent spheres (like politics, aesthetics etc.) solely in theological terms. Underpinning the new theology is thus the 'idea that every discipline must be framed by a theological perspective; otherwise these disciplines will define a zone apart from God, grounded literally in nothing'.[27] In this way the liberal method, which starts with the human being and its capacity to question and criticise, is turned on its head: there is simply no true anything apart from God.[28] Needless to say, liberalism is once again ruled out of court.

Alongside these theological criticisms of liberalism are other more popular, and sometimes even more venomous, attacks from various parts of the church. And because of their widespread appeal such attacks can have far-reaching consequences. Indeed, it is probably true to say that the last decade of the twentieth century was the time when, at least in England, theological liberalism finally lost the pre-eminence it had enjoyed for much of the postwar period. For those (apparently few) self-conscious liberals who remain, the present religious climate has become increasingly hostile. Popular religious movements,

[25] John Milbank, *Theology and Social Theology*, Oxford: Blackwell, 1990, p. 388.

[26] John Milbank, Catherine Pickstock and Graham Ward, 'Introduction. Suspending the material: the turn of radical orthodoxy', in *Radical Orthodoxy*, p. 1.

[27] Ibid., p. 3.

[28] On this, see the perceptive criticisms by Steven Shakespeare, 'The New Romantics. A Critique of Radical Orthodoxy', in *Theology* 103 (2000), pp. 163-77. See also Charles Davis, *Religion and the Making of Society*, Cambridge: Cambridge University Press, 1994, pp. 11-13.

particularly the almost ubiquitous Alpha Course originating in Holy Trinity, Brompton, and apparently now colonising churches throughout the world, market a registered-trade-mark form of Christianity as a straightforward and desirable commodity much like any other. Such a process of what John Drane has labelled 'McDonaldization'[29] requires the control of the media and the culture of success. *Alpha News* does not report backsliding. In such a climate, a theological method actually based on criticism looks questionable at the very least.

For others, theological liberalism is little short of a 'cuckoo in the nest', a concerted attempt by secularists and half-believers to take over the church (or at least the Church of England) which will ultimately subvert the host altogether.[30] The manifesto of such liberals was seen to be the 1977 collection of essays *The Myth of God Incarnate*. This, together with the Church of England Doctrine Commission report, *Christian Believing*[31] from the year before, served to question the very foundation of the Christian faith in the divinity of Christ. A recent conservative commentator points to the 'sheer audacity of the liberal programme' with its questioning of traditional beliefs which 'ultimately failed the Church of England'.[32] Or, as Adrian Hastings commented with typical hyperbole: 'the consequence of their conclusions could hardly be other than the necessity of winding up historic Christianity, with a minimum of pain to all concerned, as unacceptable to the modern mind.'[33] Others felt the whole liberal movement to be nothing short of an establishment conspiracy.[34]

These various attacks on liberalism—as well as on the Enlightenment more generally—make any attempt to recognise the positive con-

[29] John Drane, *The McDonaldization of the Church: Spirituality, Creativity and the Future of the Church*, London: Darton, Longman and Todd, 2000.

[30] Stephen Sykes, *The Integrity of Anglicanism*, London: Mowbray, 1978, p. 32.

[31] *Christian Believing*, London: SPCK, 1976.

[32] Robert Hannaford, 'The Legacy of Liberal Anglican Theology', in *Theology* 103 (2000), pp. 89-96, here pp. 92, 93.

[33] Adrian Hastings, *A History of English Christianity. 1920-1990*, London: SCM Press, 1991, p. 650.

[34] This is especially true of the strange and tragic events surrounding the Crockford's preface of 1987-88 written by Gareth Bennett, whose suicide provoked a bizarre conspiracy theory among some journalists and churchmen. On this see William Oddie, *The Crockford's file: Gareth Bennett and the Death of the Anglican Mind*, London: Hamilton, 1989.

tribution of the Enlightenment something of a risky business.[35] Indeed, many modern (or at least postmodern and postliberal) theologians have not been content with making the most of their Enlightenment lot as counselled by Leslie Houlden, and have evidently felt compelled to rebel against the fetters of that wicked villain Reason. But it must also be said that this is a rebellion in which Reason has been contorted by rhetoric into the very demonic itself. Liberalism is guilty by association with two world wars, with Nazism, with rampant individualism and every other evil (but never with its more obvious fruits – democracy, tolerance and freedom). In short, for many theologians, reason is no longer a universal and liberalism is dead. Theologians who defend the Enlightenment project may thus find themselves accused of some kind of Faustian pact (and liberals consequently become devils incarnate).

The future of liberalism

Bearing all this in mind, I will now set out a prospect for the future of liberalism. Although futurology is far from an exact science, I nevertheless want to suggest that the Kantian tradition counters some of the critiques proposed by opponents of the Enlightenment and offers a possible route forward, even if it is not without its own problems. If the Kantian picture of the Enlightenment is emphasised then the picture that emerges of the Enlightenment project is somewhat different from the caricature presented by MacIntyre. Indeed, with its emphasis on criticism, on defining the *limits* of human understanding, the Kantian Enlightenment may be far more firmly rooted in the Christian tradition than is often recognised, and may well point to the contemporary tasks of theology. Furthermore, it does not seem to me to be beyond the realms of possibility to suppose that the critical method, and more particularly the willingness to be open to criticism whatever the ideological or social constraints of the tradition (political, social or

[35] It should be remembered, however, that it was ever thus. Liberalism was the beginning of the slippery slope to anarchy. As Stephen Thomas has suggested, for the soon-to-be-sainted Newman, 'heresy admitted by latitudinarian laxity, is a canker *within*, which, when through course of time it develops into its mature form, will so weaken the Church as to make it vulnerable to dissolution. As in the early Church, Newman implies, so now, as heresy makes its way within the church in the guise of liberalism' (*Newman and Heresy. The Anglican Years*, Cambridge: Cambridge University Press, 1991, p.94).

ecclesiastical), offers a more satisfactory solution to contemporary theological—and for that matter, social and political problems—than any conceivable alternative. And it might even be the case that one of the main problems in theology stems from the fact that theologians have just not been critical enough, and have instead tended to close the debate too soon. That in itself ought perhaps to make us somewhat suspicious, something which Kant also recognised in the famous preface to his *Critique of Pure Reason*:

> Our age is, in especial degree, an age of criticism, and to criticism everything must submit. Religion through its sanctity, and law-giving through its majesty, may seek to exempt themselves from it. But they then awaken just suspicion, and cannot claim the sincere respect which reason accords only to that which has been able to sustain the test of free and open examination.[36]

Instead of the extraordinary emphasis on certainty and on rediscovering essences[37] which characterises a lot of recent theology (be it Catholic, Anglican or Lutheran), it might be suggested, following Kant, that the very object with which theology is concerned is beyond certainty; nothing we can say or feel can grasp God in her/his/its fullness. In a sense, then, truth inheres in God, and the Gospel challenge is to recognise that all that we can do is relative to this goal: all provisional truth is thus relative to the one absolute truth, but an absolute truth about which ultimately we can know only as through a glass darkly.[38] And such an understanding, I think, is a necessary concomitant of our human condition; furthermore it is deeply rooted in the Christian tradition.[39] If nobody can gain access into the heart of things, then all are

[36] Immanuel Kant, *Critique of Pure Reason* (tr. Norman Kemp Smith), London and Basingstoke: Macmillan, 1929, A xii.

[37] On this, see Stephen Sykes, *The Identity of Christianity*, London: SPCK, 1984.

[38] On this see Janet Martin Soskice, 'The Truth looks different from here, or Seeking the Unity of Truth from a Diversity of Perspectives', in Hilary Regan and Alan J. Torrance (eds), *Christ and Context*, Edinburgh: T & T Clark, 1993, pp. 43-59. This understanding of truth can be found in a wide range of liberal—and sometimes less liberal—thinkers from F. D. Maurice through to Michael Ramsey in the English tradition and Ernst Troeltsch in the German.

[39] It needs to be said that liberals have often been poor at engaging with the riches of the theological tradition. The desire for voguish solutions (as symbolised by, for instance, R.J. Campbell's *New Theology* and its heirs and successors

participants in a shared quest. There is simply no perspective available from which to glimpse the whole. Dialogue thus forms the shape of the theological task: diversity becomes inevitable and is glimpsed in the tradition and in Scripture. The cracks are not to be papered over but instead tensions, disagreements and the willingness to enter into dialogue are seen as movements towards a greater understanding of something which will nevertheless always remain incomplete.[40]

Such an inclusive, humble, open and pluralist version of theology seems infinitely preferable to the separatist, sectarian and exclusivist alternatives which seem only too willing to put an end to dialogue. In turn, the Kantian approach I have outlined[41] will engage critically in the fight against absolutism since on this analysis absolutism turns out to be the very denial of truth. Such a method makes a stand against all claims to know or to be in possession of an absolute truth, which means taking a position against the spectres of fundamentalism and absolutism wherever they emerge in the modern world. The Kantian position implies criticism, tolerance and openness, but it also at the same time stands against absoluteness, intolerance and closure. And this leads to a position which is far removed from the popular picture of liberal theology as woolly-minded and unwilling to take a stand, even if it only takes a stand in the 'deep apprehension and recognition of the *relativity* of our standpoint'.[42] There must thus be a critical (or liberal) principle built into Christianity to guard against absoluteness and idolatry. As Langdon Gilkey puts it:

in various forms of pantheism) has meant that liberals have ignored the breadth of the Christian tradition, and have often failed to enter into serious dialogue with other Christian positions. There is all too often a polemicising style of theology, which makes dialogue and debate impossible.

[40] A similar method is adopted by George Pattison in *The End of Theology – And the task of Thinking about God*, London: SCM Press, 1998. Gareth Jones also moves in this direction in *Critical Theology*, Cambridge: Polity Press, 1995. For Charles Davis too, Christianity relies on faith in a universal approached only through constant criticism and which rests at the heart of the Christian 'narrative of an argument' (*Religion and the Making of Society*, p. 110).

[41] I have explored this at greater length in my essays, 'Why the Enlightenment Project Doesn't have to Fail', in *Heythrop Journal* 39 (1998), pp. 379-393, and 'Troeltsch, Kant and the Quest for a Critical Public Theology', in *Zeitschrift für neuere Theologiegeschichte* 5 (1998), pp. 29-59.

[42] Langdon Gilkey, 'Plurality and Its Theological Implications' in John Hick and Paul F. Knitter (eds), *The Myth of Christian Uniqueness*, London: SCM, 1987, p. 47.

> A symbol or a criterion points beyond itself and criticises itself if it would not be demonic; but it also points *to* itself and *through* itself if it would not be empty, and if we would not be left centreless. The dialectic works *both* ways: relativizing the manifestation on the one hand, and so all incarnations of the absolute, and yet manifesting as well *through* the relative an absoluteness that transcends it – otherwise neither liberating praxis nor creative reflection would be possible.[43]

The very incompleteness of the Christian vision, its constant pointing towards an eschatological fulfilment, thus forces us to criticise the provisional representations of truth we have established up till the present. And this is a vision of human beings which does not separate them into sundry different types each claiming their own little bit of truth depending on where they live, on their so-called ethnic, national, or religious identity, as the rhetoric of some pluralism (and postmodernism) would have it; instead faith recognises the need for grace which destroys our efforts as mastery, at seeking to build the world on our own, always inadequate, rational construction. A liberal faith quickly becomes cosmopolitan, universalist, yet pluralist and founded on non-dominating difference. On such a view, the openness of a God in Christ who has faced uncertainty serves to prevent a regression into a state of servitude, of dependence on the props of childhood. For liberals, no alibis are allowed as human beings begin to realise their responsibilities and the finitude of their capacities. This serves as a protest against immaturity, against closure, against putting a stop to critique, against identifying God's final judgement with any partial human judgement. And in turn this leads to a theological system in which no system is or ever can be exhaustive or closed.[44]

[43] Gilkey, 'Plurality and Its Theological Implications', p. 48f.

[44] In this the most obvious secular ally is Jürgen Habermas. See esp. 'Die Moderne – ein unvollendetes Projekt', in *Kleine Politische Schriften*, Frankfurt am Main: Suhrkamp, 1981, pp. 444-64 (translated as 'Modernity – an incomplete project', in Hal Foster (ed.), *Postmodern Culture*, London and Sydney: Pluto Press, 1983, pp. 3-15. Cf. R.J. Bernstein, *Habermas and Modernity*, Cambridge: Cambridge University Press, 1985, p. 31: 'the project of modernity, the hope of Enlightenment thinkers, is not a bitter illusion, not a naïve ideology that turns into violence and terror, but a practical task which has *not yet* been realized and which can still orient and guide our actions.' On this see also Charles Davis, *Religion and the Making of Society*, esp. chapter 11.

To finish, let me point to a few implications of this liberal theological method. First, it cannot supply simple security and certainty, except, perhaps ironically, the certainty that human certainties, and that includes all unquestioned authorities and sovereign laws, are expressions of the pride that leads to premature closure. It will offer no quick fix – it is not and can never be infallible. And because of this it will never be a friend of hierarchies and the powerful, of those who might claim final authority – political, ecclesiastical or social. Such a method will resist any form of tying Christianity to a particular culture, or using it for political purposes.[45] A methodologically critical liberal theology will need to guard against over-easy identification between religion and the status quo, especially where that status quo is itself liberal.[46]

Secondly, such a method will be constantly suspicious of theological language (and here it might draw upon all manner of ideological and materialist criticism to unearth the forces at work in the production of human language and structures); and it will be equally critical of any political language which claims an authority which it can never properly have. There is thus a refusal to acknowledge the authoritativeness of human authority, the powerfulness of human power, the sovereignty of human sovereigns. Instead, human beings are asked to live not by self-reliance, but by emptying themselves of their illusory will-to-mastery, by a reliance on a trust and a hope which at its very heart can never be identified with human certainties; yet it is a certain hope which rests on questioning, on self-giving, on openness, but which resists human dominion, authority and power. Indeed, to live in this way, may be to scatter the proud in the imagination of their hearts: and that might mark the beginning of end of the Enlightenment project. The test of the future success of liberal theology—and for that matter, all other genuinely Christian theology—turns out to be whether it lives up to this challenge.

[45] Nevertheless so much liberal theology, particularly the more socially-concerned, has been utopian and distant from the realities of this world, all too ready to latch on to the next popular political notion.

[46] On this see my essay, 'The Social Doctrine of the Trinity: Some Problems', in *Anglican Theological Review* 83 (2001), pp. 239-54.

Chapter 2

What has London (or Oxford or Cambridge) to do with Augsburg?

The Enduring Significance of the German Liberal Tradition in Christian Theology

Friedrich Wilhelm Graf

In his 1824 Bampton Lectures Dr John Josias Conybeare told his Oxford audience 'that all your German theology might be buried at the bottom of the German Ocean'.[1] A year later Connop Thirlwall answered him by anonymously publishing a translation of Schleiermacher's essay on Luke. In his introduction Thirlwall declared that 'it cannot be concealed that German theology in general and German biblical criticism in particular, labours at present under an ill name among our divines'.[2] Thirlwall, who met Schleiermacher when he paid his visit to England in 1828 and accompanied him to Cambridge,[3] connected his enthusiasm for German critical theology with some polemical remarks on Oxford: 'It would almost seem as if at Oxford the knowledge of German subjected a divine to the same suspicion of heterodoxy which we know was attached some

[1] This chapter was translated by Mark D. Chapman. John Josias Conybeare, *The Bampton Lectures for the year MDCCCXXIV. Being an attempt to trace the history and to ascertain the limits of the secondary and spiritual interpretation of the Scripture*, Oxford, 1824 (cited in Keith Robbins, Protestant Germany through British eyes: A Complex Victorian Encounter, 1992 Annual Lecture, London: German Historical Institute, 1993, p. 14).

[2] Cited in F. Lichtenberger, *History of German Theology in the Nineteenth Century*, Edinburgh: T & T Clark, 1889, p. ix, note.

[3] On this see Julius Rieger, 'Schleiermachers Englandreise', in *Jahrbuch für Berlin-Brandenburgische Kirchengeschichte* 49 (1974), pp. 67-90 and Ieuen Ellis, 'Schleiermacher in Britain', in *Scottish Journal of Theology* 33 (1980), pp. 417-52.

centuries back with the knowledge of Greek.'[4] Such scepticism about German critical theology, however, was not limited to Oxford, but also occurred in Cambridge and London.

In sermons preached before the University of Cambridge, for instance, Hugh James Rose warned his congregation to be on their guard against 'that large party of men in Germany, who calling themselves Christians, have shown an anxious desire to get rid of all that is supernatural in Christianity, and to set aside the positive doctrines of the Gospel scheme, generally on the ground that those doctrines are contrary to their reason'.[5] In the reports of the young Englishmen and Scots who studied during the nineteenth century at German universities, it is easy to detect a widespread scepticism on the part of Reformed Churchmen and orthodox Anglicans towards German university theologians. When the Scotsman John Cairns came to Berlin in 1843-44, he reported to some friends at home: 'My *Sprach-Gefühl* develops, and I can fight my way through interrogations, descriptions and even debates on the Absolute, Supernaturalism and Calvinistic Dogmatic sufficiently well to bring down denunciations of the practical, unphilosophical genius of *Engländer* and the harshness and ignorant confidence of Scottish orthodoxy. The arrogance of the Germans on these points is beyond expression.'[6]

Over seventy years later in April 1915, after the first use of gas in the First World War, a pamphlet published in Birmingham spoke of the

> poison gas of Modern Thought which had spread its death-dealing doctrines far and wide ... Long before the war the German apostles of Kultur launched upon this country (and others) their 'Higher critic' theories, poisoning the minds of men in regard to the divine Inspiration and Authority of Holy Scriptures.[7]

Indeed, since the eighteenth century British theologians have fought an intense and passionate campaign against 'German liberal theology', 'theological Germanism' or 'German religion'.

Bearing this tradition in mind, my task in presenting the enduring significance of German liberal theology is especially difficult. I would neither like to present myself as a latter-day 'apostle of *Kultur*' nor send

[4] J. C. Thirlwall, *Connop Thirlwall*, London: SPCK, 1936, p. 30.

[5] H. J. Rose, *The State of Protestantism in Germany*, second edition London, 1829, pp. xxvii-ix.

[6] A. R. McEwan, *Life and Letters of John Cairns*, London, 1898, pp. 165-168.

Teutonic theological armadas to save the 'German idea of freedom'. Instead I prefer to present myself as a liberal, who, both as theologian and social historian, understands something of the particular ambiguities of German liberal theology. I seek to be a liberal theologian, but have experienced how difficult this is. Consequently I prefer to discuss what I have learnt from British and American intellectuals about the basic elements of liberal thought. I belong to the first generation born in the western sector of a divided Germany whose over-riding intellectual concern has been to understand the catastrophes of German history in the 'age of extremes', to quote Eric C. Hobsbawm. For West German academics of my generation it was a liberating and emancipating experience to learn about pluralism by reading William James or Isaiah Berlin's *Two Concepts of Liberty* of 1958. My interest in the traditions of liberal thought in Germany grew out of the question as to why most of the German protestant cultural élite (*Bildungsbürgertum*) gave such little acknowledgement to the democratic institutions of the Weimar Republic. In turn I sought to understand why, because of their cultural pessimism or their passionate criticism of modernity, they later supported, or at least passively acquiesced in, the radically anti-liberal 'German revolution' of the National Socialists. Whoever speaks as a post-war German intellectual on German liberal theology also has to try to understand the failings of this tradition. It is a commonplace to speak of the decisive victory over the long tradition of 'heretical' liberal theology by the dialectical theologians and other anti-liberal theologians after 1918. This story is, however, as with most decisive victories, simply wrong. Influential liberals continued to produce theology, and new research has rediscovered the younger liberal theologians of the 1920s and early 1930s and has shown them to have had a number of different attitudes:[8] important liberal theologians resisted the National Socialists under the banner of liberal values and many had already taken up positions of active resistance even before the Nazi seizure of power. However, some others welcomed the 'liberating' visions of the totalitarian state and supported the 'German Christians'. Here one needs to ask how it was possible to be a liberal theologian and at the same time support an anti-

[7] 'H.H.E & H.E.', 'Safeguarded', Birmingham, 1915. Cited in Mark D. Chapman, 'Anglo-German Theological Relations in the First World War', in *Zeitschrift für neuere Theologiegeschichte* 6 (1999), p. 109.

[8] See esp. Matthias Wolfes, *Protestantische Theologie und moderne Welt. Studien zur Geschichte der liberalen Theologie nach 1918*, Berlin, New York: Walter de Gruyter, 1999.

liberal political movement. Or again, what is it that is 'liberal' in liberal theology, if at the same time this leads ethically to a fundamental critique of the traditions of the Enlightenment, or if it understands human rights and individual freedom as 'western' concepts, and alien to a good Lutheran ethics?

There is, however, a further paradox. Since 1970 many American and British theologians have published important dissertations and numerous articles on German Culture Protestantism. There has been a Schleiermacher renaissance in the United States and there was a Troeltsch conference in the United Kingdom before anything comparable in West Germany. Protestant theologians in the United States and in Britain seem to undertake study in the rich but complicated history of German protestant academic theology since the late eighteenth century because it is precisely here that the classic texts of religious liberalism ranging from Schleiermacher, Ritschl, Herrmann, and Harnack to Troeltsch are to be found. Roman Catholic theologians and Jewish thinkers also understood Germany from the eighteenth to the beginning of the twentieth century as a country with strong traditions of liberal religious thought, developing influential theologies of 'reformed Catholicism' and Modernism as well as the 'scientific Judaism' of the Jewish reformers or liberal cultural Jews.

However, in academic disciplines other than theology as well as in some fields of public discourse, the opposite is the case. For political scientists, economists and many historians, Germany is understood as a country with very weak traditions of liberal thought. Political scientists have reached a widespread consensus that the dominant stream of political theory in Germany developed models of a very strong state and ideas of the Universal (*das Allgemeine*). For example, the *bonum commune*, the 'common Good' of Lutheran social ethics or Hegel's objective spirit have been much more highly prized than individual freedom or civic engagement. It is scarcely imaginable that American or British economists would invite a German to discuss the enduring significance of classical German economic thought for a globalised capitalist market economy. In the actual controversies over the different types of modern capitalism, so-called 'Rhineland capitalism' or the 'social market economies' are used as models where the spheres of economic action are severely restricted by strong corporatist institutions and legal regulations. Pure market economy, competitive capitalism and neo-liberalism are still terms of abuse for most Germans. Finally, social historians see a decisive reason for the rise of National Socialism in the relative weakness of the liberal bourgeoisie in Germany, especially in comparison to Britain and France. The failures of the Weimar Republic are almost universally explained not by the strength of the Nazis, but by the failures of the democratic tradition and especially the weakness of the bourgeois, predominantly protestant, liberals. It was this that sealed the fate of parliamentary democracy.

What then is the enduring significance of the German liberal tradition in Christian theology? To answer this question it is firstly important to decide on what theologies count as liberal. What constitutes the difference between a liberal and a non-liberal theology? What criteria do we use to classify certain eighteenth-, nineteenth- or twentieth-century theological programmes as 'liberal theologies'? If we are not simply going to repeat the partisan theological or ecclesiastical battles of the past with liberals pitched against conservatives, modernists against reactionaries (with are still just as tedious), then we need analytical tools for differentiating between theological positions. Furthermore, we need to ask why we need to pay attention to the national character of theological traditions and to look at their embeddedness in specific cultural contexts. Are the liberal theologies of English Anglicans different from those of German Lutherans or Reformed Protestants primarily because they are English? Only when we have answered such questions will it be reasonable to ask whether there is still anything to learn from German liberal theology.[9]

Theology as an interdisciplinary 'science of Christian culture'

Since 1970 in Germany, as well as in England and the USA, there has been a large number of publications on German liberal theologians. For the most part these make use of the traditional methods of intellectual history or history of theology. Such a conventional writing of the history of theology, however, is in marked contrast to the methods adopted by most of the German academics who understood themselves as liberal theologians or who were later included among the liberals. My first claim is this: it is only possible to assess liberal theology in Germany by using insights drawn from methods they used in their own theologies.

[9] In Germany, liberal theology has not only been produced by Protestants. However, it is not possible in the confines of this chapter to look at the liberal theologies of German Reformed Judaism or German Catholic Modernism. This is not to deny this importance of comparative perspectives.

At the turn of the present century German liberal academic theology developed in very close dialogue with the other cultural sciences (*Kulturwissenschaften*). Protestant theologians played an important role in the development of a new historical style of thought, which is usually understood in British and American discussions as something distinctly German. I do not want to argue now whether 'The German Conception of History' is just a (more or less problematic) 'national tradition'[10] or whether it is simply a national expression of a far more general intellectual revolution from the eighteenth century onwards. Following Troeltsch, I understand 'historicism', or more correctly 'historism' (*Historismus*), as an intellectual revolution which fundamentally changed our understanding of languages, religious traditions, cultural objects, political institutions and much else. In nineteenth-century Germany, liberal theology was part of this revolution. Liberal theologians sought to reconstruct or deconstruct religious traditions according to the current standards of historical research.

Nowadays, many theologians who are researching into liberal theology fall far behind the standards of historical methodology that had been set in Germany by 1900, for example, by Harnack and Troeltsch. Often they understand the object of their research in a consciously non-historical and purely systematic manner, and even call for a 'Schleiermacher orthodoxy' or a new 'Troeltsch renaissance'. But why should critical intellectuals need to establish new orthodoxies or practise the cult of hero worship? Instead I would like to suggest another way: theologies that since the eighteenth century have programmatically adopted the practice of historicising theological reflection should themselves be historicised.

From the late eighteenth century liberal theologians began critical study of the bible and also wrote critical histories of dogma, the church, and theology. During the nineteenth century they actively engaged in the development of historical methods, which opened up church history and history of dogma to questions of social history, psychology, ethnology or 'history of culture'. At the turn of the present century many protestant liberals understood theology as a historical and hermeneutical science of Christian culture, which did not seek to produce dogmatic norms, but rather sought to study faith as it was lived in history, and to understand popular religion.

[10] This claim has made by Georg G. Iggers, *The German Conception of History. The National Tradition of Historical Thought from Herder to the Present*, revised edition, Middletown, Connecticut: Wesleyan University Press, 1983.

If this understanding of theology is to be adopted today, then it is necessary to study modern constructivist theories of culture which do not see 'the world' or 'reality' as something simply given, but as a collection of an infinite number of signs, patterns of interpretation and images. This perspective can be traced back in German-speaking countries to the classical cultural sciences of the turn of the century, to figures like Georg Simmel, Max Weber, Ernst Troeltsch, Ernst Cassirer and Aby Warburg.[11] The primary interest of the constructivist perspective is in the cognitive maps, patterns of interpretation, stereotypes, images, symbols or language games, through which individuals or certain groups of individuals try to perceive or to construe reality. Constructivist theorists of culture look at the traditions of a social group which confer meaning, at the representations and the images of the self and of others, and also at the ways in which a social group tries to present itself as a unity both to itself and to others. Such a group might be a nation in contrast to other nations, or an organisation like the 'Modern Churchpeople's Union'. Cultural theorists try to reconstruct the symbolic boundaries and what Pierre Bourdieu has called 'procedures of exclusion' through which a certain social group or an institution maintains itself as a community. These theories of culture which are marked by a 'linguistic turn' offer new possibilities for deconstructing the ways in which different theologians or different types of theology identify themselves. When these methods are applied to the history of liberal theology they make it possible to avoid the fundamental epistemological mistake of simply affirming the self-images of liberals. Liberals have always sought to be progressive and have tried to be more modern than others, but such self-representations should not be taken for granted. It should be remembered that a large number of German liberal theologians have in many ways not been liberal at all.

'Liberal Theology': the vagueness of a diffuse term

The history of theological party names and programmatic self-designations has been inadequately researched in modern German protestantism. Terms of abuse or self-designation like 'Positive Theology', 'Conservative Theology', 'Critical Theology', 'Modern Theology', 'Confes-

[11] For a discussion of the classical cultural sciences of the turn of the century, see Otto Gerhard Oexle, *Geschichtswissenschaft im Zeichen des Historismus. Studien zur Problemgeschichten der Moderne*, Göttingen: Vandenhoeck & Ruprecht, 1996.

sional Theology', 'Neo-orthodox Theology', 'Mediating theology', 'Speculative Theology', 'Free Theology' and 'Liberal Theology' as well as movements like 'Supernaturalism' or 'Rationalism' have characterised the theological debate since the 1770s. In all these movements the dominant question has been the extent to which protestant theology has been open to the traditions of the Enlightenment, which in Germany was strongly influenced by Christianity, particularly in its protestant forms. In the controversies over the Enlightenment, the French Revolution and the attitude of the new bourgeois social groups towards the churches, the theological spectrum became so diverse in the transition from the eighteenth to the nineteenth centuries that since that time it has been possible to speak of many different theological positions.

The so-called Halle 'Neology' was the late eighteenth century self-description of moderate enlightened theologians, who criticised 'Palaeontology' or the old dogmatic way of doing theology. In 1774 Johann Salomo Semler gave the name '*liberalis theologia*' to a purely historical investigation of the New Testament unconstrained by dogmatic presuppositions. Such critical biblical research or '*theologia liberalis*' sought to make Christianity first and foremost into a religion of practical reason in contrast to the 'ecclesiastical Christianity' with its old confessions and public doctrine. In the conflict over the legitimacy of the Enlightenment in the 1770s and 80s, '*theologia liberalis*' became the party label for the Neologists and the Rationalists, that is, the theological disciples of Immanuel Kant. The early representatives of liberal theology sought to weaken the hold of the old confessions and fought for doctrinal freedom within the church. They also sought to replace the church's faith in original sin, predestination and the substitutionary atonement with a rational faith in a Creator God, moral autonomy and eternal life. 'Liberalis theologia' or 'free Theology' thus attained two meanings. The term served both as a programme for the liberation or emancipation from the tutelage of the old dogma with its fixation on creeds and confessions, and also became a self-description of a group of theologians, who sought to realise this programme by means of a new, purely philological or historical-critical understanding of the Bible, and a historical interpretation of dogma, church history and the history of theology. Consequently, Kantian theologians sometimes used the phrase 'autonomy of (practical) reason' to indicate the main purpose of 'liberal theology'. After 1789 and the conflicts over the restoration of the old political order, this emancipatory content was politicised. Influential rationalists or late rationalists pronounced after the turn of the century that whoever fought against the bondage to the letter or dogma also had to engage in the fight for freedom of opinion, freedom of the press and human rights.

In nearly all the histories of modern German protestant theology published since 1840, Schleiermacher has been called the church father of liberal culture protestantism. But it is of crucial importance to remember that he never called himself a 'liberal' or 'free' theologian. His pupils and followers consciously used the term 'mediating theology', which is something very different from 'liberal theology'. And even from among the theological followers of Schelling and Hegel a few left-Hegelians used the term 'liberal theology' after 1840. During Schleiermacher's lifetime it was another group of protestant thinkers who called themselves 'liberal theologians' or 'liberal thinkers'. Late rationalists like H. G. Tzschirner, Wilhelm Traugott Krug and Carl Gottlieb Bretschneider played an important part in the formation of an early liberal political protest movement in Germany and a more or less democratic nationalism (which at the time was an emancipatory ideology) which sought to establish a constitutional monarchy in a national state under Prussian leadership. These late rationalists sought to realise the 'Protestant Principle', which they understood primarily as criticism of hierarchy, freedom of thought, freedom of conscience, constitutional rights against the state, and participation in power through free elections and parliaments. They differentiated this political and ecclesiastical realisation of 'protestant freedom' from both Roman authoritarianism and the 'terrorist anarchy' of revolutionary democracy. In this way liberal theology became a synonym for the hope that revolutionary change could be brought about by rational reform.

It was only after 1840 that the concept of 'liberal theology' gained a partisan revolutionary meaning: the so-called 'friends of light', a radical democratic opposition group on the left wing or in many cases outside the state churches, and also left-wing Hegelian theologians like David Friedrich Strauss, understood 'liberal theology' to mean the transformation of an old obsolete Christianity into a new rational religion of humanity, or faith in the divinity of the human species-being. This more or less post-Christian use of the term 'liberal theology' gave more ammunition to the theologians of the restoration and the neo-orthodox Lutheran confessionalists in their charge, which had been levelled since the 1820s, that 'liberal theology' was not merely critical of the church, but was hostile to Christianity and anti-Christian. Here, in the guise of a theology, the religious individual or the modern human being—for conservatives the very archetype of the sinner—had taken the place of God. The accusation that liberal theology is an expression of the self-glorification of human beings has been often repeated in Germany right up to the 1930s: one need only think of Karl Barth.

After the revolution of 1848-49 some of Ferdinand Christian Baur's Tübingen students and prominent theologians founded the German Protestant Union ('Deutscher Protestantenverein') in 1863. Pre-eminently Richard Rothe used 'liberal theology' as a political weapon against the dominant alliance of confessional Lutheran orthodoxy and the restored police state. They insisted on the fundamental agreement between liberals in politics and the protestant church. For the theologians of the Protestant Union, 'liberal theology' meant not merely the battle against enforced dogmas and authoritarianism, and the domination by the church of schools and the clericalisation of politics, but also the vision of an 'imperial church' which would function as a religious analogue to the Empire established in 1870-71 as a means for integrating the different groups in the population in one true national church. Similarly, for many prominent representatives of political liberalism 'liberal theology' represented something approaching the civil religion of the new Empire. This development of the concept meant that it combined with political hopes and historical expectations which, at least when set against the background of the Enlightenment or Kantian philosophy or liberal cosmopolitanism, appear structurally illiberal and extremely intolerant. This can be illustrated from the attitude towards minorities. Many prominent liberals from the German Protestant Union asserted that Jews and Catholics could become citizens only after accepting the protestant principles of the new Empire as the cultural norm. Catholics were to deny the Pope and enter the 'ecumenical' church, which was to all intents and purposes protestant, and Jews were to be assimilated and were to convert. Many liberal theologians of the German Protestant Union thus represented a national religious ideal which was characterised not by pluralism and tolerance but by a high degree of homogeneity and at the same time a longing for a new religious unity of German culture. In contrast to the Roman Catholic and conservative protestant understanding, this religious integration of German society was not to be achieved by means of an authoritarian domination of the state by the church, but by the religious permeation of all political institutions as well as the strengthening of the unity between cultural state and church. The best example of this divinisation of the state can be found in Richard Rothe's *Theologische Ethik*, where he claimed that since the Reformation the church had receded behind the 'moral community' of the state: the 'cultural state' was the actual form of the Kingdom of God. Yet such an understanding is little more than a theological reworking of an authoritarian belief in the power of the state. What right, one might ask, has such a theology to be called 'liberal'?

In all early nineteenth-century European societies, liberals were the influential prophets of modern nationalism. This is equally true for German culture protestants and many of their theological heroes. Academic theologians like Otto Pfleiderer who organised themselves in the Protestant Union demanded what Arthur Bonus called a 'Germanisation of Christianity', in order to make Christianity attractive to those who had been alienated from the church. In their ethical teaching, most of them were extremely anti-pluralistic and intolerant, and many liberal theologians in the Empire were similarly hostile to Roman Catholics and the Social Democrats. Even those liberal theologians who voted for the left-liberal 'Freethinker' party defined Protestant freedom in terms of anti-catholicism. Nevertheless they represented a liberal ideal in their calls for the separation of church and state. However, most liberal theologians in the Empire did not seek the separation of church and state, since they regarded the state as a guarantor of academic freedom against a church dominated by conservatives.

Albrecht Ritschl, the 'History of Religion School' and other theologians associated with Martin Rade's journal *Die Christliche Welt*, did not call themselves 'liberal theologians'. Rade, Ernst Troeltsch, Otto Baumgarten and Wilhelm Bousset used the term pejoratively as a synonym for a naively optimistic bourgeois theology which failed to tackle the cultural crises of the times, such as the rise of proletarian socialism as well as the threats to the individual posed by capitalist society. As they began to see more clearly the effects of the crisis of modernity in fragmentation, pluralism and the relativisation of values, so many of them moved towards non-liberal ideologies of a new community.

The use of the term only changed in the 1920s when liberals were threatened both politically and theologically. Figures such as Rade, Harnack and Troeltsch's pupils were prepared to identify themselves as liberal theologians. The more anti-liberal movements began to dominate all spheres of intellectual life (including theology), the more weight these liberals were ready to place on basic liberal values like autonomy and freedom of conscience. Nevertheless it must also be said that even in the

1920s most liberals thought in terms of the community rather than individuality: to many, individualism was suspect.

In many ways the 'German liberal tradition' is simply an artifice. To include theologians from Semler to Mulert under the same heading makes it an extremely vague concept. There is very little common ground except a belief that theology should be open to modernity, that protestantism is the more modern, i.e. liberal, form of Christianity (which displays a deep distrust of Roman Catholics), that protestant theology must create cultural values for all Germans, that Luther is a national hero, and that conservatives are somehow morally worse than people from the same liberal tribe. Many liberals used theological language to develop utopian visions that were deeply anti-pluralistic and illiberal. The litmus test is this: most of them spoke of the '*libertas christiana*' or the autonomy of the self in grand theological language. But at the same time they used theological terms to set the limits to such freedom and to create a new social whole. 'Individualism' consequently became a term of abuse in many culture protestant organisations.

So why do we speak of 'the German liberal tradition' if it is simply an invention? As Hans-Joachim Birkner has shown, the term was a construct of the anti-liberal theologians of the 1920s, who needed a clear picture of a relatively homogenous liberal tradition, in order that they could put an end to all its heresies.[12]

Five systematic elements of German liberal theology

1. All groups of theologians who tried to be liberals were critical of the traditional patterns of authority and also sought a critical revision of the traditional confessions of faith. They accepted a religious pluralism within their church or religious community and formulated visions of the religious life which were defined not by dogma or church teaching, but by moral action or practical reason. They developed models of religious self-determination or religious freedom of the individual. Indeed individual experience became the basis for the definition of all truth. 'Individual

[12] Cf. H.-J. Birkner, 'Liberale Theologie', in Martin Schmidt and Georg Schwaiger (eds), *Kirchen und Liberalismus im 19. Jahrhundert*, Göttingen: Vandenhoeck and Ruprecht, 1976, pp. 33-42; On the history of the term 'liberal theology' see Friedrich Wilhelm Graf, 'Liberale Theologie', in *Evangelisches Kirchenlexikon*, Göttingen: Vandenhoeck and Ruprecht, 1992, vol. 3, pp. 86-98;

autonomy', however, was a very vague term. It could be defined in the strict Kantian sense but at the same time it could be used for something quite irrational. Nevertheless, there are some common threads in their understanding of the autonomous self: self-reflexive subjectivity, liberation from the immaturity of traditional forms of authority, the formation of personal identity through strong self-discipline, the growth into a personality in consciousness of the bondage to God, the call for a concrete form of freedom which was bound up with values and ideals. Religion was always considered to be the decisive element in the constitution of the personality. Such a religious experience was seen as constitutive of the individuality of the individual, with one's 'own inner life' (as for Wilhelm Herrmann) or personal interiority. By connecting religious experience and the experience of the self they established a fundamental religious pluralism: all people had their own faith. This meant that the formation of religious ideas was only secondarily related to the religious community. The classic argument is that of Schleiermacher in the *Speeches*.

2. This call for individual religious experience meant that liberal theologians could no longer develop systems of dogmatics, but instead it was only possible to describe the doctrines of the faith. A legalistic understanding of the content of doctrine was replaced by reflection on religious experience and lived religion. After the Enlightenment a non-confessional definition of the 'essence of Christianity' based on a universal philosophical concept of religion replaced the dogmatic understanding of the identity of the different confessions. Using the essence concept, the particularities of one's own tradition are shown to be in a fundamental agreement with all the monotheistic religions. Consequently, most liberal theologies have tried to open up the dogmatic claims to the absoluteness of their own faith communities to other confessions and religions. But most German protestant liberals did not give up the claims for the practical cultural superiority of Christianity (or Protestantism) above other religions, including Judaism. Since Protestantism was understood as the religion of freedom and personality it had to be regarded as the universal religion of the modern culture of individuality. There were very few (as, for instance, Troeltsch in his Berlin period) who called into question the superiority of their own tradition.

and idem. (ed.), *Liberale Theologie. Eine Ortsbestimmung* (Troeltsch-Studien, vol. 7), Gütersloh: Gerd Mohn, 1993.

3. Because they were based on individual religious experience, liberal descriptions of the doctrines of the faith were unable to develop adequate understandings of corporate identity in churches and religious communities. In this respect conservative theologians have done much better. Even in their hostile attitudes towards modernity they have to some degree been more modern than many liberals. They did not demand a new homogeneity, but indirectly accepted a pluralistic society. Church theologies, for example like that developed by Barth, may fit much better into a developed pluralistic world than classical liberal theologies.

4. Since they found it difficult to develop any strong understanding of the church, many liberals privileged other forms of reintegration of the individual into community. This might go some way towards explaining why so many liberals developed models of society where there was little room for minorities. If there is no longer any common faith, it is still possible to share common prejudices (for instance, against Roman Catholics and conservatives).

5. The liberal theologies of German culture protestantism were 'cultural theologies' as distinct from church theologies. No longer did they seek to strengthen the dogmatic uniformity of their own confessional churches, but were more concerned to integrate modern pluralist society on a religious basis. As modern society collapsed into competing world-views, so a fundamental consensus in religion became ever more pressing. Such a consensus was to be established on the basis of a rational, universally applicable faith in humanity. Since this rational Christianity was decisively determined by the Protestant tradition, most liberal cultural theologies contain a high degree of structural illiberality, despite their tolerance and openness towards differences of opinion. They understood the Kingdom of God as a well-ordered society. And as the crisis of modernity became increasingly grave, so they accepted new models of integration, in which individual freedom took second place to 'the community'. This over-emphasis of community can be prevented only if freedom is understood logically as negative freedom – and there were only a few strict Kantians who were prepared to do this.

What can be learnt from German liberal theology?

To talk about the possible relevance of intellectual traditions says more about the person doing the talking than it does about the tradition itself. Consequently, it is important to remember my own particular perspective. In the light of the history of recent German theology I am struck by the experience that liberal political institutions are extremely precarious and threatened, and that democracy will only continue to function in the long term if it continues to be supported by the people. Today as westerners we all live under the conditions of a functioning democratic order. In that respect we think under the conditions of the political success of liberal principles. In many ways we can say that liberal thought has succeeded politically, culturally and in religion. Whereas the relationship of Christianity to other religions was previously of purely academic interest, it has become an internal problem for all western societies, and many conservatives are even willing to work with liberals in this area. Consequently we might ask: why, when liberal principles have been so successful, should we still be interested in liberal theories which so often sought to undermine their success?

Does the liberal open society need the resources of liberal religion?

After the modernisation of the 1970s and the rapid expansion of global market capitalism there has been an intensified debate in all advanced societies about the high social costs of societal modernisation. The new processes which lead to cultural pluralism, the individualisation of life, together with the immigration of non-Christian groups to all the countries of Western Europe, have meant that the old premise of political theories as to what guarantees the inner stability of communal life has again become increasingly relevant. The debates between neo-liberals and communitarians are basically a continuation in a new language of the old controversies between Kantians and the representatives of an objective system of ethics like Hegel's. In all the debates over social capital, civil society, intermediate organisations and 'third ways', the basic question is this: is it possible to integrate an open society of free citizens solely on the basis of law? Or does the concept of law require some kind of what is variously called 'moral substance', 'objective spirit', 'social capital', 'objective cultural values', or a 'European cultural synthesis'?

Drawing from the German neo-protestant tradition of ethical thought this alternative can be formulated thus: on the one hand, like Kant, liberals have differentiated law from morality and insisted that the state may not intrude in the religious views and moral opinions of its citizens – this is done in order to protect the freedom of the individual and the liberty of political institutions. On the other hand, those who have maintained a system of objective ethics have claimed, primarily by criticising the so-called formalism of Kantian practical philosophy, that a free society does not create its own values but is based upon the readiness of its citizens for civic engagement. German liberal theology is still relevant in this respect, because from the end of the eighteenth century the leading question was whether the state required religion, or, more precisely, a particular form of religion, in order to function adequately. In short: does a liberal state need liberal religion in order for its citizens to cultivate a liberal conscience? Do liberals thus have to claim a certain precedence for their values in order to protect the liberality of the political system?

The modernisation of society from the late eighteenth century has been accompanied by the weakening of tradition, the destruction of the dominant ethical system and the erosion of the inherited patterns of social morality. Consequently, morality and civic virtues are notoriously weak in post-traditional societies. This leads to a precarious situation which can be politically dangerous. Modern 'risk-societies'[13] have a hitherto unknown potential for self-destruction. They require, particularly among the ruling élites, a high capacity for self-reflection. In a situation of greater power and influence there is an ever greater need for some kind of recognition of human finitude. And yet the traditional resources have been permanently destroyed by progressive modernisation. This paradox of modernisation can be formulated as follows: modern societies require an extreme measure of self-determination and autonomy of the individual. But the institutions and agencies of socialisation are unable to create an autonomous form of life out of this inner potential. Democratic open societies thus require intermediate moral agencies. They need organisations and institutions which counter this increasing moral confusion. It is the churches and other religious communities that are primarily responsible for upholding and renewing moral traditions in our cul-

[13] Ulrich Beck, *Risikogesellschaft. Auf dem Wege in eine andere Moderne*, Frankfurt am Main: Suhrkamp, 1986. English translation: *Risk society: Towards a New Modernity*, London: Sage, 1992.

ture. It is only in moral communities defined by their corporate remembering of a specific religious and moral tradition that lasting civic virtues might be formed to prevent the erosion of liberal society into a battleground of irresponsible individualism. It would thus be disastrous deliberately to destroy what is left of our religious and moral tradition. Like computer software, moral traditions are extremely fragile.

Liberals have no intention of forcing anybody into church nor of being bound by any confession of civil religion. But they have to ask whether a free democracy will survive in the future only by the cultivation of religious traditions in society which strengthen civic political responsibility, the sense of community and readiness to live by the law. These connections between free democracy and free religion (which alongside the different confessions of Christianity also includes Islam in its European form) have been drawn not just by conservative liberal protestants like Hermann Lübbe[14] or Trutz Rendtorff.[15] Even among discourse ethicists like Jürgen Habermas, who were erstwhile critics of religion, one can detect a new sensitivity for these connections between free democracy and free religion. He does not believe that 'it is possible for Europeans to understand concepts like morality and ethics, person and individual, freedom and emancipation ... without recognising the basic tenets of the salvation history of the Judaeo-Christian tradition'.[16] This presupposes the inheritance and cultivation of such thought.

The political form of parliamentary democracy has no long-term chance in a society unless its citizens are prepared to uphold the fundamental legal basis of freedom in distinct ways. To remain liberal the free state cannot itself determine the individual conscience of its citizens. In this respect this means that religious communities and other moral communities which have a tradition of active agreement with the institutional order have a decisive part to play in securing the success of freedom. If this is the case, then there are many interesting examples from the German tradition which could be used to flesh this out in more detail. The decisive point in the argument is thus the structure of the

[14] Hermann Lübbe, *Religion nach der Aufklärung*, Graz: Styria, 1986.

[15] Cf. Trutz Rendtorff, *Vielspältiges. Protestantische Beiträge zur ethischen Kultur*, Stuttgart, Berlin and Cologne: Kohlhammer, 1991.

[16] Jürgen Habermas, 'Metaphysik nach Kant', in *Nachmetaphysisches Denken. Philosophische Aufsätze*, Frankfurt am Main: Suhrkamp, 1988, p. 23. English translation: *Postmetaphysical Thinking: Philosophical Essays*, Cambridge: Polity Press, 1992. On this, see Klaus Tanner, *Der lange Schatten des Naturrechts. Eine fundamentalethische Untersuchung*, Stuttgart, Berlin and Cologne: Kohlhammer, 1993, 1993, pp. 184ff.

concept of freedom. Is freedom adequately understood solely as negative freedom? Or do we also need positive freedom? But surely, one might ask, does that not pave the way for our seduction by illiberal ideology, as Isaiah Berlin showed?

Do we still believe in the old autonomous self?

However different the theories of religion and the ethical programmes of German liberal theologians might have been, they all placed a strong emphasis on the autonomous 'personality'. To become a personality is an extremely difficult process. Personalities have to be formed. But formation (*Bildung*) is a key German concept for the hard work involved in establishing life firmly on the basis of moral principles, and it shows itself in the processes of permanent reflection of the autonomous subject. The liberal German 'personality' is possibly only a kind of dinosaur surviving from the early modern period. Whatever, at the turn of the new millennium we speak of a very different kind of free human being. In the context of globalisation we demand the flexible self or we lament the fact that a stable personal identity dissolves into hedonism, adaptability to the market and other kinds of fragmentation. The postmodern human being is a successful entrepreneur in the many different markets which make up modern life, from the world of work to the sex market. Modern human beings know that fragmentation is the watchword, and no longer seek a fixed identity for the whole of life. They surf the internet, flitter through forty television channels, search out some new basis for their fragile patch-work identities and adapt themselves to new trends and opportunities. They might be addicted to pleasure, perhaps a little melancholic, sometimes rather depressive, and every now and then even a little religious – but they do not seek after principles, and they try to work through every possible difficulty and every negative experience. Reading Kant might well be an intellectual pleasure. But living out Kant is infinitely tiresome.

In the last few years the structures of personality have become a fashionable theme among psychologists, sociologists and other analysts of culture. If their analysis of postmodern patchwork identities is correct, then the German liberal understanding of 'personality' is once again relevant. Do not the flexible human beings of late capitalism need some form of underlying certainty, which alone makes possible the recognition of the different contexts as different? Are not the symbolic languages of religion still the decisive language games which guarantee ultimate certainties and a stable framework amid this rapid change? In modern advanced and radically pluralist societies, when most individuals experience an ever-growing sense of contingency, do not the old German liberal solutions become all the more important, as they allow the individual to live with this unbounded contingency?

'The German Spirit and Western Europe'[17]

From the late eighteenth century onwards German theologians were well aware that they were different from others, and they regarded others as different from themselves. The otherness of the English was especially noticeable. Schleiermacher had already criticised them for lacking philosophical depth and for their solely pragmatic spirit, their sense of commercial values and their utilitarian calculus which they applied to everything. It would be a worthwhile task for the intellectual historian to investigate the stereotypes by which German liberal theologians from the late eighteenth century to the twentieth categorised their counterparts in Scotland and England, especially those in Oxford and Cambridge. Many of the stereotypes of 'German culture' and Anglo-Saxon civilisation which were used by intellectuals in all the warring nations in the First World War can be traced back to the theological discourse of the Enlightenment period. Indeed, national cultural stereotypes are closely connected to the images and representations used by theological elites to try to distinguish between the confessions.

In an age of increasing European integration after the end of the 'age of extremes', recalling these pictures of the enemy from the First World War might seem to many just another expression of that insane hostility to the wider world which English students in the nineteenth century observed in their German professors. But quite the opposite is the case: in the processes of European integration we need a greater degree of sensitivity towards the clash of intellectual civilisations which still exists between, on the one side, Oxford, Cambridge and London, and Augsburg, Heidelberg and Tübingen on the other side. In many of the most important debates in applied ethics British thinkers use quite different arguments from their German counterparts. As enlightened critical liberals we are well aware that our images of others, as well as those of

[17] Cf. Ernst Troeltsch, *Deutscher Geist und Westeuropa*, ed. Hans Baron, first edition, 1925, reprint, Aalen: Scientia, 1966.

ourselves, are human constructs. But we have to realise that many forms of ethical discourse, which are of vital importance in politics, make use of fundamentally different forms of rationality. An example I find fascinating is that of the philosophical and theological debate over the concept of personhood in bioethics. British and American utilitarians understand the dignity of the person quite differently from German ethicists, whose thought is still more or less dominated by Kant. Because of these different traditions they have no common understanding of what a person is, nor of what criteria can be used to determine personhood. Indeed, for many British bioethicists there are conditions when one might consider terminating a life because it no longer counts as a person. Even in an integrated Europe there is still a fundamental difference between those who understand a person with John Locke in terms of the capacity to perceive and those who understand personhood in terms of 'moral autonomy' following Kant. In this respect, liberal thinkers in Britain and liberals in Germany belong to very different tribes. Given the forces for a unified European system of regulation in many controversial areas of ethics, it is imperative that we are not merely 'nice' to one another as 'wishy-washy' liberals, but rather we must learn how to deal with dissent and with the remaining differences between cultures.

It might seem somewhat surprising that somebody from Augsburg, the city of toleration, should be reminding the English that consistent liberalism is not primarily about finding a greater harmony between all religions and world-views. Rather is about giving fundamental rights to the many dissenters, about allowing the other to be other. To demand individual freedom requires the preservation of difference and the development of a culture of conflict. Conflict, not harmony, is the real basis of freedom.

Reading British philosophers helped me a great deal in understanding the specific ambiguities of German liberal theologies. The more I read them the more Kantian I became. And as I studied Western European and American thinkers the more I secretly came to realise that it requires courage if I am going to come out into the open as a liberal. Might it not be true to say that many American and British theologians have been interested in the traditions of German liberal theology so that they can free themselves from having to engage with their own religious tradition? People who live under a liberal political system and in an open society do not need theologies that support political emancipation.

American and British theologians have discovered elements of communitarianism and a theory of material and positive freedom in the

German tradition which is fundamentally in tension with the most important traditions of political thought in the west. It annoys me how easily many theologians in Britain and America have fallen into the trap of regarding German theologians as liberal when there is so much in their thought that is blatantly illiberal. In my opinion many theologians are more interested in a mediating theology than in a genuinely liberal theology.

But we do not have to argue at this point. If religious experience is really about the individuality of the individual then we have to adopt theologies which recognise or base themselves on the inalienability of the individual. Theologians from London, Oxford or Cambridge might be interested in something quite different in the German liberal tradition than a theologian from the city of the Augsburg Confession. When Ernst Moritz Arndt thought of emigrating to England to escape Napoleonic rule, Schleiermacher responded that he could never do this himself: 'I would be no earthly use beyond the limits of Germany.' Let us take Schleiermacher seriously at this point: whoever wants to be a liberal theologian in London, Cambridge or Oxford has to do it in his or her own way, and work our precisely what it is that is to be learnt from the ambiguous positive freedom of the mainstream German liberal tradition. In any case, a contemporary Augsburg heir of this tradition, who has sought to learn from British enlightened thinkers, has no right to dictate on this matter.

Chapter 3

The Importance of Liberal Theology

Keith Ward

The liberal viewpoint

The word 'liberal' has a great many meanings, and one of the problems in speaking of 'liberal theology' is that it is very often not clear which of these meanings might be intended. I have heard some people say that liberal theologians do not believe in particular acts of God, or in miracles. Others think that liberals simply ignore Christian tradition, and accept whatever fashionable causes of the day there are as the basis of faith. And yet others, thinking of caricatures of German theologians of the nineteenth and early twentieth century like Ritschl, Harnack and Troeltsch, think that liberals interpret Christianity almost entirely in terms of moral goodness, rather than of defined dogmas, so that Jesus becomes a moral teacher, and the kingdom of God is the ideal moral community, which may come into being by human effort in the course of history.

I should say at once that I do not interpret 'liberal theology' in any of these ways, and if liberal theology has a future, it is not down one of those roads, in my opinion. Why, then, use the word 'liberal' at all? The reason is that there is a difference between forms of religious belief which permit and encourage freedom of thought and interpretation, and those which insist on rigorous adherence to defined doctrines (declared to be 'orthodox', or correct beliefs).

Obviously there is a whole range of possible positions between complete freedom to believe anything you like, and insistence on total acceptance of a set of narrowly defined beliefs. Most Christians would fall somewhere between those extremes, and towards the centre there is not much difference between liberal and orthodox believers. It is perfectly possible to be liberal and orthodox, in that middle area, accepting a set of beliefs based on authoritative revelation yet encouraging a variety of conscientious interpretations of those doctrines. To accept the term 'liberal' is to emphasise conscientious freedom of interpretation, in a carefully qualified sense, without denying the importance of tradition and authority, in an equally qualified sense, within Christian faith.

It is fairly obvious why authority should have a place in the Christian faith. Jesus taught with an authority which was absolute for his disciples. The witness of the apostles to his life, death and resurrection is fundamental to the Gospel. And for our knowledge of the God who is revealed in a new way as the Father of Jesus Christ, we depend in an essential way upon the documents of the Old and New Testament, and to a lesser extent on the reflections and traditions of the church, which is the body of Christ. To be orthodox is, minimally, to accept as reliable and trustworthy the apostolic witness to Christ, as it is preserved in the New Testament and in the life of the church.

In view of this, why should it be important to insist upon freedom of interpretation and belief, and to what extent is such freedom appropriate? Freedom of conscience has always been accepted in the Christian tradition, and it includes the freedom conscientiously to accept those beliefs which seem to oneself to be well founded and true. At the same time, some decisions about belief have always been held to place one outside the bounds of the faith. The content of the apostolic witness sets the limits of acceptable Christian belief, lacking which one places oneself outside the community of the church.

In three main ways, nevertheless, questions of belief remain open. One is that there may be more than one interpretation of the apostolic witness. A second is that there may be parts of the Bible the truth of which is not entailed by the apostolic witness to Jesus' life and teachings, which may be irrelevant to the content of that witness, and which may even seem to conflict with it. The third is that there are many things which are not part of the content of that witness, and which are therefore not settled by that authority, but which are of interest and concern to believers.

As an example of the first type of case, it may be accepted that the Sermon on the Mount' gives a generally reliable account of Jesus' teaching. But interpretations of it vary widely, from seeing it as enjoining poverty and pacifism to seeing it as asking only for consideration of the poor and restraint in self-defence. Examples of the second type would include the truth of the genealogies of Jesus in Matthew and Luke, some of the teachings on capital punishment in the Old Testament, and some passages strongly suggesting the inferiority of women in the New

Testament. Examples of the third type would be the Chalcedonian definition of the person of Christ, and consideration of the moral acceptability of possessing nuclear weapons.

What a liberal would say on such issues is that there is nothing, either in the Bible or in any set of statements by any human being or group of human beings, which declares the truth so reliably that it must be accepted by all Christians. In this they oppose those who say that either the Bible itself, or some teaching body, has the authority to declare the truth on such matters (which are not strictly part of the content of the apostolic witness) without error.

It may well be the case that one should read the Bible very carefully, and in its entirety, and that one should listen with respect to the teachings of church leaders, before presuming to form a definite opinion of one's own in such matters. It is not just a matter of saying what one thinks, without prayerful consideration of the Bible and the traditional teachings of the church. Nevertheless, there is a right and, for some, a duty (if one has the time, capacity and responsibility) to come to a conscientious decision of one's own. This is especially so in cases where there are different but well-grounded traditions of interpretation of the same basic beliefs; but sometimes changes in general human knowledge or culture will engender new problems of re-interpretation.

The Reformation background

The historical roots of such liberalism lie in the sixteenth-century Protestant Reformation, even if the Reformers might be surprised to hear it. For the Reformation saw a relocation of authority from institution to text. The Bible, available only in Greek or Latin, had been interpreted by a religious élite to a general populace which was largely illiterate. The vast majority of people had no access to the earliest available sources of Christian revelation, and so they had to rely wholly on the authority of the Church for their knowledge of the faith.

When the Bible was translated into the vernacular, it was of course still only accessible to the literate, but it was much more widely accessible, and any literate individual could now check what was said by the Church against what was written in the text. It was not what was then found that was primarily important, but the fact that the process could take place at all. The individual was given the power of judging the institution by reference to a publicly available text.

The Reformation opened the way to a wider interpretation of liberty of conscience than had been usual, by encouraging every individual to read and interpret the Bible for themselves. As John Calvin put it, 'Necessity ought not to be laid on consciences in matters in which Christ has made them free'. Calvin considered himself free to decide for himself what those matters were, and thus to decide what allegedly authoritative declarations of the church he would accept.

Whatever the political roots of the Reformation, its properly religious roots lay in this freedom of the individual to challenge the authority of any church, even his or her own. Thus the twenty first of the thirty nine Articles of the Church of England states that 'General Councils ... may err, and sometimes have erred, even in things pertaining unto God'.

This is a revolutionary principle with consequences the first Reformers might have been surprised and even shocked to see. It is a clear logical implication that, if General Councils of the Church can err, then John Calvin can err, too. Even the thirty nine Articles can err. The Bible itself remains infallible and inerrant, but anyone who reads it may err in translating or interpreting what it says. As many in the Catholic Church had feared, to put the Bible directly into the hands of the populace, and tell them they must decide for themselves who has erred in interpreting it, is to shatter the authority of any church for ever.

Of course, it is only in a certain sense that authority is undermined. Accept this principle of the 'open Bible', as it is sometimes called, and there can be no longer any infallible living personal authority in faith and morals. Yet a softer concept of authority can remain. Those who read Greek and Hebrew have greater authority in translating the text than those who cannot. Those who are familiar with centuries of reflection on the text, and who are skilled in theological discussion, presumably have an authority of scholarship. There can still be authorities, and perhaps churches have a responsibility to make known their deliberations on the sacred text, and individuals have a duty to listen carefully to them.

This is a sort of authority we are familiar with in general educational contexts. We listen to our tutors, then to learned and experienced judges, and to those whose insight and skill is clearly greater than our own. Still, we know that they are often wrong, often prejudiced in various ways, and indeed that they often dispute with one another.

So it is with the Bible. There is a reputable body of scholarship and commentary we would be wrong to neglect. But there are many traditions of interpretation, and none of them would claim to be wholly correct (or if they do, they are of course wrong). In the end, it is not true that we would be reasonable wholly to make up our own minds. But it is true that we would be reasonable to be critical in our use of authorities, seeing particularly where they disagree and why, and what their strengths and weaknesses are.

This makes very high demands on the individual. In this respect the Reformation was a positive encouragement to universal literacy, to a democratic sense of full participation in processes of decision-making, and to an acknowledgement of the legitimate diversity of human opinions. Individual Protestants may not have been very tolerant, but the whole movement of protest against the absolute authority of the church is one of the intellectual foundations of that tolerance of religious diversity which has since that time been increasingly realised in Europe, and was one of the founding principles of the United States of America.

So in England the publication of the Authorised Version of the Bible in 1611, though intended to bolster a religion established by law and to enforce conformity of religious belief throughout England, was in fact a major force encouraging the dissociation of religious belief from the authority of any institution, ecclesiastical or political, and thereby ensuring nonconformity in belief in large parts of the kingdom. The Protestant Reformation broke the unity of Western Christendom. But it also encouraged those forces of dissent and appeal to individual conscience which were to fuel the American and French revolutions. It changed the character of Christian belief by changing its focus of attention from membership of a community headed by an authoritative teaching hierarchy, to the importance of direct personal experience of God, evoked by close reading and personal interpretation of a text accessible in principle to all. That is a milestone in the religious history of Christendom no one can ignore, even if they regret it.

The nineteenth century

In the second half of the nineteenth century, another great change came over religious thought. The Protestant Reformers had denied human authority, but had retained the authority of the sacred text in full force. But with the rise of critical methods of historical study, and more rigorous techniques of textual analysis, especially in Germany, the text itself came under that close critical scrutiny that the Reformers had already applied to the Councils of the Church.

This might seem to us an entirely natural consequence of seeing that the Bible had been written by a great number of different people at different times, and had actually been collected in its present form by still other groups of people. Once criticism of human persons is allowed, one can hardly prevent it being applied to the writers and editors of texts.

There were three main contributing elements to a newly critical approach to the sacred text. One was the rise of the natural sciences. The discoveries of astronomers and geologists had shown the universe to be much bigger than the Biblical writers had supposed, and the earth to be much older than a literal reading of Genesis would suggest. These factors were fairly easily assimilable by Christians, since all one had to do was adopt a metaphorical reading of much of Scripture, which was already well accepted in principle. Nevertheless, beliefs about the nature of the earth which had been taken for granted for many years were now put in question. The Bible could no longer be seen as inerrant in every detail, without a much greater degree of metaphorical and allegorical interpretation than had been usual.

Moreover, in a universe which was now seen to be governed by apparently universal, impersonal laws of nature, it was harder to believe that God would break such laws—and in spectacular ways, like making the sun stand still—just in order to let the Israelites win a battle, or in answer to a prayer. This is not an insuperable difficulty. Isaac Newton, who virtually invented laws of nature, had no problem in believing in miracles. If God was powerful enough to make and enforce the laws of nature, God could certainly break them with impunity.

There are certainly problems about miracles. Miracles of the sort recorded in the Bible are very rare in the modern world, and some of them seem absolutely unique. Some rationale is needed of why God would perform some miracles, but not change nature in other ways, for instance to remove suffering from human life. Yet it is quite possible to accept the scientific view of a universe governed by laws of nature, and also believe that God can expand or adjust those laws for sufficiently important reasons. There is a lot that we do not yet understand about the natural world, and the influence of mental or spiritual realities upon it cannot be denied with certainty. Liberals are not committed to denying miracles. But they are committed to being prepared to look at the arguments for and against the occurrence of miracles, and to not accepting the mere fact of their being reported in Scripture as evidence that they did occur.

More difficult was the impact of Darwin's formulation of the theory of evolution by natural selection. *The Origin of Species* was published in 1859, and while it was welcomed by many Anglican clergy, including especially Charles Kingsley, it threw doubt on the doctrine that God had a good purpose in creation, and that divine providence governed the affairs of earth. Natural selection seems a very accidental, almost random process, and the universal struggle for existence which Darwin saw in nature did not seem consonant with the rule of a benevolent God.

Nevertheless, nature can be viewed in a more benevolent light than it is by some advocates of evolution. The process of evolution can be seen as a striving for fuller life, and a process which has a natural propensity to generate consciousness and moral responsibility. It does not have to be seen as unforeseen accident. But what was thrown into doubt was the general biblical worldview of a world of angels and demons who are battling for the souls of human beings, quite recently ejected from Paradise, and waiting expectantly (some of them, anyway) for the end of the world and the return of the Saviour on the clouds. The scientific world-view was more compatible with an idea of a supremely rational God who had set up the general laws of the universe and let them work themselves out over vast stretches of time, extending into a distant cosmic future of which this earth is only a tiny part, but who did not specifically create human beings as its centre and goal. Some views of God's providential action would also have to be amended, to allow for the elements of random mutation in evolution, and the morally neutral nature of basic genetic laws. So the world-view of the Bible was put in question, and by those who accept the findings of the best natural science of the day, the Bible came to be regarded as a product of a scientifically naive time and culture, and not the very words of an omniscient God, who provided hitherto unknown information about how the world began and about early human history.

The second critical element was the rise of history as a science or rigorously evidential discipline, and of new techniques of textual analysis. Once the Bible was seen as a collection of ancient documents, and analysed like any other such collection, it came to be seen in a new light. It remained an extraordinary and compelling text, but one began to see more clearly the piecemeal nature of its construction, and the culturally influenced beliefs of its writers. No longer could the four gospels be regarded as various aspects of one harmonious total narrative of the life of Jesus. Instead, they were seen as four very different documents written for different groups, expressing different interests, and putting things in rather different ways. It might still be possible to say that the Bible was inspired, but the human forms and limits of that inspiration became very much more apparent.

Thirdly, as philosophers increasingly rejected the authority of the church, criticism of the Bible from a moral point of view became more pointed. F. D. Maurice's rejection of eternal Hell on moral grounds was one instance of such criticism. Other examples would be some Biblical attitudes to women, to sexuality, and to political authority, to which one might add an apparent lack of concern with those issues of global justice and social inequality which moved the great English social reformers like John Stuart Mill.

It is important to see that such criticism was not the rejection of the Bible in favour of some secular viewpoint. It was a probing of traditional interpretations (e.g. that women should not have authority over men), in the light of more basic moral principles of the New Testament (that Christ liberates from the letter of the law, offers fulfilment to everyone without exception, and declares God's love to be without limits). The general consequence was that the letter of many Biblical texts (stoning homosexuals to death, perhaps) could be rejected in favour of general, more basic Biblical principles (of respecting humanity in everyone). Such a process is not by any means confined to liberals, but liberals, who insist on the right of responsible private interpretation, will probably have less difficulty in rejecting literal interpretations of Scriptural passages.

So the Bible came to be generally seen, not as the last divine word on the nature of things, on what actually happened in history, and on the great moral issues facing humanity. Rather, it was a collection of documents which was often mistaken in its understanding of the physical cosmos, which routinely incorporated legend and mythology into its accounts of historical fact, and which often expressed the rather limited moral outlooks of the culture in which it was promulgated.

Liberal theology and revelation

It might well be felt that this was a change so great that religion could not survive, and there were many, like Auguste Comte, who predicted its imminent demise. The change was certainly a major blow to classical Protestantism, with its strong emphasis on the inerrancy of Scripture. From that time on, Christians found themselves divided in a new way, not into Catholic and Protestant, but into traditional and liberal. The traditionalists wish to insist on a supreme teaching authority, either Church or Bible, which could be trusted in every detail and on every topic. Liberals accept the general findings of the natural sciences, try to take account of critical discussions of Scripture in historical and textual matters, and accept the possibility of formulating new moral insights in new social contexts. As I have said, liberals can be very conservative. But the final test is this: if they accept, for instance, the Genesis account of creation, the high reliability of the biblical historical records, and the correctness of the Bible's moral teaching, it is because they think these things are true, not because they accept them on authority. They do not say, 'This is the case because the Bible says so, and the Bible cannot err'. They say, 'These accounts can be defended by informed scientific opinion, historical scholarship, and moral argument. This confirms the reliability of the Bible in these respects.'

An unfriendly critic might try to say that liberals are subjecting revelation to the bar of Reason, as though the Word of God could be judged by human beings. This criticism is, however, so unfriendly that it is positively unjust. Revelation is not in question. It is accepted that God discloses the divine nature and purpose to human beings, who do not just make up these things by speculation or imagination.

There is a question, however, about the nature of revelation. Does it consist in the promulgation of sentences in a natural language? Or is it more a matter of a personal disclosure of the being of God, whether that occurs in inner experience or in an objective event, as interpreted by a prophet? It could, of course, be both, and many people think that it is. But it seems a very natural interpretation of Christian faith to say that revelation is given primarily in a person, in the person of Jesus. It is in the life, death and resurrection of Jesus, and in the experience of the

Holy Spirit which transformed the lives of the disciples after Jesus' resurrection, that God acts to disclose the divine nature and purpose in a new way. The objective historical events of Jesus' life and death are important, though to be taken as religious phenomena they have to be seen as disclosing God, which involves a specific personal attitude, a receptivity to such disclosure. The inner experience of renewal in the Spirit is also important, and it both depends upon and evokes a passionate commitment in those who experience it.

It thus seems that the model of Christian revelation is a personal discernment of the presence and activity of God, in the person of Jesus and in the community of disciples which gathered in memory of him. The only records we have of that discernment are to be found in the New Testament, and so the New Testament becomes the essential witness to the revelation of God in the person of Jesus. Because it consists of many documents, including occasional letters, written by many authors in the light of local problems and conditions, it is reasonable to expect that it will express many rather different and culturally conditioned viewpoints, not excluding some restrictions of vision and blurred or somewhat embroidered memories. This expectation is corroborated by the texts themselves, which contain varying accounts of the events of Jesus' life, differing in detail, while agreeing on the basic facts and their general significance.

Though this may seem the natural view to take of Christian revelation, it was not clearly and explicitly formulated until Friedrich Schleiermacher propounded his view that all Christian doctrines are founded upon personal experience, the experience of 'God-consciousness' as evoked by the Spirit and fully and definitively expressed in Jesus. This was not a matter of subjecting revelation to the bar of Reason. Indeed, Schleiermacher was explicitly rejecting Immanuel Kant's interpretation of Christian faith (and Kant was not a practising Christian) in exclusively rational and moral terms. Kant did want a religion without revelation, but Schleiermacher set out to propose an alternative view which would preserve a proper place for revelation, and would replace speculative Reason by personal experience. If there has to be a general term to cover late eighteenth and early nineteenth century attitudes to religion, it would be Romanticism rather than Rationalism.

The attempt was not at all to make the Christian faith conform to Reason – that was more characteristic of Anselm and Aquinas than of Ritschl and Harnack. In fact one of Harnack's criticisms of traditional dogmas was that they were too rationalistic, formulated in terms of Hellenistic philosophy, and Ritschl rejected reason as a source of religious truth. Both Harnack and Ritschl distrusted 'mystical' experience, and stressed the moral claims of Christian faith, and the central place of intuitive value-judgements. This form of German liberal theology was thus based on seeing revelation as a unique form of disclosure, either an 'intuition of the infinite' (by which Schleiermacher meant an apprehension of the infinite, not some sort of subjective feeling), or of supreme value (Ritschl). They stressed that revelatory experience must involve personal commitment and take place in community – thereby distinguishing it, they thought, from what they called the 'mystical' type of experience, which they saw as individualistic and morally indifferent. One can only conclude that those who accuse these liberals of trying to subordinate faith to reason cannot have read them at all.

Of course liberal Christians do not have to believe what Schleiermacher, Ritschl, or Harnack believed. Nonetheless, if the heart of liberalism lies in not accepting the authority of humans or of scriptural texts as unquestionably binding, a liberal must have some account of revelation which is not propositional (consisting in divine provision of inerrant sentences). An account in terms of a unique type of faith-discernment, closely associated both with personal value-commitment and with a tradition of such discernments preserved in a distinctive community, is in my view likely to be the most adequate. And that is precisely what the classical liberal theologians provided.

The future of liberal theology

Such an account of revelation would explain how one can be critical of all forms of authority (that is, not accepting their particular pronouncements without question and proper enquiry), and still assent to a faith which is firmly founded on an alleged historical revelation from God which, because it happened so long ago, can only be known to have occurred on authority. We criticise the people who tell us of it. We criticise the text which claims to record it. By what right, then, can we believe it?

For traditional thinking there is some institutionalised group or some particular text that sets out doctrines of faith that are exclusively, irrevocably and absolutely true. Revelation is embodied in propositions all of which are finally definitive for the faithful. The liberal view, though not all liberal Christians need put it exactly like this, is that revelation is not exclusive, unrevisable and inerrant in this propositional way. The liberal interpretation in some ways returns to older, very early Christian traditions which stressed much more the mystery of faith, and the symbolic nature of Christian language and imagery. Revelation is basically a self-disclosure of God. Just as God is beyond direct literal description, so disclosures of God cannot be exhaustively defined in particular propositions. The self-disclosure of God is an unveiling of the living reality of God to those whose eyes have been opened by the Spirit to perceive it.

On this view, the church does not preserve revelation by formulating correct propositions. It is a community or tradition which preserves revelation by evoking anew in each generation the self-disclosure of God which originated in and through the person of Jesus. This can be evoked by ritual, imagery, and poetry better than by quasi-scientific definitions. And the central mysteries of faith are safeguarded by words which leave open the possibility of such self-disclosure, rather than by requiring assent to certain culturally influenced sets of concepts.

The Bible does not preserve revelation by giving factually correct accounts of ancient history or of abstruse philosophical problems. It is a text used by a community to help re-evoke a specific discernment of God which is associated with the life of Jesus, and which has been handed down, elaborated and reinterpreted in every generation. The puzzle about how one can treat as authoritative a text which is subject to continual critical scrutiny is resolved by seeing that the authority of the text lies in its use by the community to express and evoke present discernments of God. Discovering more about the circumstances in which the texts were written, the cultures to which they originally spoke, and the variety of insights that their writers expressed, can and should increase their power to stimulate personal discernments in the community which receives them as an authentic and tested vehicle of divine self-disclosure.

If doctrines are means to expressing and evoking disclosures of the divine, they need not be taken as exclusive and irrevocable. Indeed, it becomes rather odd to take them in that way. Particular doctrinal formulations will be interpretations of the primary text or of extrapolations from it, issued at a specific time and place, and will display the cultural limitations and insights of that time and place. One would thus expect that very different cultures would generate different formulations of doctrine. Doctrines will, in other words, change and develop, as human understanding, one hopes, increases by continued reflection on the primary text, in its relation to ever-changing contexts of knowledge and experience.

Liberal Christians can seek to take account of this by, for example, encouraging a search for reformulations of eucharistic doctrine which might overcome old hostilities between Catholics and Protestants. They may also see that once an understanding of faith as acceptance of exclusively correct propositions is given up, one can no longer simply say that the Christian faith has the only truth, and that all others are wrong. If faith is response to a disclosure of the divine in this community, then why should there not be different disclosures of the divine in other communities?

Communities of faith can be seen as communities of discernment and empowerment. They consist of people who (or some of whom at least) have discerned the divine through some originative person or event, and who have found themselves empowered to new life-transforming commitments by that discernment. In the texts and rituals of their community, the originative events, continued reflection upon them, and long and varied experience of living in response to them, are expressed in largely symbolic, metaphorical ways.

The Christian churches are communities which discern the divine in and through the life of Jesus. That life is expressed, both in the New Testament and in the devotional life of a particular church, in largely symbolic ways, so as to have the function of evoking further discernments, requiring in turn new symbols and metaphors, as the community extends through time.

Christians will naturally claim that these discernments are authentic, and that they bring forms of empowerment which transform, enrich and fulfil truly human lives. But they need not, and perhaps should not, claim that as a result they have unique access to a set of irrevocable philosophical or moral truths. To be sure, some truths will be implicit in Christian practice, but it may be extremely difficult to state in clear propositions exactly what these are, and almost impossible, given the limitations of human understanding, to state them in ways not subject to further revision.

It also becomes impossible to deny the possibility of such discernments to those who are not Christians, but who similarly claim revelations of the divine. Non-Christian faiths come to be seen, not as sets of beliefs which contradict Christian beliefs, and are therefore mistaken, but as sets of symbols for discerning the divine which are indeed different from Christian symbols, but do not necessarily contradict them.

Even where contradictions do exist, so that Christians are bound to affirm the distinctive veracity of their own beliefs, there might still be much for Christians to learn from the insights of other traditions, however ambiguous or limited they may be thought to be. The Second Vatican Council of the Roman Catholic Church recognised this, in propounding clearly, for the first time in official Roman Catholic statements, that non-Christians may be saved, and that the Holy Spirit is at work invisibly in the hearts of all men and women. To be sure, they added that the fulness of truth is still to be found in the Roman Catholic Church. But the seeds of a recognition of a genuine plurality of religious traditions, as different communities of faith rooted in distinctive symbols for discerning and mediating the divine, had been sown.

The move to a more symbolic, discernment-evoking interpretation of faith is more unambiguously made in much Protestant thinking of the mid-twentieth century, but should not be thought of as a distinctively Protestant phenomenon. It is found in the Roman Catholic theologians Karl Rahner and Hans Küng as well as in the Anglicans and Protestants, Ian Ramsey, John Macquarrie, John Hick and Maurice Wiles in England, and Paul Tillich in America. It is not the preserve of extreme radical thought. It is more a product of a growing global awareness, the astonishing increase in modern scientific knowledge, together with an increased sensitivity to the distinctive character of religious language, all of which characterise the mid-twentieth century. In such a cultural situation, religion is separated off from science as a distinct form of human culture, and faith becomes the passionate commitment to a symbolically expressed discernment of supreme value, rather than assent to a set of irrevocably true propositions. The many religious faiths are seen as parts of the whole religious history of humanity, and Christianity is one community of discernment among others, not the only source of religious truth. A major goal of religious practice is to realise wholeness of life for all, rather than the salvation of a few chosen elect. And the role of the Christian church is seen to be that of a particular community called to serve the world in love, rather than to claim sovereignty over the political rulers and philosophers of the world.

It could be argued that liberal theology marks the decay of Christian faith, and an inevitable journey of our culture towards full secularism. But that journey has been undertaken precisely because traditional interpretations have been tried and found intellectually and spiritually wanting. The crucial question for the religious life of the modern world is whether Christianity in any of its forms can continue to capture hearts and minds as it has done for two thousand years, or whether it will be superseded by something else – as it already has been in the eyes of many. A liberal faith is one that is committed to a quest for the truth about ultimate reality, and for a way of turning from egoism towards relationship with supreme value, but also fully open to the intellectual and moral challenges of a consciously global society. It is the great strength of Christian faith that more than two hundred years ago it clearly established liberalism as a movement which was seen to spring from the very heart of Christian faith in Jesus as the personal revelation of God, and in the Spirit as the divine agent of dynamic change and new creative insight.

Liberal theology is not a movement which belonged to nineteenth-century Germany, a movement rooted in a shallow optimism about human progress and an arrogance about the powers of human reason, but which has now been superseded. It is instead a movement which looks for the roots of faith in a discernment of the infinite God which occurred in a new way through Jesus, and which still carries the challenge to every generation to evoke its own life-changing discernments through participation in the communities which spring from that paradigmatic source. It places faith above reason, worship above speculation, and moral and spiritual commitment above doctrinal correctness. It accepts above all the ambiguity of the human heart and the myopia of the human intellect, even as they respond to the self-disclosure of God which is the source and goal of faith. Such a humble, trusting, self-critical but passionately committed faith is desperately needed in a world which longs for spiritual experience but is in danger of losing touch with its religious traditions. For that reason, liberal theology has a future which is assured, and which can contribute in a positive way to the renewal of Christian faith in the world of the third millennium.

Chapter 4

'But who am I?'

The Question of the Theologian rather than the Question to the Theologian

David A. Pailin

Introduction

In this chapter 'liberal theology' primarily refers to that form of theological reflection found in Britain that seeks to show that what it presents is both meaningful and significant in the contemporary situation and credible according to the appropriate forms of rational truth-testing for such understanding. It has antecedents in the long tradition of natural theology found in British thought, from the late seventeenth century, that declines to regard any supposed religious authorities, be it in the form of institutional decisions or religious texts, as determinative, and attempts, more or less successfully, to establish the content and truth of basic theistic belief by considering the character of human experience of the world in which people find themselves. This type of liberal theology is thus to be distinguished from another type of theology also called 'liberal theology' that starts from something supposedly authoritative given in the tradition or practice of faith and then seeks to apply to it more or less 'liberal' modes of critical interpretation and application. One of the demands upon both the liberal theology as here understood and, *mutatis mutandis*, the exegetical form of liberal theology, however, is that it should manifest and warrant itself as significant for human beings in the world today. This chapter focuses on some of the implications of this demand, the satisfaction of which is critical for the future credibility of theological understanding.

Theology and mumbo jumbo

A cartoon by Steve Bell in the *Guardian* in February 1999 portrayed Tony Blair as an irate teacher sending Glenn Hoddle[1] out of the room for 'peddling the wrong kind of mumbo jumbo'. On the blackboard behind Blair is written:

> 'Virgin Birth √ OK
> Transubstantiation √ OK
> Dead babies go (unchristened) to Limbo √ OK
> Reincarnation X Not while I'm alive'[2]

The cartoon expresses how many people affected (perhaps one might say infected) by the secularism of the day regard much of what they think they hear (and probably do hear) when they listen to theologians.[3] It seems to them to be 'mumbo jumbo', albeit a high class of mumbo jumbo with an impressive degree of abstruseness. What often puzzles them is why theologians become so excited about it and why, in particular, some theologians condemn what other theologians say as being nonsense. Not only to secularist outsiders but also to many struggling, with Anselm, to understand faith from within, such theological disputes appear to be a case of the pot calling the kettle black. Do any of the assertions make sense? And if they do, what kind of a sense is it?

In case one doubts this description of theology, consider what sense and significance the following assertions may be expected to have for people whom one might meet in the train, especially those who are aware of what current cosmological, biological, and epistemological investigations inform us about the cosmos and about our understanding of it: 'maker of heaven and earth, and of all things visible and invisible', 'begotten, not made, being of one substance with the Father', and 'came down from heaven and was incarnate by the Holy Spirit of the Virgin

[1] Hoddle had been the coach for the English football team but had lost his post after allegedly suggesting that deeds in former lives might explain why some people were disabled.

[2] The *Guardian*, 2 February 1999, p. 16.

[3] It would be exaggerating to say when they 'read' what theologians write as hardly any of them would read what deserves to be classed as theology, in distinction from the pseudo-religious fantasies peddled by popularising writers from 'the aliens have landed' type through purveyors of the occult to vapid forms of psychologism.

Mary';[4] or 'the Catholick Faith is this: That we worship one God in Trinity, and Trinity in Unity; neither confounding the Persons: nor dividing the Substance' and 'it is necessary to everlasting salvation: that he also believe ... that our Lord Jesus Christ ... is God and Man; God, of the Substance of the Father, begotten before the worlds: and Man, of his Mother, born in the world; ... of a reasonable soul and human flesh subsisting'.[5] Or one might ponder the notorious example of a medieval debate about how many angels can dance on the point of a pin. When, against satirists, it is pointed out that the issue is not a recondite debate about topology but a question about whether angels have spatial extension, the clarification does not seem to make a solution to the debate any more important for life in today's world.

It may seem a cheap trick to lampoon theology by quoting ancient creeds and medieval debates. While, however, contemporary theology is typically too verbose to provide a source of neat quotations to make the same point, to those not professionally engaged in it, it often appears to be manifest mumbo jumbo. In *Human, All Too Human: A Book for Free Spirits*, Friedrich Nietzsche remarks

> When on a Sunday morning we hear the bells ringing we ask ourselves: is it possible! this is going on because of a Jew crucified 2000 years ago ... A god who begets children on a mortal woman; a sage who calls upon us no longer to work, no longer to sit in judgement, but to heed the signs of the imminent end of the world; a justice which accepts an innocent man as a substitute sacrifice; someone who bids his disciples drink his blood; prayers for miraculous interventions; sin perpetrated against a god atoned for by a god; ... how gruesome all this is wafted to us, as if out of the grave of a primeval past! Can one believe that things of this sort are still believed in?[6]

If theologians are not haunted by this remark, they ought to be.

[4] The previous three quotations are statements from the so-called Nicene Creed.

[5] The previous two quotations are from the *Quicunque Vult* or so-called Creed of St Athanasius.

[6] Friedrich Nietzsche, *Human, All Too Human: A Book for Free Spirits*, tr. R. J. Hollingdale, intro. E. Heller, Cambridge: Cambridge University Press, 1986, §113, pp. 65-6.

Criteria for significant belief

How then are statements of belief, in particular statements expressing Christian faith, to be shown to be authentic, meaningful and credible? Various criteria can be and have been suggested. It may then be argued that statements of belief that satisfy such criteria are thereby shown to be significant. Among such criteria are the following ten.

The first two are found in two short but packed works in which Maurice Wiles explores *The Making of Christian Doctrine* and *The Remaking of Christian Doctrine*.[7] In the earlier of these works, having examined the factors influencing the development of doctrine (in particular the roles of scripture, worship, and the experience of salvation), he concludes that 'the test of a true development in doctrine is not whether it preserves' the original forms of what was once held but whether it 'continues' the doctrinal objectives of the Church 'in a way which is effective and creative in the contemporary world'.[8] Wiles then takes up in the later work the challenge of suggesting where such development may currently lead the doctrines of God, the person and work of Christ, grace, and the Holy Spirit if it be guided by the twin 'aims' (or 'objectives') of 'coherence' and 'economy'. The former requires the theologian to check that her or his affirmations are in some appropriate way 'consistent with each other'; the latter that what is maintained is warranted by the evidence. As Wiles himself acknowledges (and as his critics bewailed), the application of these objectives may lead to 'the pruning of some luxuriant growths that have come to be highly valued'.[9]

The third and fourth criteria are presented in an important essay by Schubert Ogden, 'What is Theology?' Ogden maintains that the adequacy of a theological statement of 'the Christian witness' as 'decisive for human existence' is shown by the way it satisfies 'the two criteria of appropriateness and credibility ... in the given situation'. While Ogden's own interpretation of the former criterion may be deemed too narrow in requiring a theological statement, in order to be authentically Christian, to represent 'the same understanding of the faith as is expressed in the "datum discourse" of normative Christian witness', the basic de-

[7] Maurice Wiles, *The Making of Christian Doctrine: A study in the principles of early doctrinal development*, Cambridge: Cambridge University Press, 1967; *The Remaking of Christian Doctrine*, London: SCM Press, 1974.

[8] *The Making of Christian Doctrine*, p. 177.

[9] *The Remaking of Christian Doctrine*, pp. 17-18. Anticipating the reaction of unfriendly critics, Wiles states that these aims are not 'euphemisms for "rationalism" and "reductionism"'.

mand (namely, that what claims to be a statement of the Christian faith be identifiably *Christian* in some pertinent way) is not obviously controversial.[10] The other criterion, that of credibility, requires the theological statement to satisfy 'the relevant conditions of truth universally established with human existence'.[11]

Gordon Kaufman's analysis of the constructive character of the concept of God at the heart of theological understanding proposes, fifthly and sixthly, the criteria of the tests of relativising and of humanising. A proper concept of God is that of an absoluteness that relativises all else and accordingly calls 'into question everything we do and are and experience'. Putting our concerns in their proper perspective and demanding of us 'continuous criticism of ourselves, our values and ideas, our activities and customs and institutions', it undermines all idolatrous tendencies 'to identify our wants and programs with God's will'. Nevertheless, 'at the same time' it is also to be 'apprehended as ultimately humane and beneficent, that which fulfills and completes our humanity; and that in which we can put our full confidence' since it affirms truly human(e) values and promises 'ultimate human realisation or fulfil-

[10] Ogden's demand that the touchstone for the criterion of appropriateness be the original 'datum discourse' does not necessarily conflict with Wiles's denial of the need to preserve the early formulations of the faith since Ogden also recognises the necessity of demythologising the 'datum discourse' (whatever it be determined to be) in order to understand it in the contemporary world. On the other hand, while the criterion of appropriateness itself may not be controversial, the use of a criterion of this type as the decisive one for determining the nature and content of theology, as in views of theological understanding put forward by Gustav Aulén, Anders Nygren (with reference to Wittgensteinian views of understanding), and George Lindbeck (with reference to postmodernist views of understanding), is open to radical challenge. See David A. Pailin, 'Theological Truth within the Circle? Evading the Spider's Parlour', in André Cloots and Santiago Sia (eds), *Framing a Vision for the World: Essays in Philosophy, Science and Religion*, Leuven: Leuven University Press, 1999.

[11] Schubert M. Ogden, *On Theology*, San Francisco: Harper and Row, 1986, pp. 4-5; see also Schubert M. Ogden, *Doing Theology Today*, Valley Forge: Trinity Press International, 1996, p. 9: systematic theology must show that its witness 'is appropriate to Jesus Christ, in the sense that what is thought, said and done ... suitably expresses the experience of Jesus that is properly Christian', and that it is 'credible to human existence, in the sense that what Christians think, say, and do in bearing it is worthy of belief, practically as well as theoretically, by any woman or man simply as a human being'.

ment'.[12] As such it gives both orientation and motivation to human being.[13]

A seventh criterion that must be met by theological expressions of theistic faith, if their claims to be significant are to be seen to be warranted, is highlighted by Hans-Georg Gadamer's hermeneutical point that 'every age has to understand a transmitted text'—or, we may add, an inherited system of theological understanding—'in its own way'. What is received only makes sense as and so far as it can be and is applied to current situations. Such 'application' neither follows nor is an accidental part of understanding what is being considered; it is a necessary component of the act of understanding itself.[14] It thus follows that in order for theological statements to show themselves not to be mere verbiage, they must be perceived to be applicable to current modes of human being, individual or social.

The requirement of applicability leads to (or perhaps itself includes) a further, eighth, criterion. This is that if theological expressions of Christian faith are to show themselves to be authentic, meaningful and credible, they must satisfy what I sometimes refer to as the 'Bright Hour Test'. The 'Bright Hour' are a group of elderly ladies who meet regularly. Those who presume to address them about faith's understanding should bear in mind that while none of them has had any formal higher education, they do have a huge amount of experience of life. If, therefore, what is said to them is to be significant, it needs to make sense of what they find in that experience to be the case—to apply faith, that is, to a world and to events which they can identify as being real, not to spin what their experience identifies as fairy-tales about a cloud-cuckoo land of pietistic imagination. As the members of the Bright Hour show, one does not have to be able to articulate the formal principles of empirical verification and falsification to be able to recognise whether what is being asserted about the significance of faith makes sense of the situations in which people actually find themselves.[15]

[12] Gordon D. Kaufman, *An Essay on Theological Method*, third edition, Atlanta: Scholars Press, 1995, pp. 67-8 (first edition, 1975, pp. 53-4).

[13] Cf. Gordon Kaufman, *In Face of Mystery: A Constructive Theology*, Cambridge, Mass.: Harvard University Press, 1993, p. 47.

[14] Hans-Georg Gadamer, *Truth and Method*, London: Sheed & Ward,1975, pp. 263, 289; see also William C. Placher, *Unapologetic Theology: A Christian Voice in a Pluralistic Conversation*, Louisville: Westminster/John Knox Press, 1989, pp. 112-13.

[15] Cf. Kaufman, *In Face of Mystery*, p. 30: 'If God is to be the ultimate point of reference for understanding and orienting *us* in the world in which *we* live,

A ninth criterion for significant theological understanding is highlighted by John Henry Newman's contrast between 'real' and 'notional' forms of apprehension and assent. In the *Grammar of Assent* he maintains that since 'what is concrete exerts a force and makes an impression on the mind which nothing abstract can rival', it is important for the effectiveness of faith for believers to apprehend that on which it is focused as a reality rather than as what may be described as a *mere* idea.[16] While this requirement may be treated as a development of the criteria of applicability and actuality, it is sufficiently important to deserve drawing separate attention to it. For instance, while historical reports provide evidence that in the past presentations of the death of Jesus as an atoning sacrifice or as a ransom from fiendish captivity or as a defeat of powers of darkness gripped people as speaking to their condition as they perceived it and as announcing its proper remedy, for many people today such traditional models no longer describe what they can apprehend as a reality for and in their existence. Whatever the theological significance of that death, at best such models are now apprehended by them as abstract notions. As such they have little or no 'bite'. If they are to be effective, faith statements need to find forms of expression that people grasp as referring to brute realities.

Finally, and most importantly of all,[17] there is, tenthly, the criterion of verifiability.[18] It is important to show that what is theologically affirmed can for good reasons be held to be true. While, as with the other criteria that have been mentioned, there are many debatable issues about how this criterion is to be implemented in practice, the most fruit-

then our contemporary experience and knowledge and problems must themselves function as a criterion to be taken into account in criticising conceptions of God received from tradition and in formulating notions adequate for today.'

[16] John Henry Newman, *An Essay in Aid of a Grammar of Assent*, London: Burns, Oates, & Co., 1870, p. 34.

[17] 'Most importantly', that is, for those who consider that truth-questions are legitimate and, to a significant degree, answerable – and those postmodernists who reject that this is so seem to imply that faith claims and theological assertions are to be classed as affirmations shared by the members of self-selecting intellectual ghettos but as having no verifiable relationship to what is actually the case. As with the scepticism that asserts that it is unqualifiedly 'true', such a position arguably contradicts itself by absolutising the essential relativity of understanding that it is concerned to highlight. For more on this, see Pailin, 'Theological Truth within the Circle? Evading the Spider's Parlour'.

[18] Although Ogden's criterion of 'credibility' may be considered to have already covered the test of verification, I consider that since it is determinative, it merits independent mention.

ful procedure seems to be that which seeks to show that the theological understanding under review makes sense of reality as a whole in a way that appears to be less beset with problems than any alternative way of understanding.[19] Admittedly such a test rests on the principle of rationality, namely that things ultimately do make sense and make sense in a manner that human beings are capable of perceiving, but this is a principle that underlies all attempts at understanding, even of those who conclude that things do not ultimately make sense. It also presupposes that the inescapable conditioning of understanding does not make the general demand for rational justification impossible, a presupposition that underlies the conviction that there is a basic and not merely an intra-systemic difference between some cases of truth and error.

If theology is to evade the charge of presenting mumbo jumbo, however long-standing and however esoteric that mumbo jumbo may be, it cannot evade the demand that it show that what it puts forward satisfies each of the above ten criteria in a rationally significant manner. A statement of belief that fails to satisfy any one of them is shown thereby to be an importantly deficient expression of the Christian faith. While the failure may not show that the statement must thereupon be consigned to the waste bin as rubbish, the failure does show that it faces a serious problem in establishing its significance.

Is anything else needed for belief to be significant?

While theological understanding may accept the demand that it justify itself by the ten criteria and while it may make an impressive attempt to meet them, it may still be that what results does not thereupon immediately secure recognition as significant. Why is this? Why is it that, even if it succeeds in satisfying these tests, theology may still fail to impress? Even if satisfying the criteria prevents people from superficially dismissing it as mumbo jumbo, they may nevertheless not see it as anything more interesting than words, ideas and theories that do not stir them. Is this because something important is lacking?

In *Honest to God* John Robinson writes of areas of 'traditional Christian expression', particularly concerned with devotion, that 'have *not* rung a bell' with him and with others he has come to know but

[19] Cf. David A. Pailin, 'The Credibility of Theism: The Question of Verification', pp. 203-28, in idem, *Probing the Foundations: A Study in Theistic Reconstruction*, Kampen: Kok Pharos, 1994.

rather 'have simply left one cold'.[20] Later he quotes George Macleod's reference to a 'bankrupt corner' in people's libraries. This contains works that have been acquired in the persistent hope that sometime something will actually help. Each in turn, however, has failed.[21] Today this may be the experience of those who open theological works. What are hoped to provide resources to be quarried turn out, for many at least, to have nothing to offer. Why do these books taken up in hope fail to deliver what is wanted?

The answer may be that those who read them had unreal expectations about what such books could provide. Alternatively, it may be that those who acquired them have since abandoned them because they have come to suspect that theology peddles childish illusions – and they want to grow up.[22] In the particular case of liberal theology,[23] it may also be that the secularism of the age has pushed people into one or other of two ghettos that deny the possibility of reasonable belief, the ghetto of scepticism and the ghetto of credulity. As a result, like others who have sought to establish a rationally credible form of theological understanding,[24] those who produce liberal theology find that they affirm too much to please the sceptics and too little to please the credulous.

Nevertheless, although such responses may throw light on some of the reasons why liberal and other forms of theology that avoid being completely ignored are suspected by many people of offering either straightforward mumbo jumbo or pretentious speculative ideas, there may be a further and deeper reason why theology is considered not to be a significant form of understanding, even of religious faith. It is argu-

[20] John A. T. Robinson, *Honest to God*, London: SCM Press, 1963, p. 19.

[21] Ibid., p. 95.

[22] While Sigmund Freud's arguments to justify his view of religion as an illusion may be judged unconvincing, the interpretation itself seems convincing to many people.

[23] As mentioned in the opening paragraph of this chapter, by 'liberal theology' is meant those who inherit that tradition of rational theological understanding whose English forebears in the seventeenth and eighteenth centuries were those who sought to identify and establish what it is 'reasonable' to believe.

[24] It is a fate that has affected the reputation of a liberal theologian of a previous age, Herbert of Cherbury. Richard Baxter, for example, comments that Herbert's position was 'too low' for those who accept divine revelations as 'certain verities' but 'too high for the atheistical sensualists of his age' (*The Practical Works of Richard Baxter*, London, 1830, vol. 21, p. 522). A similar judgement is made by John Leland (in spite of his hostility to Herbert) in his *View of the Principal Deistical Writers*, London, 1754, vol. 1, pp. 7, 13.

able, at least in many cases, that something vital is missing from its reflections. Before, then, we are tempted to engage in complex rational arguments to show what is and what is not properly to be judged to meet the ten criteria outlined above, we should consider whether the basic problem is that liberal and other forms of theological understanding typically tend to forget what they are about.

The suspicion that this may be the case has bothered me for some time. Recently it was highlighted when I read a sermon delivered to members of the House of Commons. While the preacher was primarily concerned to discuss the doctrinal disagreements within Christianity that have led to 'many large Volumes and Discourses written' about Christology, he points out the error of 'Bookish Christians, that have all their Religion in writings and papers,' and 'think they ... cannot possibly miss the way to Heaven; as if Religion were nothing but a little *Book-craft*, a mere *Paper-skill*'.[25] They need to recognise that the truth about the Christian faith is that

> He is a true Christian indeed, not he that is only *book-taught*, but ... he that hath the Spirit of *Christ* within him, ... Ink and Paper can never make us Christians, can never beget a new nature, a living principle in us; ... Cold Theorems and Maxims, dry and jejune Disputes, lean Syllogistical reasonings, could never yet of themselves ... convey the living notions of heavenly Truths to us.[26]

Just as a painter may give a likeness of a rose but 'can never paint the scent and fragrancy,' so 'words and letters' cannot give 'the Life, Soul and Essence of any Spiritual Truths'.[27]

Christianity, which is defined as '*the knowledge of Christ*', in practice is a matter of 'keeping his Commandments'; it does not '*consist merely in a few barren Notions, in a form of certain dry and sapless opinions*'. This is because

> *Christ* came not to possess our brains only with some cold opinions, that send down nothing but a freezing and benumming influence upon our hearts. *Christ* was *Vitæ Magister*, not *Scholæ*: and he is the best

[25] Ralph Cudworth, 'The First Sermon; or a Discourse on I JOHN Chap. II. Vers. 3, 4', in *A Discourse concerning the True Notion of the Lord's Supper. To which are added Two Sermons*, Third Edition, London, 1676, pp. 39-40.

[26] Ibid., p. 40 ; cf. pp. 52-3.

[27] Ibid., p. 41.

> Christian, whose Heart beats with the truest pulse towards heaven; not he whose Head spinneth out the finest cobwebs.[28]

While the preacher makes it clear that he is no immured believer who rejects 'free and ingenuous enquiry into all Truth, according to our several abilities and opportunities,' and that he does not defend 'captivating and enthralling our judgments to the Dictates of men', what he does oppose is

> the dispiriting of the life and vigour of our Religion by dry Speculations, and making it nothing but a mere dead *Sceleton* of *Opinions*, a few dry bones without any flesh and sinews tied up together, and the mis-placing of all our zeal upon an eager prosecution of these, which should be spent to better purpose upon other objects.[29]

To prevent misunderstanding about the theological concerns and competence of the House of Commons, it should be noted that this sermon was preached to the members (or to those of them that were still there) over 350 years ago[30] by Ralph Cudworth. Its points, however, are still pertinent.[31] As we consider the future of theology, whether it be liberal or any other kind, the sermon reminds us that authentic faith, and so authentic theology as it seeks to investigate, expound, revise and justify the understanding that identifies (but does not constitute) the core of faith, is about the foundations of people's lives.

When authentic, faith pervades and moulds all the aspects of personal and social living. It cannot be separated from them as if it were a distinguishable and perhaps an optional feature – as if it were more like belonging to a lacrosse team or choosing to eat yoghurt than like drinking water or sharing a language. Indeed, evidence of the decline of authentic faith in the eighteenth century is provided by the way in which the word 'religion' (which Cudworth uses to refer to the life of faith)

[28] Ibid., p. 43.

[29] Ibid., p. 45. Presumably, in modern terms, Cudworth is holding that there is nothing wrong with intellectual endeavour so long as it be not an antiquarian and pointless study of texts and problems that contribute nothing significant to the enhancement of life today.

[30] On 31 March 1647.

[31] It is arguable that Cudworth should have taken the points that he makes in this sermon more to heart in his later years. His *True Intellectual System of the Universe*, which was published in folio in 1678, has 917 pages of text and another 87 pages listing the contents in double columns. Furthermore, what was published is only the first part of what was projected; the rest of the work never appeared.

came, particularly in Protestant thought, to refer to something that could be abstracted from the other aspects of actual life and treated as an isolatable phenomenon. This development may have been helped by the way in which theology was studied as ideas that are to be argued about but that are divorced from life as actually lived. In contrast to this, where faith and theology have been and still are properly appreciated and understood, they are seen to be connected with how people actually live in every aspect of being who they are.[32]

The works of Kierkegaard and of those influenced by him may be held to provide powerful evidence that the existential character of theological understanding has not been overlooked by theologians. In the twentieth century, it has played an important part in the work of major theologians. Karl Barth, for instance, writes that 'a very precise definition' of the Christian view of theology requires the 'complex term "The-anthropology"'. This is because 'an abstract doctrine of God has no place in the Christian realm, only ... a doctrine of the commerce between God and man'.[33] For Rudolf Bultmann, 'theology speaks of God because it speaks of man as he stands before God'.[34] In another article he affirms that 'faith does not mean to accept the proclamation of God's forgiving love and to be convinced of its truth in general, but rather to regulate one's life by it'.[35] Paul Tillich is concerned to make clear that faith, as 'the state of being ultimately concerned', affirms the ultimacy both of its object and of the subject's concern focused on that object. As shown by his interest in the relations of faith with culture, and in particular with what current forms of art and psychoanalysis reveal about the human condition, he emphasises that faith is 'an act of the total personality' that 'happens in the center of the personal life and includes all its ele-

[32] A disturbing corollary of this is that when faith is apprehended as providing the basis of life, people can get extremely passionate about it. Faith is a dangerous matter. When taken seriously and not tempered by a proper use of rational reflection, it can lead to conviction being perverted into bigotry and fanaticism.

[33] Karl Barth, 'Evangelical Theology in the Nineteenth Century', in *The Humanity of God*, London: Collins, 1967, p. 9. 'The-anthropology' is a term coined from combining *theos* (God) and *anthropos* (the human).

[34] Rudolf Bultmann, 'Liberal theology and the latest theological movement', in Robert W. Funk (ed.), *Faith and Understanding I*, tr. Louise Pettibone Smith, London: SCM Press, 1969, p. 52.

[35] Rudolf Bultmann, 'Faith as Venture', in idem, *Existence and Faith: Shorter Writings of Rudolf Bultmann*, tr. and intro. Schubert M. Ogden, London: Hodder and Stoughton, 1961, p. 56.

ments'. As 'an act of the personality as whole, it participates in the dynamics of personal life'.[36]

Nevertheless, while these comments indicate that the existential dimension has not been overlooked,[37] discussions of this dimension of theological understanding generally seem to be concerned more with talking *about* the structure of human existence than with dealing with the actualities of what it is to live, and with uncovering how faith enhances the actual quality of life. They resemble a physiologist's analysis of what constitutes health in principle rather than a description of how to be healthy and what it is like to enjoy being so. Those engaged in developing theological understanding may retort that the implied criticism of theology being made here is unfair: since theology is a second-order study *about* faith rather than a firsthand experience of the state of faith, it is fated in this respect to be systematically inadequate in its treatment of faith – just as the study of physiology is different from being alive. This response is justified to some degree.[38] Nevertheless, it may be that theology need not be as inadequate in its treatment of faith as it often is, especially when examination indicates that on many occasions it is not about *faith* but about *reports about* faith and about *analyses of* faith. As talk about living is not to be confused with living, so it is important for theological understanding to remember that faith's primary concern is with living and not with talk about living.

This leads to the question posed in the title to this chapter: 'But who am I? – The question of the theologian rather than the question to the theologian'. The subtitle reminds us that Christian theologians have

[36] Paul Tillich, *Dynamics of Faith*, New York: Harper & Brothers, 1957, p. 4. If there were space, the works of Martin Buber, John Baillie and H. H. Farmer could provide other examples of the recognition of the existential dimension of theological understanding.

[37] Tillich's works in particular evoked a response from many non-theologians who, in a way that they did not completely understand, felt that these works spoke to them. I remember an incident in the late 1950s when a Texan rancher appeared at the Dean's office in a theological seminary, put a wad of dollar bills on his desk and said, 'That's for anyone who can help me understand what this Tillich is saying'! A few years later in Britain the large sales of John Robinson's *Honest to God* showed that a number of people were interested in theology if they thought it might be saying something that made sense to them.

[38] It is a point that many thinkers forget. The result is that academic studies are widely criticised as emanating from those that dwell in ivory towers and that do not perceive that they are thereby insulated from the brute actualities and rich pleasures of real life.

spent much time trying to understand and develop the answer to Jesus' alleged questions 'But who do people say that I am? ... But who do you say that I am?'[39] These are questions *to* the theologian. They may be interesting; they may be critically important. Attempts to answer them deal, sometimes in very sophisticated ways, with the abstract complexities of incarnational and trinitarian theology. It is important, however, that the theologian should also ask of herself or himself and to seek to get the reader also to ask of himself or herself a question of a different logical category, namely, 'But who am I?', with the intention of raising questions about what the faith being examined means for life as actually lived. That is the question *of* the theologian. Failure to answer it may be the reason why theology is regarded as presenting 'either straightforward mumbo jumbo or pretentious speculative ideas'. And, although answering it does not demand that the theologian deliver a personal confession,[40] it does demand that the theologian critically examine the theological understanding of faith from the perspective of what she or he, as a person, may find that he or she can endorse as real from her or his own experience as well as from the experience of others.[41]

The question *of* the theologian is a basic component of theological enquiry. It confronts theologians with questions about the significance of what they are discussing. Furthermore, when theologians ensure that they explore this dimension of theological understanding in terms that show that they know what it is to live, they may find that what they affirm begins to be treated seriously as what they say evokes resonances in their readers' experiences of living. It is a point illustrated by George Eliot's description of an incident in the impulsive and passionate existence of Maggie Tulliver when she reads Thomas à Kempis:

> She knew nothing of doctrines and systems – of mysticism or quietism: but this voice out of the far-off middle ages, was the direct communica-

[39] Cf. Matthew 16: 14-15.

[40] Privacy is to be respected far more than many religious groups seem to appreciate.

[41] It is this requirement of any fully adequate theological understanding that makes it difficult for theologians to investigate, expound, criticise and revise a faith that they do not share, even more one that they consider to be grossly wrong. That it is difficult, however, does not mean that it is impossible but the demands of empathetic appreciation are great – just as the demands for critical examination are great where the theologian is sympathetic to what is being examined.

> tion of a human soul's belief and experience, and came to Maggie as an unquestioned message.[42]

It is an insight that was perceived by the Buddha when he held that one should follow what one finds in one's own experience to be the way, not what others (including the Buddha) teach:

> Do not be satisfied with hearsay or with tradition or with legendary lore or with what has come down in scriptures or with conjecture or with logical inference or with weighing evidence or with liking for a view after pondering over it or with someone else's ability or with the thought 'The monk is our teacher.' *When you know in yourselves*: 'These things are wholesome, blameless, commended by the wise, and being adopted and put into effect they lead to welfare and happiness,' then you should practise and abide in them.[43]

This is a proper and necessary extension of the Bright Hour Test. Faith and its theological understanding must not only satisfy the demand that it speak about the world that people recognise as the one that they inhabit, it must also show that it reports what gives to life in that world meaning and satisfaction.[44]

Faith as self-understanding

If it be correct to hold that a vital dimension of theological understanding is the appreciation that, as Cudworth puts it, Christ came to be '*Vitæ Magister*, not *Scholæ*', it may be that theologians need to take more seriously than they have tended to do works like those written by Harry Williams following his decision 'that alongside of teaching academic theology I would try to ask myself in what way a doctrine of the creed or a saying of Christ had become a part of what I am'. Deciding

[42] George Eliot, *The Mill on the Floss* (1880), Harmondsworth: Penguin Books, 1985, p. 384.

[43] Quoted from the *Kalama Sutta* in Stephen Batchelor, *Buddhism without Tears: A Contemporary Guide to Awakening*, London: Bloomsbury, 1997, p. 1, italics added.

[44] It was a point that I remember being made by Whitfield Foy in a sermon on Trinity Sunday in Cambridge in the mid-1950s. Having spent some time on the theological details of the doctrine of the Trinity, he stopped and asked, 'But what is the point of all this for how we pray and how we live?' Unless it had such point, it had no place in Christian self-understanding. I cannot remember his answer but his question has stayed with me.

that the pulpit was the obvious medium for discussing what he then discovered, he 'resolved' that he

> would not preach about any aspect of Christian belief unless it had become part of my own life-blood. For I realized that the Christian truth I tried to proclaim would speak to those who listened only to the degree in which it was an expression of my own identity. Previously, it seemed to me, I had often been like a man who, while perhaps he enjoyed a good tune, was essentially unmusical and who attempted from the books he had read to describe the quality of Beethoven's quartets. And I wondered how much I had thereby contributed to the emptying of the Churches by making the Christian gospel appear unreal and irrelevant to people's lives.[45]

The consequence was that not only in two volumes of sermons but also in a number of other works[46] Williams provides perceptive explorations of how faith is related to the way in which persons actually live, and of what faith does mean and what it could mean for them. While the passage just cited indicates that Williams writes only of those things to which he can testify from own experience, his description of which in retrospect is at times hilarious,[47] the importance of his contribution to theological understanding[48] is not that it is the testimony of an individual's experience but that it is theology that speaks from living to living. In doing this it does not turn theology into the consideration of a supposedly distinct area of awareness called 'religious experience', as if this were isolatable as a distinct mode of human experience, comparable to

[45] H. A. Williams, *The True Wilderness: A Selection of Addresses*, London: Constable, 1965, p. 8.

[46] They include H. A. Williams, *True Resurrection*, London: Mitchell Beazley, 1972; *Poverty, Chastity and Obedience: The True Virtues*, London: Mitchell Beazley, 1975; *Tensions: Necessary Conflicts in Life and Love*, London: Mitchell Beazley, 1976; *The Joy of God: Variations on a Theme*, London: Mitchell Beazley, 1979; *Some Day I'll Find You: An Autobiography*, London: Mitchell Beazley, 1982; 'Theology and Self-Awareness', in A. R. Vidler (ed.) *Soundings: Essays concerning Christian Understanding*, Cambridge: Cambridge University Press, 1962, pp. 67-101; and 'Psychological Objections', in D. M. MacKinnon, H. A. Williams, A. R. Vidler, and J. S. Bezzant, *Objections to Christian Belief*, London: Constable, 1963, pp. 35-56.

[47] This is particularly the case with some of the incidents that he mentions in his autobiography.

[48] For this is what it is in spite of complaints by some 'academic' theologians that what Williams presents is not theology but psychologically influenced counselling using religious and theological notions as metaphors, e.g. using the notion of 'resurrection' as a metaphor for new life – as if this is not what the interaction of the divine with the human is about.

but different from other modes of human experience. It is, rather, a form of theological understanding that investigates the significance of faith for the life of a person as a whole, for a person, that is, whose experience has aesthetic, physical, intellectual and emotional qualities. It deals with such issues as the way in which authentic faith enhances life rather than diminishes it, evokes confidence and wholeness rather than fear and disintegration, exposes the silly games and pretences by which people hide from the truth about themselves, challenges people to live life to the full, and encourages people to take on the frightening demands of love in the assurance that to do this is to resonate with the heart of being. It also highlights the 'humorous potential' inescapably involved in theological enquiry as human beings make fools of themselves with portentous statements about what is thereby shown only too clearly to be ineffable.[49]

Although this is not the occasion to try to give a summary of the insights to be found in Williams' works – and a desiccated academic survey would suggest (much doubtless to Williams' own wry amusement) that I have not internalised the point that I am trying to make, a few samples may hint at their flavour. Aware that 'religion is to a large extent what people do with their lunacy: their phobias, their will to power, their sexual frustrations',[50] he points out that faith should not be used, as it often has been, 'as an attempt to escape from the ambiguities and anxieties which belong inevitably to being human' when the Christian faith is that 'God took the fullness of humanity upon Himself'.[51] God constitutes 'the self I am ... as its deepest centre': we have to discover God in us 'in the warmth and sweetness, and dryness and terror of actual living'.[52] To portray the love of God in terms of consolation in suffering is to corrupt it into 'bad chocolate-box art' whereas, like 'the very greatest art', 'its *métier*' is 'to give life', not to make sense of what is beyond our understanding.[53] Religion that offers its god as a source of goodies and is entertained as 'a species of insurance, sedation or joy-popping cannot fail to betray its devotees'.[54] When the devout despair and find themselves 'in a state of what they imagine is total unbelief,' what in fact they may have 'ceased to believe in is their own idea of God

[49] *Some Day I'll Find You*, p. 214. These comments apply, *inter alia*, to works about the conditioning and foundations of theological judgements.

[50] Ibid., p. 109.

[51] *True Wilderness*, p. 13.

[52] *The Joy of God*, pp. 22f, 24; cf. *Some Day I'll Find You*, pp. 242-3, 253.

[53] *The Joy of God*, p. 105.

[54] Ibid., p. 20.

as the buttress of their own religious egos, and it is *God* who has smashed up their ideas of Himself in order to destroy their false fabricated religious identities'.[55] For the self-consciously religious person the way to life may be through death to 'slavish subservience to a tyrannical idol' into resurrection to the 'freedom' to discover the 'richness of being' one's self.[56] And in evoking that change, God may encounter people in all kinds of unexpected places – for Williams himself awareness of God's redemption has come in the unconventional English colony in Tangiers,[57] in watching Judy Garland in *A Star is Born*, in visiting a dying young man, and at a performance of the *Nutcracker*.[58] In discussion after a public lecture at Manchester University in 1981 he suggested that a performance by Rowan Atkinson might be more helpful to the personal growth of visitors to London than listening to the capital's preachers! At the end of his autobiography, Williams quotes Unamuno as saying 'God forbid you peace and give you glory' and then comments:

> Nothing is for nothing. You always have to pay for what you get. Without pain there can be no birth; without death no resurrection. In that necessity the ideal and the actual are reconciled and seem to belong inescapably to each other.[59]

But, lest this seem too forbidding, note that he writes at the end of *Tensions* that 'all the contradictions, conflicts, and tensions' of life 'must be ... positively welcomed and joyfully received' since it is only then that we discover 'how laughable they are. And although we are still on our journey, when we laugh we know that really we have already arrived. The party has begun and we are there.'[60]

[55] Ibid., p. 64.

[56] *Some Day I'll Find You*, p. 191; cf. *Poverty, Chastity and Obedience*, p. 99.

[57] *Some Day I'll Find You*, p. 248. This was 'to the amusement of the more material among the clergymen of the Cambridge establishment and the pious horror of the others'!

[58] Ibid., pp. 250-1.

[59] Ibid., p. 383.

[60] *Tensions*, p. 120.

The implications for theological understanding

If, in order to be fully adequate, theological reflection is to take seriously the dimension of self-understanding that has been illustrated by reference to the works of Harry Williams, it does not follow that it must become wholly a matter of religiously conceptualised considerations of the nature of human being as personal. Recognition of the personal dimension in theology does not mean that theology has no other dimension than that of personal discovery and guidance. What, however, should result from tackling the question 'But who am I?', as asked *of* the theologian, as part of theological reflection is that the results of such reflection, if successful, should be seen to be concerned with the understanding, fulfilment and significance of human being. In that case it will not be easy to dismiss authentic and adequate theology as mumbo jumbo. Furthermore, theological discussion—and the religious faith linked with it—will be characterised in five ways.

First, it will become clear that the justification for theological understanding necessarily involves a pragmatic component. The question 'But who am I?' as asked *of* the theologian (and of all others who may not regard themselves as theologians but who claim authority to guide others in understanding and developing religious faith) raises the issue of authority and justification. By what authority do theologians speak? At least since the early seventeenth century there have been legitimate doubts about the status of those who arrogate to themselves authority to instruct others on the basis of expertise in a community's scriptures and traditions and, even more, on the basis of their membership of some mutually-authorising and self-regulating clique within the community of faith. By having to confront the question 'But who am I?' theologians will be forced to appreciate that in developing their views, they must pay attention to what those views mean for how people actually live. Even though, as postmodernists (and many before them) emphasise, all understanding is relative, the Achilles' heel of attempts to impose views based on cultural and institutional inheritance is the brute stubbornness of what is experienced. Reality is not what we decide that it is; in the end illusions and delusions are exposed for what they are. Among the matters, therefore, to which theologians should pay attention is whether what they present justifies in practice their claim that it gives understanding, fulfilment and significance to actual human being. Admittedly, theological understanding that claims to be informed by and warranted by actual experience will be somewhat messy, prejudiced and relative—for this is the character of our apprehension of experience. It will, however, be linked to what people find important in their lives.

Secondly, the question 'But who am I?' as asked *of* the theologian rather than addressed to the theologian makes clear the importance of the concrete. A danger with liberal as much as with conservative and radical theology is that is presents abstractions and plays at interesting intellectual games with ideas while the world passes by. Cudworth points out that unless we make it our own in practice

> The Gospel ... cannot save us; no more than that Physician's Bill [*sc.* prescription] could cure the ignorant Patient of his disease, who, when it was commended to him, took the Paper only and put it up in his pocket, but never drank the Potion that was prescribed by it.[61]

Theologians need to take to heart Karl Marx's remark that 'the philosophers have only *interpreted* the world, in various ways; the point, however, is to *change* it'.[62] Marx's own writings show that he does not deny the importance of understanding (or 'interpretation'): his point is that understanding is not an end in itself. Its important role is to show how life can be transformed for the better. This is a view of intellectual activity that is particularly pertinent when theologians discuss the so-called problem of evil. As Gustavo Gutiérrez insists in his study of Job, theological reflection is a second-order activity: the primary issue is 'to do God's will and allow God to reign' through 'contemplation and practice together'.[63] Hence what is most important is not to give a theoretical understanding of evil but a practical response to those who suffer. Or, as Wendy Farley insists, while 'theodicy cannot explain away evil or make evil into any good', what is important is to 'illuminate the radical love of God' so that people

> come to burn with incandescent compassion for the world, to feel the grief of the world without being destroyed by it, without being paralysed against resistance by despair. Instead they are empowered for the work of resistance.[64]

[61] Cudworth, 'The First Sermon', in *The True Notion of the Lord's Supper*, p. 53.

[62] Karl Marx, 'Theses on Feuerbach', § XI, in Karl Marx and Friedrich Engels, *On Religion*, New York: Schocken, 1964, p. 72.

[63] Gustavo Gutiérrez, *On Job: God-Talk and the Suffering of the Innocent*, tr. Matthew J. O'Connell, Maryknoll: Orbis Books, 1987, p. xiii.

[64] Wendy Farley, *Tragic Vision and Divine Compassion: A Contemporary Theodicy*, Louisville: Westminster/John Knox, 1990, p. 133.

When theology directs and inspires action for good, it may well cease to be dismissed as mumbo jumbo.[65]

Mention of the problem of evil draws attention to a third characteristic of theology that pays attention to the question 'But who am I?' as asked *of* the theologian. This is the need for theological reflection to expose the false presuppositions (and hence the unanswerability) of certain questions that people insist on asking and which theologians are consequently tempted to try to answer. When Jessica aged three looks at some photographs of her grandfather as a child and then asks, 'Where was I?', it may be difficult to get her to accept that the presupposition of her question (namely, that she was *somewhere* at the time that the photographs were taken) is radically mistaken and so the question is unanswerable. Nevertheless, while such a reply may not be easy to explain to her, adults should have no difficulty with it. What is worrying, however, is that adults do insist on asking similarly mistaken questions and that theologians fall into the trap of trying to answer them. One major example is the question of the meaning and purpose of events.

To return to the edition of the *Guardian* with which this chapter opened, it is interesting to read that Hoddle said to a reporter that

> there has to be some reason why some people suffer in the world and others do not ... why some people have the terrible misfortune to be born disabled while others like me are born healthy. There has to be some reason for it all.[66]

But there may be no reason. Certain events come about by the chance interaction of processes, each of which is intelligible but whose interaction is totally accidental and unpredictable; other states are the product of quantum indeterminacies that appear to be statistically ordered but individually random. In such cases there is no reason, intention or purpose for those individual events having happened as they did. Attempts to make sense of them in such ways are doomed to

[65] This is a view of theology that religious institutions often overlook. I found it hard to credit a report that when the Russian revolution was under way senior members of the Russian Orthodox Church were absorbed in a dispute about liturgical colours *until* I sat in a Methodist Committee debating the colour of the covers of new liturgical booklets while a missile crisis was coming to a head.

[66] The *Guardian*, 2 February 1999, p. 1.

fail. If some theory does seem to make sense of them, it is because it imposes meaning on what is intrinsically meaningless. Theological reflection that considers the question 'But who am I?' not only must make sure that it investigates genuine questions; it must also expose bogus ones, however obstinate people may be in asking them and in demanding that they be answered. An important part of self-awareness is discovering one's limits – and this includes, most importantly for theological understanding, the limits in principle of what makes sense.

That there are events which do not make sense does not, however, show that human life is worthless. A fourth characteristic of theology that emerges when it faces the question 'But who am I?' is the perception that theological understanding—as faith itself—is about living, not about theorising, and that authentic living is characterised by confidence in the worth of individual human being in the face of the uncertainty of an unpredictable future. Although faith is often examined in terms of beliefs that are assents to propositions, whether explicitly or implicitly theological, its presentation is seriously inadequate when it fails to appreciate that faith is essentially (even though not wholly) concerned with affirming the significance of each self as an existing entity, an affirmation grounded in God's awareness of and concern for each individual.

Fifthly, and finally, questions are only genuinely answered by assertions that can warrantably claim to be true. Accordingly another characteristic of theology that takes seriously the question 'But who am I?' is that it seeks to satisfy the demand to justify the claims that it makes in reply. Theological understanding cannot evade the suspicion of being mumbo jumbo unless it can provide rationally convincing grounds that it is not peddling attractive illusions and seductive delusions. As has been suggested, one of great contributions to theology made by those such as Harry Williams is the exposure of the silly games that people confuse with authentic faith in God. Theologians displaying their latest theological fashions need the child who sees, giggles, and announces that 'the Emperor has got no clothes on'. Furthermore, while this is not the place to go into the nature of the appropriate truth tests, they involve satisfying the ten criteria for significant belief that were mentioned earlier. Although the satisfaction of those criteria on its own may not be sufficient to persuade people that theological understanding is important, when that understanding has taken proper account of its existential dimension, it is crucial for showing that the result deserves to be taken seriously. In the quotation from the *Kalama Sutta* cited previously, it is important to note the 'know' as well as the 'in yourselves' when the Buddha speaks of acting on the basis of what 'you know in yourselves' to be good.[67] Theological understanding that takes seriously its existential dimension needs the authorisation of being seen to be significant, comprehensible and rationally justified. If and so far as it succeeds in meeting these demands it will clear itself of the suspicion of peddling mumbo jumbo, whether that mumbo jumbo be of the wrong sort or of the right sort.

Conclusion

I suggest, then, that those engaged in pondering the future for 'liberal theology', whatever basket of notions and practices that label applies to, should consider whether one factor in ensuring that it has a future is that it ask and seek to answer in terms of the faith that it is seeking to identify, revise, develop and expound the question 'But who am I?' – and remember that it is asked *of* the theologian rather than addressed *to* the theologian. Theologians who offer a credible answer to that question as part of their theological understanding may thereby avoid uttering what people hear as mumbo jumbo, whether it be about Christology, ritual or the fate of individuals, and move some way towards realising a perception of the character of authentic faith that was presented to the members of the House of Commons in 1647. Sadly, one result of reading theologians of past times like Ralph Cudworth is that one learns that their faults are perpetuated much more than their (occasional) insights are taken to heart.

[67] See above, n. 43.

Chapter 5

The Revival of Liberal Modernism

Paul Badham

Liberal English Modernism developed out of the need for Christian thought to come to terms with the findings of literary and historical criticism of the Bible and the acceptance of evolutionary theory during the latter half of the nineteenth century. It was continuous with the 'Broad Church Movement' which preceded it, and it particularly identified with the largely Anglican Society now known as 'The Modern Churchpeople's Union' which was founded in 1898. When I first started to research for a book to celebrate the Centenary of this society,[1] I assumed it would primarily be a work of church history because English Modernism is generally held to have been an important movement in the twenties and thirties, but to have since been superseded, replaced initially by the work of Barth and the Niebuhrs and later by more radical schools of thought. But on reading through the works of the English Modernists I realised that this was an entirely false position. It is not they who are out of date – rather it is their opponents. If one looks coolly at the views for which the Modernists were pilloried seventy years ago one finds either that they are now almost universally accepted by mainstream Christians, or they are at the leading edge of contemporary theology.

Let me start by looking at the Modernists' approach to the question of human salvation. Their starting point was that if one takes seriously historical and literary criticism of the Bible, together with the findings of evolutionary biology and anthropology, then one cannot believe in the literal historical fall of the first man and woman. Consequently, one cannot believe that their 'original sin' had led to the corruption of all their descendants. Consequently, their descendants cannot be said to 'deserve' everlast-

[1] *The Contemporary Challenge of Modernist Theology*, Cardiff: University of Wales Press, 1998.

ing damnation after death. And if none is damned then none is to be saved from damnation by putting their trust in the atoning death of Christ. In short, the Modernists rejected the whole of the traditional schema: there never was an aboriginal fall, substitutionary atonement is an immoral idea and the doctrine of hell a legend. Instead, the Modernists believed that God had been revealed by Christ to be like a loving Father who is always ready to accept and forgive his prodigal children.

This classic liberal position is usually held to have been refuted as an unacceptable watering down of authentic Christianity by the withering judgement of Richard Niebuhr, who characterised Liberal Modernism as teaching that: 'A God without wrath, brought men without sin, into a kingdom without judgment through the ministrations of a Christ without a cross.'[2] Sixty years later it is by no means clear that Niebuhr was right, for few today still think in the categories of sin, wrath and judgement. Modern Evangelicals experience considerable embarrassment in talking about the cross of Christ. In the past it was something to 'glory in', because Christians believed that the cross had made an absolutely decisive difference to human destiny. The early Christians believed that the human nature of the dying Jesus had been like the bait placed on a fish-hook (St Gregory of Nyssa) or in a mouse-trap (St Augustine) in order to deceive the devil into swallowing Christ's divinity which could then destroy the devil's power. Later Christians thought that it was not the devil's power, but the wrath of God from which Jesus' death had saved us. According to St Thomas Aquinas, Luther and Calvin, the death of Jesus had been 'a sacrifice by which God was *placated*'. As long as one could think in such terms it would indeed be glorious to know that this propitiation had been achieved and God's wrath averted.[3] There was a very powerful message in the much-loved Good Friday hymn:

He died that we might be forgiven,
He died to make us good,
That we might go at last to heaven,
Saved by His precious blood.

However, although such hymns continue to be sung, even Conservative Evangelicals reject the theology behind them. Archbishop George Carey, in

[2] H. Richard Niebuhr, *The Kingdom of God in America*, Chicago: Willett Clarke and Co., 1937, p. 173.

[3] Hastings Rashdall, *The Idea of Atonement in Christian Theology*, London: Macmillan, 1925, pp. 305, 333, 375, 411.

his otherwise very conservative *Canterbury Letters*, explicitly denies that a ransom was paid to either the devil or to God. He describes such pictures as sterile, immoral, and out of character with what we know of God.[4] Similarly staff members at some Evangelical theological colleges who contributed to John Goldingay's collection of essays on the *Atonement Today*, were also unanimous in rejecting older views of the atonement either in terms of a ransom paid to the devil or as the Son appeasing or propitiating the wrath of God the Father.[5] But without any realistic sense of a ransom being paid somewhere, what meaning is left in keeping the language of redemption? Carey has no answer to this except to say that traditional terminology about the atonement 'can't be put to definitive analysis'.[6] David Ford agrees: 'There is something about the reality of salvation that resists an overview.'[7] Stephen Sykes explores the same predicament accepting that although 'phrases and sentences' associated with the older atonement beliefs are 'the common coin of the Church's worship', explanations of such terms are 'not obvious'. Consequently, if an 'inquirer without a religious background but with an instinct to be disputatious were to demand one, we might quickly be in some difficulty'.[8] Sykes' use of the phrase the 'common coin of the Church's worship' is interesting. As I remember Don Cupitt remarking once, much Christian language today is like a currency which is no longer in circulation but which people interested in antiques still collect. The language of sacrifice and ransom would seem good examples of such currency.

There is, however, one understanding of Jesus' death in contemporary theology which does seem meaningful, and which has become increasingly popular. This is that God was 'wholly present' in Jesus' suffering on the cross and that this illustrates the way in which God always shares in and is present in the darkest afflictions of humanity.[9] This was the view held by all the leading Modernists who saw the death of Christ as a parable of the way God suffers with us. Today this understanding of the cross has been endorsed by the 1996 Church of England Doctrine Commission report on *The Mystery of Salvation* as the 'only ultimately satisfactory response to

[4] George Carey, *Canterbury Letters*, London: Kingsway, 1998, p. 165.

[5] John Goldingay (ed.), *Atonement Today*, London: SPCK, 1995.

[6] Carey, *Canterbury Letters*, p. 165.

[7] David Ford, *Self and Salvation*, Cambridge: Cambridge University Press, 1999, p. 4.

[8] Stephen Sykes, *The Story of Atonement*, London: Darton, Longman and Todd, 1997, p. 5.

[9] Carey, *Canterbury Letters*, p. 167.

evil'[10] and most contemporary Christians think this is what Christianity is all about.

Likewise, almost all contemporary Christians join with the same report in rejecting the idea of an everlasting hell. At first sight this claim might seem difficult to reconcile with the fact that the latest Roman Catholic Catechism teaches 'the sad and lamentable reality of eternal death also called hell'. However, this assertion is at once qualified by the claim in the next section that 'it is also true that God desires all men to be saved' and 'for God all things are possible'. Consequently, the Catechism concludes: 'At the end of time the Kingdom of God will come in its fullness ... and God will be all in all'.[11] A similar situation occurs in Archbishop Carey's *Canterbury Letters*. He also speaks of hell but immediately follows this with talk of the wideness of God's mercy which will embrace all humanity, so that in the end God will be all in all.[12]

The response of the Churches to the death of Princess Diana provides the clearest picture of what Christians today really believe about sin and salvation. From the perspective of traditional Christian teaching she was a married woman who had separated from her husband and was 'living in sin' with another man. But apart from two fundamentalist Sunday School teachers who attracted great press opprobrium, no Church leaders spoke of her as a sinner. Instead she became a contemporary Icon of the Virgin, Mother, and Martyr archetypes. She had been the virgin bride of the Prince of Wales, then the mother of a future king and finally she had been martyred by the wicked press. At her funeral Archbishop Carey prayed for her Muslim lover Dodi al-Fayed 'in certain hope of resurrection to eternal life'.[13] This was in spite of the fact that Dodi al-Fayed manifestly embraced neither Christian belief nor Christian morality. As for Diana herself, Cardinal Hume made it clear that she was en route for heaven where 'God locks us for ever into that endless now of God's ecstatic love'.[14] Thinking back to Niebuhr's famous saying: it becomes clear that in relation to Dodi and Diana both Cardinal and Archbishop agree that 'A God without wrath brings men without sin, into a kingdom without judgment through the ministrations of a Christ without a cross'. And in accepting Dodi and Diana in this way it is clear that both Cardinal and Archbishop spoke for almost

[10] Cited in Carey, *Canterbury Letters*, p. 167.

[11] *Catechism of the Catholic Church*, London: Chapman, 1994, pp. 240-1.

[12] Carey, *Canterbury Letters*, pp. 220-33.

[13] *The Sunday Times*, 7 September 1997, and also the BBC CD of the Funeral.

[14] *The Sunday Times*, 7 September 1997.

the entire Christian community of modern Britain.

Turning from Niebuhr, let us consider why Karl Barth rejected Liberalism. His basic position was a total denial of the validity of Natural Theology and of religious experience as potential sources for knowledge of God. Barth's rejection of Natural Theology on theological grounds was matched by an equally firm rejection of the discipline from the dominance of logical positivism in British philosophy following A.J. Ayer's youthful firework, *Language, Truth and Logic.* Consequently, for two generations hardly any theologians or philosophers had any real time for the subject. Indeed in 1968 when Ian Ramsey left the Nolloth Chair of the Philosophy of the Christian Religion it was proposed that the Chair be abolished on the grounds that the Philosophy of the Christian Religion was no longer a worthwhile subject. Fortunately the proposal was resisted and the appointment first of Basil Mitchell and then of Richard Swinburne to the Nolloth Chair played a major role in reviving the idea that philosophical thought could help to justify religious belief and illustrate the coherence of Christian theism.

However, the biggest reason for the revival of Natural Theology has been the way some modern scientists have latched on to it. As Keith Ward observed, 'Just when philosophers had thought that the argument from design was gone for ever, the physicist brings it back again'.[15] The reason for this, according to Russell Stannard, is that 'the very latest revelations of science, instead of posing fresh difficulties, have led to new harmony, and the methods of investigation used in science and religion, far from being opposed to each other in their outlook, are in many ways similar'.[16] Paul Davies goes even further, insisting that in the light of the new physics we can legitimately claim that 'science offers a surer path to God than religion'.[17]

Before this sea-change took place among some scientists, many, perhaps most, philosophers of religion believed that the arguments for God's existence had been definitively answered by Hume and Kant and there was little mileage in refuting them except as an introductory exercise for first year philosophy students. For example Kai Nielsen, a Canadian philosopher and a convinced atheist, wrote in 1971 that philosophers who took

[15] Keith Ward, *The Turn of the Tide: Christian Belief in Britain Today*, London: BBC Publications, 1986, p. 45.

[16] Russell Stannard, *Science and the Renewal of Belief*, London: SCM, 1982, Cover.

[17] Paul Davies, *God and the New Physics*, London, J.M. Dent, 1983, p. ix. See also *The Mind of God*, London, Simon & Schuster, 1992.

the claims of religion seriously were 'very much in the minority and their arguments have been forcefully contested'.[18] But nearly twenty years later Nielsen's estimate of philosophical attitudes has changed. He believes that 'Philosophy of religion in an Anglo-American context has taken a curious turn in the past decade ... what has come to the forefront ... is a group of Christian philosophers of a philosophically analytic persuasion, but hostile to even the residues of logical empiricism or Wittgensteinianism, who return to the old topics and the old theses of traditional Christian philosophy and natural theology'.[19] We should of course notice that Nielsen describes this development as 'curious', indicating that he himself is unconvinced by it. We should also note that philosophers not engaged in the current discussions in the philosophy of religion often remain unaffected by it. Nevertheless, if we are looking simply at the current status of the arguments for the existence of God, it is interesting to note Richard Purtill's evaluation of the scene: 'All the traditional arguments have able and respected defenders and if there is not a consensus in favour of philosophical arguments for God's existence it is no longer true that there is a consensus against'.[20]

The point is that the current scientific consensus that the Universe began quite literally from nothing is more compatible with the Christian claim that God created the Universe out of nothing than any previous scientific picture. Secondly, that the Universe appears to have been very 'finely tuned' for the emergence of life and mind is very compatible with Christian belief in a divine designer. Consequently, there has been a flood of books from philosophers of religion looking again at the cosmological and teleological arguments for the existence of God and a host of works of a metaphysical kind have flowed from many of the leading mathematical physicists. In fact, according to Astronomer Fred Hoyle, 'while most scientists claim to eschew religion, it actually dominates their thoughts more than it does the clergy'.[21]

Religious experience is also re-emerging as a key factor in current theological debate. This is partly because the research of people like David Hay, Michael Argyle and the Alister Hardy Research Centre has shown just how common religious experience still is. According to David Hay, 56%

[18] Kai Nielsen, *Contemporary Critiques of Religion*, London: Macmillan, 1971, p. 19.

[19] 'Foreword' to K. Parsons, *God and the Burden of Proof*, New York: Prometheus 1989, p. 7.

[20] Richard Purtill, 'The Current State of Arguments for the Existence of God', in *Review and Expositor* 82 (1985), p. 521.

[21] Davies, *The Mind of God*, p. 223.

of postgraduate students claim to have had a religious experience which influenced them, while in his most recent work he has shown that spirituality is natural to primary school children.[22] From a philosophical perspective the revival of interest in religious experience is very important because Basil Mitchell, Richard Swinburne, and Caroline Frank Davis all argue that it is religious experience which provides the most important evidential foundation for religious belief (just as Dean Inge claimed in his discussion of *Christian Mysticism* in 1918). However, to take Christian religious experience seriously inevitably leads to taking equally seriously the purported experiences of people from other world faiths. It is no accident that John Hick moved from claiming that it was personal religious experience which made theistic belief rational to his later pluralist vision in which all the world faiths are seen as different human responses to the one divine Reality. But this is also in some ways reminiscent of the view of William Temple who claimed that the divine Logos was at work in all the great traditions so that 'by the Word of God—that is to say by Christ—Isaiah, and Plato, and Zoroaster and Buddha conceived and uttered such truths as they declared. There is only one divine light and every man in his measure is enlightened by it'.[23]

Another example I wish to give of the contemporary value of Modernism is the importance Modernists attached to the historical Jesus, and of how the doctrine of the Person of Christ can be understood in the light of modern knowledge. It is notorious that on the historical side the English Modernists had a penchant for Adolf von Harnack's work *What is Christianity?*,[24] which left the impression that the supernatural and miraculous elements in the Gospels can largely be dispensed with but that what matters for Christians should be what historical research can postulate as the most likely reconstruction of the original teaching of Jesus of Nazareth. In the history of thought this was superseded by almost sixty years of scholarship which tended to emphasise how little we can know for certain about the historical Jesus, but that this hardly mattered since what was important was not the Jesus of History but the Christ of Faith disclosed through the preaching of the Church. Hence not only was the quest of the historical Jesus seen as a blind alley, but the Christological questions raised at the Conference at Girton in 1921 and elsewhere came to be seen by a subse-

22 David Hay, *Religious Experience Today*, London: Mowbray, 1990, pp. 54, 82, 83 and *The Spirit of the Child*, London: Harper Collins, 1999.

23 William Temple, *Readings in St. John's Gospel* (1943), London: Mowbray, 1963, p. 9.

24 Adolf von Harnack, *What is Christianity?* (1901), London: Benn, 1958.

quent theological generation as irrelevant to the person of faith.

However, the wheel has turned full circle in that in recent years there has been a powerful reawakening of interest in the historical Jesus. E. P. Sanders, one of the most respected New Testament specialists today, has characterised the period 1910-1970 as a time when scholars tended to argue that we knew very little about the historical Jesus whereas 'in recent decades we have grown more confident'.[25] Sanders's own position is that 'There are no substantial doubts about the general course of Jesus' life: when and where he lived, approximately when and where he died, and the sort of thing he did during his public activity'.[26] His own study of *The Historical Figure of Jesus* gives the fullest and most detailed account of the emerging consensus, which is backed up both by the detail of his other works and by the comparably positive conclusions of other scholars such as James Dunn, N. T. Wright, and Leslie Houlden.[27] This confidence does not extend to any rehabilitation of the miraculous and supernatural elements discarded by earlier Modernists and Liberal Protestants. Sanders comments on popular contemporary views of New Testament miracles that 'none of this is accurate'[28] and it is a commonplace that most scholarly works on the historical Jesus either ignore the supernatural elements altogether or discuss them simply as aspects of the thought-world of that time.[29] However, the historical figure of Jesus has re-emerged as a major focus of discussion for the rediscovery of authentic Christianity.

Similarly, over the past twenty years the meaning of the doctrine of the incarnation has been one of the most vigorously debated areas of Christian theology, just as it was at the height of Modernist controversy of 1921. Most of the principal proponents then as now wished to affirm that Jesus was truly divine while at the same time being like us in all respects save sin, and also a completely unified person. The point at issue has al-

[25] E. P. Sanders, *The Historical Figure of Jesus*, Harmondsworth: Penguin, 1993, p. 10.

[26] Ibid., p. xiii.

[27] James Dunn, *The Evidence for Jesus*, London: SCM, 1985; N. T. Wright, *The New Testament and the People of God*, London: SPCK, 1992; *Who was Jesus?*, London : SPCK, 1992; J. L. Houlden, *Jesus, A Question of Identity*, London: SPCK, 1992.

[28] Sanders, *Historical Figure*, p. 134.

[29] For example, books explicitly about the historical Jesus ignore the birth narratives entirely. Cf. E. Fuchs, *Studies of the Historical Jesus*, London: SCM, 1964; J. Robinson, *The New Quest of the Historical Jesus*, London: SCM, 1966; E. Käsemann, *Essays on New Testament Themes*, London: SCM, 1964.

ways been what the claim 'Jesus is God' actually means. Christians have always recognised that throughout the period of Jesus' life, God continued to be ever-present throughout the Universe upholding all things in being. Likewise, Jesus as a human being never exhibited that unlimited power, boundless knowledge and total self-sufficiency (aseity) that is integral to Godhead. Instead he confessed to ignorance, suffered, died, and was buried. In what sense then is it possible to speak of God as being present in Christ?

In this context the Modernist proposals of 1921 seem to have a real contribution to make. They affirmed then what more modern scholarship has also confirmed, that Jesus had no sense of being divine but that people did become aware of God through him. The Modernist solution was the concept of a 'degree Christology'. It is a fact of human religious experiencing that in the presence of holy people others become aware of God through them. The more holy the other is, the more likely it is that it will reveal God to us. Hastings Rashdall suggested that in Jesus this quality we partially sense in all human being was present to the nth degree.[30] Understood this way it can truly be believed that God was really present in Christ and yet at the same time it also remains true that Jesus was fully human. This understanding of the incarnation is of particular importance in the inter-faith context. It places Jesus within the continuum of human religious experiencing, rather than being totally distinct and alien from the rest of humanity. It would make the divinity of Christ a concept which could, if understood in this sense, be potentially acceptable to Jews, Muslims and Hindus. For each of these religions believes that Prophets, or Gurus or other sanctified people can reveal something of God to other human beings. The problem with the classic account of the incarnation is that it is hard to see that God could be revealed in the language of a human life unless the awareness of God in that person's life was akin to that which we all are capable in principle of experiencing. A degree-Christology solves that problem and discussion of this theory should be re-incorporated into the current debate.

My final example concerns the nature of the future life. Historical Christianity taught a literal understanding of bodily resurrection based on an absolutely literal understanding of the resurrection of Jesus. According to the fourth Anglican Article of Religion: 'Christ did truly rise again from death, and took again his body, with flesh, bones, and all things pertaining

[30] Hastings Rashdall, *Philosophy of Religion* (1910), reprint, Westport: Greenwood Press, 1970, pp. 180-81.

to the perfection of Man's nature; wherewith he ascended into heaven, and there sitteth.' What happened to Jesus' body then was seen as revealing what would happen to his followers at the end of time when the 'particles composing each individual's flesh' will be collected together, the sea will 'give up its dead', the cannibal restore the flesh he had borrowed, and 'the identical structure which death had previously destroyed would be raised to new life'.[31] This understanding of Jesus' Resurrection and its implications for us was affirmed in the Apostles' Creed, with its dual assertion of the Resurrection of Jesus and of the resurrection of the flesh (*carnis*).

In my study of the Modernists I discovered that there was an absolutely blazing controversy in 1922 when several leading Modernists criticised such views and urged the Church of England to remove talk of 'resurrection of the flesh' from the Apostles' Creed. Today among contemporary Christians these issues are all simply a non-starter. Stephen Davis, a relatively conservative thinker who has written or contributed to three books on the resurrection in recent years, comments that in the course of all his theological reading about the resurrection in the past ten years he has come across no scholar today who thinks of the resurrection of Jesus in terms of the resuscitation of Jesus' corpse.[32] Yet that was precisely the starting point for historic Christianity. As for belief in the resurrection of the flesh as a future destiny for human beings this belief has so completely vanished from contemporary Christianity that many Christians today simply have no idea that this is what the Apostles' Creed actually says in the Latin. Apart from some Jehovah's Witnesses tracts, I know of no contemporary defence of such a view.

The significance of these changes has been somewhat concealed by the almost universal habit today of translating *Resurrectionem Carnis* as 'Resurrection of the Body' and then re-interpreting this to mean that after death people will be given new and quite different 'spiritual bodies' to serve as vehicles for their self-expression and development in heaven. And the only bond of union between present and future bodies is that they will be 'owned' successively by the same personality. This is the view adopted by the Church of England Doctrine Commission in 1938 and by the Roman

[31] Collated from Rufinus, *Apostles' Creed*, § 42; Revelation 20:13; Augustine, *City of God*, 22.20; Rufinus, § 43.

[32] S. Davis, D. Kendall, and G. O'Collins, *The Resurrection: an interdisciplinary symposium on the Resurrection of Jesus*, Oxford: Oxford University Press, 1997, p. 133.

Catholic Bishops of Holland in their 1965 Catechism.[33] A similar view was expressed by the 1996 Anglican Commission on Doctrine which, despite vigorously defending the language of resurrection against the language of immortality, then went on to insist that the 'essence of humanity is certainly not the matter of the body, for that is continuously changing. ... What provides continuity and unity through that flux of change is not material but (in a vague but suggestive phrase) the vastly complex information-bearing pattern in which that material is organised. That pattern can surely be considered the carrier of memories and of personality'.[34] What happens at death according to this theory is that 'Death dissolves the embodiment of that pattern, but the person whose that pattern is, is "remembered" by God, who in love holds that unique being in his care'. However there must at some point be a 'fuller realisation of God's purpose for us all'. This will come with 'the resurrection of the body'. But 'it is not to be supposed that the material of the resurrected body is the same as that of the old'.[35]

What I have demonstrated by these examples is that if we look at what the classic Modernists believed in the 1920s we find that far from their thought being superseded, in reality it has come to be accepted within the life of the Christian Church today. What has survived from traditionalism is a preference for traditional terminology, but if we go behind the words and explore the beliefs they are being used to convey, we find that a Modernist understanding is presupposed even by Christians who would regard themselves as the heirs of very different theological traditions.

[33] *Doctrine in the Church of England*, pp. 209; The Bishops of the Netherlands, *A New Catechism*, London: Burns and Oates, 1967, pp. 473, 474, 479.

[34] The Doctrine Commission of the Church of England, *The Mystery of Salvation*, London: Church House Publishing, 1996, pp. 10-11.

[35] Ibid., pp. 191-2.

Chapter 6

Reconsidering Pluralism: The Diversity of Ethical Goals

Steve Else

Although the final significant flowering of liberal theology is generally agreed to have ended in the first half of the last century, its influence is clearly discernible in the variety of forms of religious pluralism. I understand 'liberal theology' to be the attempt to ground religious enquiry in something other than tradition, and this usually involves a greater than usual willingness to learn from the many branches of secular culture, such as philosophy, the natural sciences, and anthropology. Pluralism draws on this heritage in that it has provided arguments for its conclusions derived from moral philosophy, political conceptions of 'justice', epistemology, and so on. Therefore, the continued well-being of liberal theology is to a certain extent tied up with the success of pluralism: both have a commitment to expanding the boundaries of possible truth-claims.

This chapter focuses on the ethical side to this issue. In *An Interpretation of Religion*,[1] John Hick wrote the following:

> The great ... [religious] ... traditions ... exhibit in their different ways a soteriological structure which identifies the misery, unreality, triviality and perversity of ordinary human life, affirms an ultimate unity of reality and value in which or in relation to which a limitlessly better quality of existence is possible, and shows the way to realise that radically better possibility. This may be by self-committing faith in Christ as one's lord and saviour; or by the total submission to God which is *islam*; or by faithful obedience to the Torah; or by transcendence of the ego, with its self-centred desires and cravings, to attain *moksa* or Nir-

[1] *An Interpretation of Religion: Human Responses to the Transcendent*, London: Macmillan, 1989.

> vana... [T]hese are variations within different conceptual schemes on a single fundamental theme: the sudden or gradual change of the individual from an absorbing self-concern to a new centring in the supposed unity-of-reality-and-value that is thought of as God, Brahman, the Dharma, Sunyata or the Tao.[2]

This passage is a useful summary of the ethical element of Hick's well-known pluralistic philosophy of religion, in which the religions of the world are different, but equally valid, perspectives on the same ultimate reality known as 'the Real'. This ethic revolves around the concept of salvation/liberation, which is universal in its application: Hick believes that each of the world religions is designed to promote the transformation of the moral outlook of their individual adherents, from lives lived with no concerns other than the selfish, to ones in which high value is placed upon the interests of other people and the wider environment.

However, a precise and detailed analysis of this allegedly 'pluralistic' ethic, reveals anomalies which would appear to cast serious doubts upon the veracity of its rhetoric. As Hick's work has been at the forefront of debates about religious pluralism for some time now, the importance of these findings, both for pluralism and liberal theology, should not be underestimated.

The pre-axial religions

Hick describes as the 'axial' the period from roughly 800 - 200 BCE, when many of the great world faiths took on more or less the form in which we now recognise them, under the influence of revolutionary teachers and prophets such as the Buddha, Zoroaster, and the writers of the Upanishads and the Bhagavad Gita. In line with this, he uses the term 'pre-axial' to refer to 'both the "primal", "pre-literate", or "primitive" religions of stone-age humanity and the now extinct priestly and often national religions of the ancient Near East and Egypt, Greece and Rome, India and China';[3] and 'post-axial' to refer to the religious traditions, such as Christianity and Islam, which came to prominence after the axial period.

[2] Ibid., p. 36.
[3] Ibid., p. 23

He gives a clear and generally accurate description of the pre-axial religions. They are 'centrally (but not solely) concerned with the preservation of cosmic and social order':[4]

> Pre-axial religion has both psychological and sociological dimensions. Psychologically it is an attempt to make stable sense of life, and particularly of the basic realities of subsistence and propagation and the final boundaries of birth and death, within a meaning-bestowing framework of myth. This serves the social functions of preserving the unity of the tribe or people within a common world-view and at the same time of validating the community's claims upon the loyalty of its members. The underlying concern is conservative, a defence against chaos, meaninglessness and the breakdown of social cohesion.[5]

Hick points out that the pre-axial religions do not have, because of this wish to maintain order, any hope, similar to Christian eschatology, for 'a radically new, different and better existence, whether in this life or in a further life to come'.[6]

This is a component of the concept of salvation/liberation, which is Hick's central criterion for valid religions. But note the following: 'Whereas pre-axial religion was generally concerned to keep life on an even keel, post-axial religion has been concerned with salvation/liberation'.[7] This strongly implies that the pre-axial religions were not concerned *at all* with salvation/liberation, and so, by Hick's own logic, are not valid religions.

Additional statements of his only strengthen this objection. The 'new movements arising in the axial period exhibit a soteriological structure which stands in marked contrast to the relatively simple world-acceptance of pre-axial religion'.[8] In *God and the Universe of Faiths*,[9] he says that the burst of religious creativity which marked the shift between the two periods can only be attributed to 'the pressure of the divine Spirit upon the human spirit'. This can easily be read as saying that, in helping us to mature as a race, the Spirit made us see that we had outgrown the pre-axial religions.

[4] Ibid., p. 22.

[5] Ibid., p. 23.

[6] Ibid., p. 28.

[7] Ibid., p. 12.

[8] Ibid., p. 32.

[9] *God and the Universe of Faiths: Essays in the Philosophy of Religion*, London: Macmillan, 1973, p. 135.

In the light of this, his account of religious history reads very much like a natural selection of religions (or what Gavin D'Costa calls 'chronological confessionalism'[10]): noting that the 'relatively primitive religions' have mostly disappeared, he decides that 'from the standpoint of religious faith the only reasonable hypothesis is that this historical picture represents a movement of divine self-revelation to mankind'.[11] As humanity has matured, so has its conception of ultimate reality. The most valid religions, those that have survived up to the present day, are those that emphasise salvation / liberation.

It is only fair to point out that Hick repeatedly claims that he does not believe the pre-axial religions to be invalid, or less valid, religions. It 'would be hazardous to assume that human life is more truly centred in the Real' in the post-axial than in the pre-axial period.[12] It is the case that 'the same divine reality has always been self-revealingly active towards mankind',[13] so all religions are expressions of human contact with the same ultimate reality.

However, as has been shown, the actual mechanics of Hick's system pull in the opposite direction to his protestations. His concept of salvation/liberation mitigates against the inclusion of the pre-axial religions in his pluralistic philosophy of religion.

Buddhism

In *Death and Eternal Life*,[14] Hick bemoans the fact that scholars writing on the topic of life after death 'have dismissed the eastern religious point of view with little more than token discussion'; but with the definition of salvation/liberation as 'the transformation of human existence from self-centredness to Reality-centredness' he himself seems to have treated the religions of the East in a similar fashion.

In Buddhism especially, a strong emphasis is placed upon escape from *dukkha* - universal suffering. Although this is believed to have secondary effects in the field of morality, i.e., a healthy person will be

[10] *John Hick's Theology of Religions: A Critical Evaluation*, London: University Press of America, 1987, p. 141.

[11] *God and the Universe of Faiths*, p. 138.

[12] *An Interpretation of Religion*, p. 164.

[13] *God and the Universe of Faiths*, p. 138.

[14] *Death and Eternal Life*, London: Collins, 1976, p. 12.

more amenable to moral instruction,[15] it is still the case that a significant amount of Buddhist morality is devoted to the reduction of personal suffering *per se*. The motives lying behind this are 'selfish', though for the Buddhist there are no pejorative connotations to this.

Hick's presentation of salvation/liberation does little or no justice to this aspect of Buddhist morality. The words and phrases he uses—'love, compassion, self-sacrificing concern for the good of others, generous kindness and forgiveness'[16]—are all on the altruistic side of the equation. This is in evidence in his conception of the final, post-death state to which all human life is moving: 'this interpersonal potentiality of selfhood seeks its full realisation in a society of selves each wholly open to the others in a perfect mutuality in which egoity has been transcended'.[17] The point in the future towards which we should all strive is that which constitutes the final release from the characteristics of existence as separate individuals: 'the perfecting of personal individuality is a transcending of it'.[18]

Nowhere in his published writings does Hick give a sustained treatment, and affirmation of the idea that one has a duty to care for and cultivate one's self. In a system containing such an eschatology, such a task may be impossible. The nearest that he gets to this is when he writes that the morality he has outlined 'is not an alien ideal imposed by supernatural authority but one arising out of our human nature'; there is nevertheless still something contradictory in this, as immediately after this one is told that this morality is 'always in tension with other aspects of that nature'.[19] This can surely only refer to the selfish sides of our nature, and so goes no way to capturing the sort of ethic recommended by Buddhism, where a major part of the effort is directed towards the escape from suffering, and is therefore a 'selfish' end.[20]

[15] Cf. the following aphorism of Friedrich Nietzsche: '*Seducing into love* – We have cause to fear him who hates himself, for we shall be the victims of his wrath and his revenge. Let us therefore see if we cannot seduce him into loving himself!' (*Daybreak: Thoughts on the Prejudices of Morality*, Cambridge: Cambridge University Press, 1982, tr. R.J. Hollingdale, § 517).

[16] *An Interpretation of Religion*, p. 325.

[17] *Death and Eternal Life*, p. 51.

[18] Ibid., 459.

[19] *An Interpretation of Religion*, p. 325.

[20] There are problems with Hick's presentation of Buddhism, and Hinduism, in general. In *IR*, he summarises the outlook of each of them in a few pages. However, I would argue, as would many scholars of these traditions, that

Recognising difference

This issue points to the conclusion that different systems of religious ethics promote different goals. Other examples spring to mind. Some religions have a strong tendency to asceticism, and presuppose that society and the world in general are things to be escaped from, as they can only hinder the achieving of moral virtue. This is a feature of forms of Jainism, Buddhism, and Christianity, amongst others; in Gnosticism, this world is believed to be the creation of evil forces. But other religions declare that the problems to be encountered in the world are to be faced, and that in the final analysis man is a social animal. This feature is particularly evident in Liberation Theology, which has used Marxist ideology to expose hidden injustices within society, and which urges us to live in, not flee, the everyday world. It is extremely doubtful whether both of these religious ends could be achieved, as they pull those who follow them in opposite directions.

Another example is the intellectual and psychological rigour gained by the meditative techniques utilised in Zen Buddhism and Hinduism. Very few religious traditions promote intense meditation on such esoteric subjects as non-duality, and so their adherents would not be able to gain the benefits of these insights. There is no inherent paradox in, for example, a follower of one of the primal religions of Africa learning in this way, but it would be difficult, as their tradition is lacking the skills to allow them.

The mechanics of Hick's moral philosophy stand in the way of recognising this diversity of religious ends. One finds the suggestion that there is in fact no real diversity at all, that behind all the *apparently* different ethical philosophies, rituals, and practices, the same process—salvation/liberation—is taking place. By virtue of being a generalisation, it focuses on common elements but fails to capture those of an idiosyncratic origin. For an avowed pluralist, someone who wishes to take seriously the variety of ethical reflection, this must count as a serious limitation.

'Buddhism' and 'Hinduism' are not terms like 'Christianity' or 'Islam', but rather like, for example, 'philosophy'. Within the history of Western philosophy alone, there are thinkers as diverse as Democritus, Plato, Thomas Hobbes, Gottlob Frege, Charles Fort, Robert M. Pirsig, and Nietzsche. This radical diversity is mirrored in Buddhism and Hinduism. I am grateful to Keith Ward for his thoughts on this issue.

The very *raison d'être* of the pluralistic enterprise is supposed to be to respect difference, to affirm the realisation that, because they arise out of differing contexts, religions and their component traditions will, to a greater or lesser extent, be idiosyncratic in nature. But the way in which Hick has constructed his philosophy of religion leaves no room for pluralism in the true sense of the word, only a pretence.

In his book *Salvations: Truth and Difference in Religion*,[21] S. Mark Heim speaks of the need to recognise what he calls 'the diversity of religious fulfilments'. He goes so far as to give this metaphysical support, that is, he proposes that ultimate reality is so constituted as to support the validity of the variety of ethical goals, even into the after-life. This has the advantage of avoiding the implication, common to exclusivist theories of religion, that the vast majority of people are wasting their efforts, and that common to inclusivist theories, that most people are greatly deluded as to the ends they are striving for. Heim's underlying assumption seems to be that since the Creator made the world with a great degree of diversity, there is something wrong with denying this natural state of affairs.

Perhaps it is time to lay to rest the ghost of speculative metaphysics, and to resist the temptation to construct meta-theories. Although most religious discourse is a form of speculative metaphysics, a pluralism of the sort propounded by Hick is a bridge too far, in that it allows the pros of pluralism (the recognition of difference) to be outweighed by the cons (generalisation).

Ironically, it is Hick's insistence that none of the religious traditions be ultimately wrong that is the source of the lack of respect paid to each one: if there is no possibility of being wrong about important matters, then there is also no possibility of being correct about them either. This means that no significant assertions are made by any tradition, and their voices are muted; the meta-theorist *tells them* what they are really saying. To correct this, to affirm the validity of each perspective, religious traditions must be allowed the possibility of *being wrong* in the statements they make. After all, part of what is meant by 'maturity', especially in the West with its critically-honed sensibilities, is realising and accepting (a) that others do not, and do not want to, think and act as we want them to, and (b) that we will at times be wrong about things ranging from the trivial to the vitally important.

[21] *Salvations: Truth and Difference in Religion*, Maryknoll, New York: Orbis, 1995.

Without the detrimental influence of a meta-theory, a recognition and affirmation of difference can be given, which in addition will provide a motive (as if one were needed) for detailed study of traditions unfamiliar to oneself. Once it is realised that religions do say different things, rather than the same thing under different guises, then every committed seeker after truth will be drawn to religions other than their own, in order to learn new things.

It may well be, as Paul Heim suggests,[22] that in the after-life some religious goals are deemed to be more important than others (he calls this 'ontological ordering'). But we should be wary of making this decision too early, by identifying the supposed 'core' of all religious ethics. Such an evaluation is at best speculative, and works against the pluralist's stated aims: instead of allowing each person or group of persons to put forward their point of view without shame, it adds the caveat that it must somehow be re-evaluated or 'purified' before it can join public debate. The challenge is to encounter, cope with, and affirm diversity, not to hide from and condemn it, or to suggest that, in the final analysis, it does not really exist. Only if this is achieved will there be any lasting ethical resonance in the term 'liberal theology'.[23]

[22] 'Salvations: A More Pluralistic Hypothesis', in *Modern Theology* 10 (1994), p. 348.

[23] In this essay I have been quite critical of Hick's position, but I would not want the reader to finish with an overly negative view of his work. His influence on the philosophy of religion in the latter half of the twentieth century is virtually unparalleled, and in my experience he always asks the right questions, even if I do not agree with his answers. I would also like to take this opportunity to express my gratitude to him for the interest he has taken in my research, which has included a number of personal discussions of this topic, and his providing me with a bibliography of his works and critical responses to them.

Part Two

Liberal Theology and Education

Chapter 7

Liberal Theology and Transformative Pedagogy

Peter C. Hodgson

A postmodern liberal theology

The topic of this chapter is the contribution of liberal theology to a transformative pedagogy for our time. More broadly I am interested in exploring the connection between liberal theology and liberal education. Liberal theology is generally thought to be dead, the product of modernity, displaced by 'postliberal theology' or no theology at all in the age of 'postmodernity'. Similar claims do not seem to be made about liberal education or liberal arts. Perhaps we are moving into an age of 'postliberal education'.[1] but if so it is scarcely something to be welcomed, as some people have welcomed the advent of postliberal theology. While I believe that significant connections exist between liberal education and liberal theology, my argument is not that the latter might be resuscitated through association with the former. Rather my first premise is that liberal theology is not in fact dead. It has survived in and through the transition from modernity to postmodernity and the critiques of neo-orthodoxy, dialectical theology, and postliberal theology. Of course it

[1] Elaine Graham, in her challenging response to this chapter, describes several signs of the 'commodification' of pedagogy in the market-driven culture of our time. When liberal education has become the province of the leisure industry, while universities are dominated by vocational training, we should know that we have arrived at the condition of postliberalism in education. Graham does not welcome this development but believes that the fact of it renders the achievement of the goals I advocate all the more problematic. I acknowledge the impact of her analysis—a heavy dose of reality, perhaps, by contrast with my utopian tendencies—but I am then compelled to argue with even greater urgency for a new vision of the liberal agenda in education and theology.

has not remained unchanged in this process; one of its qualities is its openness to change. Its characteristic marks must be revisioned for the twenty-first century. What I am advocating is a *revisionary, postmodern liberal theology* as opposed to a postliberal, countermodern theology. I am not exactly an 'impenitent liberal', as Alec Vidler remarked when he retired in 1967,[2] for I think that penitence is something that the liberal traditions must practise just as profoundly as any other human intellectual effort, but I do believe that there remains a great resource of truth and insight in these traditions that should not be lost, and I happen to believe that the term 'liberal' is wonderfully appropriate.

My first step is to explain what I mean by a 'postmodern liberal theology'. Then I will identify five marks of a liberal theology for today. Thirdly, I will consider some of the connections between liberal theology and liberal education. Finally, I will set forth elements of a transformative pedagogy that can be shown to have religious or spiritual implications, implications that are best appreciated, in my judgement, by a revisionary theological liberalism.[3]

The term 'postmodernity' is bandied about loosely these days with a wide array of meanings. Paul Lakeland has brought some admirable clarity to bear in his book *Postmodernity: Christian Identity in a Fragmented Age*.[4] Basically, he says, the postmodern elements in our contemporary world are all manifestations of a breakdown in the 'givens,' in the fundamental coordinates of experience – time, space, and order. This does not mean that these co-ordinates simply disappear; rather their old fixed, stable, structures have collapsed and are being replaced by something new which is fluid, relative, permeable, expansive or elastic, more like a net or a web (an image introduced by Quine) than a building with foundations.[5] Accordingly, some of the elements of the 'postmodern sensibility' are that it is nonsequential, noneschatological,

[2] Quoted by Peter Baelz in D. W. Hardy and P. H. Sedgwick (eds), *The Weight of Glory. A Vision and Practice for Christian Faith: The Future of Liberal Theology. Essays for Peter Baelz*, Edinburgh: T. & T. Clark, 1991, p. 15.

[3] On the latter point see Peter C. Hodgson, *God's Wisdom: Toward a Theology of Education*, Louisville: Westminster/John Knox, 1999. Portions of this chapter draw upon materials contained in this book and are used with the permission of the publisher.

[4] Minneapolis: Fortress Press, 1997.

[5] Ibid., pp. 2-5. On W. V. O. Quine's image, see Nancey Murphy, *Beyond Liberalism and Fundamentalism: How Modern and Postmodern Philosophy Set the Theological Agenda*, Valley Forge, Pa.: Trinity Press International, 1996, pp. 88-9.

nonutopian, nonsystematic, nonfoundational, and, ultimately, nonpolitical. 'The postmodern human being', writes Lakeland, 'wants a lot but expects little. The emotional range is narrow, between mild depression at one end and a whimsical insouciance at the other.'[6]

This is not an especially attractive picture, and one of the services provided by Lakeland is to show how different types of postmodernity emerge in response to it. There are, in the first place, the *true or radical postmoderns,* who celebrate all these negations, are content to live without cultural orientation in a kind of existential vacuum, are radically historicist (no self, no history, no book, no God, as Mark Taylor puts it),[7] and regard knowledge to be purely a function of power, desire, and self-interest. These are the heirs of Nietzsche, Foucault, and other recent French thinkers. At the other end of the spectrum are the *countermoderns,* for whom modernity itself is the problem (its liberalism, moral relativism, secular humanism, etc.), and who celebrate its demise as an opportunity to reaffirm traditional truths and values, not by returning to precritical forms but by embracing a postcritical theory of knowledge and language, drawn especially from Wittgenstein, which emphasises the function of language in forming distinctive patterns of life. Finally, in the middle are the *late moderns* or *critical postmoderns,* who live critically in the postmodern world, affirming some of it (the decentring of the human person, Western culture, and Christ), challenging other parts of it (its relativism, atheism, aestheticism), wanting to carry the unfinished project of modernity forward but in a vastly changed cultural world, principally in the form of communicative reason, discourse ethics, situated freedom, drawing upon either pragmatism (James, Dewey, and their heirs), critical social theory (Habermas), or a holistic philosophy of relationality and process (Hegel, Whitehead).[8]

The kind of revisionary, postmodern liberal theology that I am advocating belongs in the latter camp, but it accepts the valid criticisms brought against traditional liberalism by the other two camps. From the radical postmoderns it accepts the critiques of philosophical foundationalism, cultural Eurocentrism, and the notion of God as a metaphysical 'supreme Being'. From the countermoderns, most forcefully represented today by the postliberal theology of the Yale school, it accepts the critiques of culture-Protestantism, evolutionary optimism, individualism,

[6] Lakeland, *Postmodernity,* pp. 8-9.

[7] Mark C. Taylor, *Erring: A Postmodern A/theology,* Chicago: University of Chicago Press, 1984.

[8] Lakeland, *Postmodernity,* pp. 10-12, 42-3, 45.

subjectivism, ahistorical antitraditionalism. It acknowledges with H. Richard Niebuhr the possibility of liberalism's 'disinherited mind', the theoretical loss of the fundamental principles of Christianity. But as Niebuhr points out, this was more characteristic of liberal theologians in the early years of the twentieth century in America than it was of the great theologians of the nineteenth century, and Niebuhr himself at the end of his career was moving toward a positive reassessment of the liberal tradition.[9]

The tendency to caricature and stereotype liberal theology goes back, unfortunately, to the other Niebuhr, Reinhold, who, when pressed, could not identify a single thinker who actually fitted the monstrous system of liberal ideas he conjured up in *Christian Realism*.[10] In my judgement, George Lindbeck's characterisation of liberal theology as 'experiential-expressivist' is also a stereotype,[11] not as egregious as Reinhold Niebuhr's, although some of Lindbeck's students have been less careful than he. I do not intend to respond here to Lindbeck since others have done so effectively. I am inclined rather to follow the advice of Richard Niebuhr, who used to quote F.D. Maurice to the effect that it is better to take seriously what persons affirm than what they deny.

So what did and does liberal theology affirm? This is not an easy question to answer. There are any number of liberal theologies, some good, some bad, some indifferent. One of the problems is that few if any of the theologians most directly associated with the liberal theology movement in Germany, Britain, and the United States at the end of the nineteenth and the beginning of the twentieth century were truly great thinkers, thinkers of the first rank. There were certainly some very competent thinkers, mostly forgotten or slandered,[12] and some near greats – Albrecht Ritschl, Adolf Harnack, and Wilhelm Herrmann in Germany, Auguste Sabatier in France, Charles Gore and later William

[9] H. Richard Niebuhr, 'Next Steps in Theology' (The Cole Lectures, 1961), in William Stacy Johnson (ed.), *Theology, History, and Culture: Major Unpublished Writings*, New Haven: Yale University Press, 1996, pp. 6-8.

[10] This was first pointed out by Daniel Day Williams. See L. Harold DeWolf, *The Case for Theology in Liberal Perspective*, Philadelphia: Westminster Press, 1959, pp. 11-13.

[11] George Lindbeck, *The Nature of Doctrine: Religion and Theology in a Postliberal Age*, Philadelphia: Westminster Press, 1984, pp. 31-2.

[12] See Claude Welch's careful accounting in *Protestant Thought in the Nineteenth Century,* 2 vols., New Haven, Yale University Press, 1972, 1985, vol. 2. pp. 221-38. See also Lloyd J. Averill, *American Theology in the Liberal Tradition*, Philadelphia: Westminster Press, 1967.

Temple in Britain, Walter Rauschenbusch and William Adams Brown in the United States. But the tradition of liberal theology is not limited to these thinkers in this time period. It is much broader and deeper, going back to the Enlightenment and continuing to the present day; and it includes some truly great thinkers. My own list starts with the philosophical heritage of Immanuel Kant and especially G. W. F. Hegel, and it includes Friedrich Schleiermacher, S. T. Coleridge, Horace Bushnell, Josiah Royce, and Ernst Troeltsch. These are the theologians and philosophers of the nineteenth and early twentieth centuries who have most influenced me. Troeltsch in particular stands out as a model: his only partly-executed reconstruction of theology at the beginning of the twentieth century might help to guide us into the twenty-first. My list continues with several thinkers who represent the left wing of dialectical theology and who were deeply influenced by the liberal tradition: Paul Tillich, Rudolf Bultmann, Richard Niebuhr, Paul Ricoeur, and Gerhard Ebeling. There is also an important trajectory of British liberalism from Gore to Temple, F.R. Tennant, Ian Ramsey, Charles Raven, Alec Vidler, John Hick, and Maurice Wiles. I am appreciative of the early and mid-twentieth century Chicago school (Shailer Mathews, Henry Nelson Wieman, Bernard Meland, and Bernard Loomer). Leaping ahead to our own time, the revisionist theology associated with Chicago, Harvard, and Vanderbilt (David Tracy, Langdon Gilkey, Brian Gerrish, Gordon Kaufman, Francis Fiorenza, Edward Farley, Sallie McFague, and myself) stands very much in the liberal tradition. Process theology (Daniel Day Williams, Schubert Ogden, John Cobb) is a liberal theology with its roots in Whitehead and Hartshorne (and, for Ogden, in Bultmann). Feminist and liberation theologies share many of the central concerns of the liberal tradition, recontextualised in a much more diverse cultural and intellectual situation. These are the resources upon which I shall be drawing as I think about the possibility of a postmodern liberal theology for today.

I am striving for a balance, a comprehensive or mediating theology that affirms *both* past and future, subject and object, immanence and transcendence, contemplative and practical reason, *both* reason and revelation, tradition and experience, unity and plurality, identity and difference, concreteness and universality – or, in a word, both Christ and culture, related to each other in such a way that is mutually transformative.[13] I am not willing to limit this work of mediation just to

[13] This places me in the trajectory of Bushnell, Troeltsch, and H. R. Niebuhr, specifically of Bushnell's theology of 'Christian comprehensiveness', of

apologetics, as Lakeland suggests,[14] while conceding systematic theology to the postliberals. The marks of a liberal theology for today that I have in mind ought to be incorporated into new efforts at theological construction.

Marks of a Liberal theology for today

A free and open theology

Liberal theology is above all a *free* theology – 'a free theology of Catholic and Protestant modernism,' as Troeltsch expressed it.[15] This is why the term 'liberal' is so appropriate. 'Liberal' (*liberalis*), as Martha Nussbaum suggests,[16] means something that is 'fitted for freedom' and *makes* for freedom. As such it has not only political and pedagogical but also theological implications. Theologically speaking, what makes for freedom is above all God, the One who *is* freedom ('the Free,' *das Freie,* a nomenclature highlighted by both Hegel and Barth[17]) and who *gives* freedom

Troeltsch's theory of new cultural configurations (*Neugestaltungen*), and of Niebuhr's ideal of 'balance'. See Horace Bushnell, 'Christian Comprehensiveness' (1848), in H. Shelton Smith (ed.), *Horace Bushnell,* New York: Oxford University Press, 1965, pp. 106-26; Ernst Troeltsch, 'Ethics and the Philosophy of History', in Baron F. von Hügel (ed.), *Christian Thought: Its History and Application,* London: University of London Press, 1923, pp. 37-129; and Niebuhr, *Theology, History, and Culture,* pp. 4-9, 18. The German 'Mediating Theology' of the nineteenth century also lies in the background. Bushnell preferred the term 'comprehensive' to 'liberal', since the latter could, he thought, be taken to connote indifference to truth and thus to be simply negative, insipid, and impotent. In my view, it need not be taken in that sense at all, although it is the characteristic caricature of it.

[14] Lakeland, *Postmodernity,* pp. 85-92.

[15] Ernst Troeltsch, 'Religion and the Science of Religion' (1906), in Robert Morgan and Michael Pye (tr. and ed.), *Ernst Troeltsch: Writings on Theology and Religion,* Louisville: Westminster/John Knox, 1990, pp. 119-20.

[16] Martha C. Nussbaum, *Cultivating Humanity: A Classical Defense of Reform in Liberal Education*, Cambridge, Mass: Harvard University Press, 1997, pp. 30-5, 293-300.

[17] See G. W. F. Hegel, *Lectures on the Philosophy of Religion*, ed. and tr. Peter C. Hodgson et al., Berkeley, Los Angeles and London: University of California Press, 1984-87, vol. 1, p. 114 *et passim*; and Karl Barth, *Church Dogmatics*, ed. G.W. Bromiley and T. F. Torrance, vol. 2:1, Edinburgh: T. & T. Clark, 1957, § 28.3. Insofar as Barth is a 'theologian of freedom', he too in a surprising way

(who engenders 'the progress of the consciousness of freedom' in history).[18] As the Apostle Paul eloquently expresses it in Romans, chapter 8:19-23, God gives freedom to creation as a whole, thus setting it free from its 'bondage to decay', and to God's children in particular, human beings, who are to obtain the 'glory' of freedom (the *doxa* of *eleutheria*). If you want a proof text for liberal theology, this is it. John Habgood captures this beautifully in his remark that, while there is no 'identikit' for being a liberal, it is possible to recognise 'some whose lives have clearly been shaped by the gracious liberality of God, and who display its marks in their own liberality toward all that God has made'.[19] Both aspects of this statement need equal emphasis. The earlier liberalism tended to stress the latter at the expense of the former, and that is a valid criticism of it, for the ultimate source of human freedom is precisely God's 'gracious liberality.' There is a divine liberality as well as a human liberality, and the two are profoundly interconnected.

This means that the freedom of liberal theology is not simply or primarily a negative freedom—freedom from the constraints of tradition, confession, institution, external authority—although such freedom is a necessary condition of truth and conscience. More than this, it is a positive freedom – *freedom for*, or *openness to*.[20] Openness to what? To whatever presents itself or reveals itself in the Bible, in Christian tradition, and in the whole of experience – in personal experience, in nature, in one's own culture and religion, in the often-wrenching cultural transitions of one's time, and in the great cultural and religious traditions of humankind as a whole.[21] Confidence in the

contributes to the liberal tradition. On this, see Clifford Green (ed.), *Karl Barth: Theologian of Freedom*, Minneapolis: Fortress Press, 1991, pp. 11-12.

[18] G.W.F. Hegel, *Lectures on the Philosophy of World History. Introduction: Reason in History*, tr. H.B. Nisbet, Cambridge: Cambridge University Press, 1975, p. 54. Ernst Troeltsch argued that 'free personality' constitutes the 'Christian principle,' and that redemption, as the upraising of the divine Spirit in human history, entails liberation and rebirth on the part of humanity. See *The Christian Faith (Glaubenslehre)*, tr. Garrett E. Paul, Minneapolis: Fortress Press, 1991, pp. 230-1, 235-6, 274-7.

[19] John Habgood, 'Reflection on the Liberal Position', in Hardy and Sedgwick (eds.), *The Weight of Glory*, p. 12. Peter Baelz, for whom this work is written, says that in the context of catholicism 'liberal' 'expresses the manner in which God's grace, freely given, is freely received' (p. 16).

[20] Welch emphasises the sense of 'openness' that characterised many of the late nineteenth-century liberals (*Protestant Thought*, vol. 2, pp. 223, 229).

[21] See DeWolf, *The Case for Theology in Liberal Perspective*, pp. 13-14.

gracious liberality of God means that we can and should be open to wherever the marks of this liberality are displayed in nature, culture, and history. There is no single, foundational mark, but a hermeneutical interplay of marks whereby truth, freedom, and grace are apprehended again and again by human beings in different times and places. For Christians, the marks centre upon Christ but are not contained within Christ. An open theology is above all a theology of the Spirit.

A critically constructive theology

Liberal theology is a *critical* theology. Such criticism is a byproduct of its openness and thus its freedom. In the light of God's gracious liberality, theologians must be critical of all established orthodoxies, partial truths, seductive idolatries, and parochial judgements. They must also learn to be self-critical, reminding themselves that all constructions and systems, including their own, are but human products, called forth in response to what presents itself in experience, but mirroring it only dimly. They must learn that it is always necessary to 'think more', never to rest content with what has been accomplished, in theory or in practice. Critical consciousness is a prophetic, iconoclastic consciousness, constantly aware of the deep difference between finite forms and infinite, inexhaustible truth. This is the Kantian element in liberal theology. It certainly does not mean that liberal theology is indifferent to the truth and is merely neutral, tolerant, permissive, or relativistic. By contrast with this standard caricature, liberalism has a deep passion for truth but also recognises the complexity of the question of truth.

Part of the task of thinking more is to take up the task of *reconstruction* after every deconstruction.[22] The goal of liberal theology is not to destroy or lose the heritage of the past but to preserve and appreciate it; and it understands that this can be accomplished not by fruitlessly holding on to old forms but by allowing them to pass over into new and different ones. This requires a new construction, seeking new symbols to replace overused and worn-out ones,[23] attending to new circumstances and new insights never imagined in the past. While such a construction is a human effort, if it is a genuine and honest effort and if we have faith in God's gracious liberality, we have grounds for confidence that our construction is a response to something real that is

[22] See Peter C. Hodgson, *Winds of the Spirit: A Constructive Christian Theology*, London: SCM Press, 1994, chs. 1, 3, 4.

[23] See Niebuhr, *Theology, History, and Culture*, pp. 19-33.

presenting itself. Truth will come out through the testing of these constructions in a community of free and open discourse. In the final analysis we have no alternative. We cannot know truth directly, and we cannot dwell humanly in the world without undertaking such constructions, fragile and fallible though they be. We cannot live simply with the silence of a negative theology but must strive for a balance between negation and affirmation, apophasis and kataphasis.

An experiential theology

Liberal theology is an *experiential* theology. This is certainly one of the classic marks of theological liberalism. The liberal theologians believed that all religion is rooted in experience, both immediate and mediated, concrete and universal. Experience is the matrix in which religion occurs.[24] This could be understood in a foundational way, as postliberal critics have charged,[25] but it need not be. The matrix of experience is more like Quine's web than a stable building. It is multidimensional and interactive, fluid and elastic. Theologians must be open to the totality of experience: empirical, sensible, emotional, intuitive, intellectual, aesthetic, cultural, revelatory. The revelation of God's gracious liberality occurs through certain root experiences that reverberate in history, are mediated by texts and traditions, and interact with the personal experience of interpreters and their communities.[26] Experience in all its forms, including that of emotions and feelings, puts us in touch with what is real, objective, powerful, abiding.[27] Schleiermacher was convinced that the feeling of utter dependence is elicited by the ultimate Whence and Whither of existence and is not a projection of a private state. William James and Josiah Royce came to a similar conclusion, as have recent pragmatic theologies.

The liberal theologians also recognised that there is a science of experience—a term that initially came from Hegel as a way of characterising his phenomenology of Spirit, but that was appropriated by the new, empirical human sciences at the end of the nineteenth century—

[24] For an excellent study, see Wayne Proudfoot, *Religious Experience*, Berkeley and Los Angeles: University of California Press, 1985.

[25] See Murphy, *Beyond Liberalism and Fundamentalism*, chap. 1.

[26] See my *Winds of the Spirit*, chs. 1-2.

[27] See Niebuhr, *Theology, History, and Culture*, pp. 34-49.

psychology and sociology of religion, comparative history of religions.[28] It is these sciences of religion that helped to fuel the emergence of religious studies in secular universities. I believe that a postmodern liberal theology must incorporate within itself the science of religion (including literary and cultural as well as psychological and sociological studies) as an essential critical moment, just as religious studies must incorporate within itself a theological engagement with the truth- and reality-claims of the faith-traditions under investigation. Experience *critically engaged* can serve to mediate between religious and theological studies. The goal here, as Troeltsch clearly recognised,[29] is to establish relations of *consonance* and *coherence* between science and religion, experience and faith, as opposed to a foundationalist deduction of one from the other, or a separation of them into hermetically sealed realms.

A visionary theology

Liberal theology is a *visionary,* spiritual, holistic theology. Vision entails an awareness and appreciation of the mystery at the heart of reality. It represents the mystical dimension of theology by contrast with its empirical, experiential dimension; it entails intellectual as compared with sensible intuition, the ability to see or intuit or imagine the whole in the parts, the universal in the concrete. It requires a heightening of imagination, an ability to discern and interpret figures, to create new concepts out of revisioned symbols. If Schleiermacher is the modern patron saint of experiential theology, then Hegel and Coleridge are the modern saints of visionary, spiritual theology. The two strands come together in Troeltsch, clashing and fusing.

Theology can be visionary in both apophatic and kataphatic forms – both the negative theology of Pseudo-Dionysius and Kierkegaard and the speculative theology of Hegel. Its visions can be philosophical, spiritual, aesthetic, utopian, political or a combination of these. What is called for in our own time, I believe, is a postmetaphysical speculative-political theology, one that can articulate a holistic ontological vision, an interpretation of reality that connects nature and spirit, psyche and culture, the aesthetic and the ethical, the personal and the political, and

[28] See Troeltsch, 'Religion and the Science of Religion', in *Writings on Theology and Religion,* pp. 82-123.

[29] Troeltsch, *The Christian Faith,* pp. 73-84, 195-204.

that does so in the form of an open, nontotalising metanarrative.[30] What is required is not simply a methodological or cultural-linguistic holism, as postliberals claim,[31] but an ontological holism, perhaps even (God forbid!) an 'ontotheological' holism, or better a 'cosmotheandric' holism.[32] We do not necessarily need a singular genius to produce such a vision, helpful as that might be, but a group of people networking together. Given the enormity of the task in the greatly expanded horizons of postmodernity, it is hard to imagine how any individual could accomplish it alone. Whatever might be achieved along these lines today will have more the character of a collage or quilt, a bricolage, than of a finished tapestry.

A culturally transformative theology

Finally, liberal theology is a *culturally transformative theology.* This is the ethical mandate of classical liberalism, radicalised by the postmodern critiques of late-modern bourgeois capitalist culture. Culture-Protestantism is no longer a possibility for us, and its evolutionary optimism was already severely criticised by Troeltsch. Troeltsch himself sought a new cultural synthesis, a *Neugestaltung,* a transformative ethic of cultural values.[33] His awareness of the colossal power of human evil and of the tragic dimension of existence led in his final writings to

[30] On this way of reading Hegel, see Cyril O'Regan, *The Heterodox Hegel*, Albany: State University of New York Press, 1994; O'Regan attends especially to Hegel's stance in the mystical tradition and to his speculative metanarrative; Robert R. Williams, *Recognition: Fichte and Hegel on the Other*, Albany: State University of New York Press, 1992, esp. ch. 11 on Hegel's holism; and Michael Theunissen, *Hegels Lehre vom absoluten Geist als theologisch-politischer Traktat*, Berlin: Walter de Gruyter, 1970. See also the introduction to my anthology, *G.W.F. Hegel: Theologian of the Spirit*, Edinburgh: T & T Clark, 1997, esp. pp. 4-11.

[31] See Murphy, *Beyond Liberalism and Fundamentalism*, chs. 4-5. Murphy also calls for a 'metaphysical holism' in ch. 6, but what she offers there, drawing upon some postmodern cosmologies and philosophies of science, seems impoverished by comparison with the philosophical wealth of Hegel or Whitehead.

[32] See Raimon Panikkar, *The Cosmotheandric Experience*, Maryknoll, N.Y.: Orbis Books, 1993.

[33] See Troeltsch, 'The Ethics of Cultural Values', in *Christian Thought*, pp. 69-99. For his general cultural assessment just before his death in 1923, see the whole of sections 2 and 3 of this book, which contains lectures he was to have delivered in England.

an ethic of struggle, patience, compromise, hope without illusions, realism without cynicism and despair. That good might, from time to time, be brought out of evil, that culture might be transformed, ambiguously and fragmentarily, requires faith in God's providence.[34] The same hopeful realism, this same striving for human freedom and flourishing often in the face of overwhelming odds, is characteristic, I believe, of the greatest liberal thinkers. Today liberal theology must also be a liberation theology. The very name *liberal,* 'making for freedom', requires it. Thus in terms of Richard Niebuhr's Christ-and-culture typology, it is not really the 'Christ *of* culture' that fits this deeper liberal tradition but 'Christ the *transformer* of culture'.[35]

I believe that the transformation works both ways. Despite its negative features, there are some transformative potentialities in postmodern culture. Good theology ought to be able to identify these elements, strengthen them, work with them, separate them from the cultural dross that clings to them. God's truth is being revealed through them as well as through our all-too-familiar theological sources. In *Winds of the Spirit* I sought to identify three of these elements—the emancipatory, the ecological, and the dialogical quests of our time—and to bring the resources they offer to bear in a revisioned constructive theology.[36] Each of them requires us to think about God, Christ, and the Spirit differently and with new insight: the Transformer is being transformed in the process of transformation. Is this not what a radical theology of incarnation requires? God is actually becoming God through interaction with, embodiment in, the world.[37]

The work of cultural transformation is the responsibility not only of religion but of politics, the arts, and education. These seem to be failing as miserably in our time as religion itself. This is why we sense a deep cultural crisis. Politics has become a game of power, image, and deception with virtually no social conscience; the arts have been displaced by media and entertainment; education is riven by culture wars and disci-

[34] See Troeltsch, *The Christian Faith,* pp. 174-94, 204-23, 253-9.

[35] See H. Richard Niebuhr, *Christ and Culture,* New York: Harper & Bros., 1951, chap. 6. Niebuhr associates this 'conversionist' model with F.D. Maurice, who stands with at least one foot in the liberal tradition. Claude Welch connects Maurice and Horace Bushnell with what he calls 'critical orthodoxy' (*Protestant Thought,* vol. 1, chaps. 10-11).

[36] See *Winds of the Spirit,* chs. 5-8.

[37] Ibid., chap. 11. See also Sallie McFague, *The Body of God: An Ecological Theology,* Minneapolis: Fortress Press, 1993, chaps. 5-6.

plinary jealousies. Yet there are hopeful signs here and there, and religion has the potentiality of playing a prophetic role within each of these other cultural activities. I would like now to explore the linkage of liberal theology and liberal education in the common work of cultural transformation. Here the hopeful signs may prove more promising than expected.

Liberal theology and liberal education

Liberal theology and liberal education: the connection between these two forms of liberalism seems obvious but has rarely been discussed. Let us start with liberal education. I am helped especially by Martha Nussbaum's wonderful book, *Cultivating Humanity: A Classical Defense of Reform in Liberal Education* (1997). She writes that 'an education ... is *liberalis,* "fitted for freedom" ... only if it is such as to *produce* free citizens, citizens who are free not because of wealth or birth, but because they can call their minds their own'. She traces this idea back to Seneca, who argued against the assumption of his time that only gentlemen of the propertied classes are 'fitted for freedom'. Thus liberal education has immediate political implications. It produces free citizens who are able to participate in democratic governance and who 'have ownership of their own thought and speech'. Such people are not uncritical moral relativists, nor do they simply scoff at older traditions. They start from convention and tradition, says Nussbaum, 'viewing it as essential food for the mind. On the other hand, they do not confuse food with the strength in the mind that the food is supposed to produce.' It is through such strength of mind that 'they hope to advance from the cultural narrowness into which we all are born toward true world citizenship'. Through the broadest possible community of discourse and enquiry, they hope to make informed judgements about truth and value.[38]

Adapting a phrase from Seneca, Nussbaum suggests that the basic purpose of liberal education is 'a cultivation of the whole human being

[38] Nussbaum, *Cultivating Humanity,* pp. 293-4. Two earlier authors set forth very similar definitions of liberal education: Howard Lowry in *The Mind's Adventure: Religion and Higher Education,* Philadelphia: Westminster Press, 1950, ch. 3; and Robert Ulich, 'The Meaning of Liberal Education', in Christian Gauss (ed.), *The Teaching of Religion in American Higher Education,* New York: Ronald Press, 1951, ch. 2. The other contributors to the latter volume (Gauss, Howard Jefferson, Kenneth Morgan, and J. Hillis Miller) are also helpful.

for the functions of citizenship and life generally'. She believes that this 'noble ideal' has been tried in the United States 'to a degree unparalleled in the world', and she is relatively hopeful about its present prospects, despite the persistence of severe problems, such as the scarcity of full-time teaching positions, institutional cost-cutting, and the prevalence of a corporate mentality among administrators and a vocational mentality among students. Precisely in the midst of these problems, she believes that 'never before have there been so many talented and committed young faculty so broadly dispersed in institutions of so many different kinds, thinking about difficult issues connecting education and citizenship', struggling 'to reason well about urgent questions and to engage the hearts and minds of their students in that search'.[39]

The cultivation of humanity requires the *transformation* of humanity, that is, a change from one condition to another. This is the basic conviction behind the classical idea of *paideia,*[40] from which Nussbaum's 'cultivation' derives. Paideia is a formation that is simultaneously a transformation; something like a 'conversion', a 'metamorphosis' is required. Education, like religion, transforms human beings from self-centredness to reality-centredness.[41] We can almost use the words of the Apostle Paul in saying to cultivated, educated persons: 'Do not be conformed to this world, but be transformed by the renewing of your minds' (Rom. 12:2). Precisely what it is that we are to be transformed *from* and *to* remains a matter of discussion. Is it *from* conformity to this world and its values, from cultural narrowness and human self-centredness? Do these mean essentially the same thing? What is it that holds human beings captive to something false, narrow, and idolatrous? Paul says that what we are to be transformed *to* is discernment of 'the will of God'; but he adds that God wills 'what is good and acceptable and perfect'. What do these things mean? What is the good? What is virtue? What is truth or perfection? What is reality? In addressing these questions education takes on a religious, spiritual quality, whether explicitly recognised or not. For most of Western history, religion and education were

[39] Nussbaum, *Cultivating Humanity*, pp. 2-3, 8-9.

[40] See Werner Jaeger's three-volume study, *Paideia: The Ideals of Greek Culture*, New York: Oxford University Press, 1943-4.

[41] This expression is used by John Hick to characterise the fundamental character of salvation/liberation in religion. See *The Metaphor of God Incarnate: Christology in a Pluralistic Age*, Louisville: Westminster John Knox Press, 1993, p. 136; and *An Interpretation of Religion: Human Responses to the Transcendent*, New Haven: Yale University Press, 1989, p. 14.

closely associated. They split apart in the modern era. Does postmodernity offer the prospect of putting them back together – but on a thoroughly nonparochial, religiously nonpartisan, intellectually open, and culturally plural basis?

This was a question that was discussed by several thinkers during the 1950s and 1960s.[42] With the emergence of religious studies departments in the 1960s and 1970s, the primary emphasis was on making the study of religion conform to the paradigm of the research university. Not much thought was given to the question whether liberal education as such and as a whole might have a religious dimension, and if so what that might be. Only recently has this question been seriously addressed once again.[43] Before turning to it in the final section of this chapter, I want to introduce an idea that was suggested by E. Harris Harbison.[44] In his paper, Harbison asked two questions: 'Can a liberal education be a Christian education?' 'Can a Christian education be a liberal educa-

[42] See esp. Howard Lowry *The Mind's Adventure*; Robert Ulich, 'The Meaning of Liberal Education' and Harris Harbison, 'Liberal Education and Christian Education', in Edmund Fuller (ed.) *The Christian Idea of Education*, New Haven: Yale University Press, 1957.

[43] During the past decade a host of books has been published on the connection between liberal education and the study of religion: Frank Reynolds and Sheryl Burkhalter (eds), *Beyond the Classics? Essays in Religious Studies and Liberal Education*, Atlanta: Scholars Press, 1990; George M. Marsden, *The Soul of the American University: From Protestant Establishment to Established Nonbelief*, New York: Oxford University Press, 1994; George M. Marsden and Bradley J. Longfield (eds), *The Secularization of the Academy*, New York: Oxford University Press, 1992; Philip Gleason, *Contending with Modernity: Catholic Higher Education in the Twentieth Century*, New York: Oxford University Press, 1995; Douglas Sloan, *Faith and Knowledge: Mainline Protestantism and American Higher Education*, Louisville: Westminster John Knox Press, 1994; Mark R. Schwehn, *Exiles from Eden: Religion and the Academic Vocation in America*, New York: Oxford University Press, 1993; Merrimon Cunninggim, *Uneasy Partners: The College and the Church*, Nashville: Abingdon Press, 1994; Denise Lardner Carmody, *Organizing a Christian Mind: A Theology of Higher Education*, Valley Forge, Pa.: Trinity Press International, 1996. A number of these works are reviewed by Daniel Sack, 'Struggling for the Soul of the American University: Studies on Religion and Higher Education', in *Religious Studies Review* 23 (1997), pp. 35-39. Several recent issues of *The Journal of the American Academy of Religion* have been devoted to this topic.

[44] In *The Christian Idea of Education*, pp. 60-100. A number of other notable essays are found in this volume, which contains papers presented at a seminar at Kent School in 1955.

tion?' He summarised his conclusion as a paradox: 'A liberal education can be illumined by Christianity provided that the Christian education which complements it is liberal.' For 'Christian' we could equally well read 'religious'. A liberal education can be illumined by religion, said Harbison, because its provision of *hindsight* and *foresight* to students must be supplemented by *insight,* and that is the domain principally of religion. But the religious and/or Christian education that complements liberal education must itself be liberal. It must be true *education* and not *catechesis,* which is ordinarily dogmatic, domineering, divisive, sectarian. Unfortunately, what has passed for education in much of Christian history has really been catechesis. Are there, Harbison asked, liberal alternatives in this history? He found them in the Brethren of the Common Life, in Erasmus, in Comenius, in Milton, and in Dostoievsky. Harbison was a historian of the Renaissance and Reformation, not a theologian, and he did not think to look to the traditions of liberal theology in the nineteenth and twentieth centuries. Here is an approach to religious thought and practice that is intrinsically appropriate to liberal education and that can help to elicit the transformative potential, the spiritual insight, that is potentially present in such education.

One further aspect of the connection between liberal theology and education which cannot be developed in this chapter is that liberalism found in the figure of Jesus a paradigmatic teacher. Jesus taught not by way of catechesis but by telling stories which drew people out of petty preoccupations and narrow traditionalisms into a larger vision, a vision of God and of God's kingdom as radically transformative. He was truly an educator. The effect of this teacher on people's lives was also transformative, and thus it is not surprising that the earliest Christological models of redemption were pedagogical. Jesus not only taught but embodied the way, the truth, and the life. As such he was believed to be a divine teacher, the one through whom God teaches, for God is the ultimate teacher. This ancient Christian conviction has the possibility of being newly articulated by a postmodern liberal theology.[45]

Elements of a transformative pedagogy

One of my purposes in addressing a theology of education has been to discover whether there are emergent themes in late modern and postmodern pedagogical theory that might be pointing in the direction of a

[45] See *God's Wisdom: Toward a Theology of Education*, ch. 4, § 2.

recovery of the religious dimension of education. I shall present five such elements:[46] education and life-formation, the rhythm of education, constructive and interactive knowledge, connected and imaginative teaching, and education as the practice of freedom. Each can be shown to have points of contact with the marks of a postmodern liberal theology outlined earlier.

Education and life-formation

Education and life-formation emphasises what we have just been discussing, that education both forms human beings, makes it possible for them to live humanly in the world, and transforms them towards an end or vision of human flourishing. John Dewey and others have argued that education is a necessity of life because living things are able to maintain themselves only by constant renewal. For human beings, this entails not only the renewal of physical existence through reproduction but also 'the re-creation of beliefs, ideals, hopes, happiness, misery, and practices'.[47] 'Education, in its broadest sense, is the means of this social continuity of life.' Above all, it is the 'ineluctable facts of the birth and death of each one of the constituent members in a social group [that] determine the necessity of education'. For just this reason, it would seem, education takes on a sacral or religious quality. Religion focuses on events, beliefs, practices intimately associated with the boundary experiences and transitions of life, the points at which the fundamental mystery of life itself is most directly experienced, points at which the holy is encountered: birth, natural endowment, family, cultural formation, achievement, failure and renewal, death. Education is a life-enhancing practice. It is the means by which a newly-born infant is nurtured through a laborious process into becoming a free, responsible, thinking, acting human being; it is the means by which persons become productive and self-supporting, and the means by which they learn (if at all) how to grow old and die.[48] Without it, human existence is simply

[46] These themes are developed at length in *God's Wisdom,* chap. 3. Used by permission of Westminster/John Knox Press.

[47] John Dewey, *Democracy and Education: An Introduction to the Philosophy of Education* (1916), New York: The Free Press, 1966, ch. 1.

[48] Gabriel Moran (in *Showing How: The Act of Teaching,* Valley Forge, Pa.: Trinity Press International, 1997, pp. 37-9) argues that the verb 'to teach' means 'to show' (from an Anglo-Saxon root meaning 'sign,' 'symbol') – to show

inconceivable, and thus education is a root experience of life. Dewey himself does not pursue these religious implications, but his analysis seems to cry out for them. The connection of life-formation with the experiential character of liberal theology seems evident.

According to Dewey, what enables beliefs and aspirations to be communicated and appropriated is 'the action of the environment in calling out certain responses'. In other words, the 'medium' in which individuals live leads them to see and feel one thing rather than another, to have certain plans and adopt specific beliefs; it gradually produces in them a disposition to action. The words 'environment' and 'medium' denote for Dewey a continuity of interactions more than physical surroundings. But 'environment' cannot be adequately designated as simply the 'conditions' that promote or hinder the characteristic activities of a living being. This pragmatic approach does not resolve the question of the ontological status of environment, whether it is spiritual as well as natural, cultural as well as social. Human beings dwell in a transcendental horizon that they call 'world,' not just environment, and the constitution of world cannot be settled by a pragmatic theory of knowledge.[49] Ontological and religious questions may be bracketed but they do not thereby disappear. It seems rather flat to say that the ultimate source of life-formation is simply 'environment' or 'social conditions'. Nor is it satisfactory to say that this is as far as social science can take us, as if that disposes of the matter.

Another suggestive and recent approach to education as life-formation, including both social and intellectual formation, is that taken by political scientist Charles W. Anderson.[50] He argues that the public purpose of the university is to initiate the young into the way of life of a people, while its intrinsic purpose is to find out what can be done with the powers of mind.[51] Here he is embracing a perspective that runs from Plato and Aristotle through Kant and Hegel. With respect to both these functions—initiating into life and drawing forth the powers of mind—

someone how to do something. What teaching and education ultimately show us is 'how to live and how to die'.

[49] Dewey, *Democracy and Education*, pp. 11-15. See, for example, Martin Heidegger's analysis of 'being-in-the-world', in *Being and Time*, tr. Joan Stambaugh, Albany: State University of New York Press, 1996, pp. 49 ff.

[50] Charles W. Anderson, *Prescribing the Life of the Mind: An Essay on the Purpose of the University, the Aims of Liberal Education, the Competence of Citizens, and the Cultivation of Practical Reason*, Madison: University of Wisconsin Press, 1993.

[51] Ibid., pp. 44-58.

education is up against a fundamental mystery. The power of mind is uncanny. Where and what is it? Is it strictly an individual power that we try to draw forth, as contemporary theories of education primarily assume? Are we just interested in personal interpretations, feelings, views? Or is the aim to bring students to see what all humans can see, what we can understand in common? Is mind individual, or universal, or somehow both? What is the 'way of life of a people' into which we are initiating students? Is it simply an arbitrary and contingent social product? Where do its values and virtues come from? How are we able to recognise justice and injustice when we see them? To be sure, education cannot be based on the idea of knowing universal truth directly but rather must attend to the partial, contingent, inadequate truths encountered in everyday teaching. 'Yet recurrently', Anderson continues,

> during the routine process of getting an education, one should glimpse the possibility that something big is going on here, that in some respects, astonishingly, the universe is *comprehensible* and that we all do have a fundamental sense of right and wrong. One need not dwell too long in such regions. The university is really not the place to sit all day enraptured, contemplating the eternal verities. This power is better captured in sidelong glances. As natural beauty can overwhelm us only in brief doses, and then it is best to get back to hiking, or paddling, or chopping wood, so natural law and the universality of mind is something it is best to come upon, unexpectedly, in all sorts of odd places, in the course of doing other things.[52]

Here Anderson captures the religious dimension that is present in all education, especially when teachers recognise that they are initiating their students into a way of life and drawing forth the powers of their minds. I agree with Anderson that it is probably best to come upon this region unexpectedly, in the course of doing other things, and that it is unwise to dwell in it too long. But disciplined reflection upon it is also necessary if education is to reach its goal, and such reflection is only caricatured if it is represented as sitting 'all day enraptured, contemplating the eternal verities'. The disciplines of theology and religious studies do in fact exist, where what is encountered unexpectedly in odd sorts of places in other regions of study is thematised on its own account. The university *needs* these disciplines if its educational purpose is to be attained.

[52] Ibid., pp. 90-92.

The rhythm of education

The rhythm of education is an expression introduced by Alfred North Whitehead. By 'rhythmic' he means 'the conveyance of difference within a framework of repetition'. Mental growth cycles repeatedly through three stages, which he named 'romance' (discovery, direct experience, immediacy), 'precision' (disciplined knowledge, mastery of technique, differentiation), and 'generalisation' (fruition, synthesis, freedom).[53] Education consists of a continual repetition of these cycles in each unit of study, but the cycles also mark the advance of persons from infancy into adulthood. Romance is the stage of first apprehension, when subject matter has the vividness of novelty, unexplored connections, and wealth of material. It occurs principally in the stage of early adolescence (ages 8-13), when a rich world crowds into the child's life and basic skills in language and arithmetic are acquired, but education will go stale if the leaven of romance and the excitement of discovery are lost. Precision comes at the time of secondary education (ages 13-18), when mastery of language is acquired along with precision in the basic tools of science. Generalisation is the goal of university education. It should presuppose the particulars and start with general ideas, studying their application to concrete cases. The student should attain a 'wide sweep of generality', which is not abstracted from concrete fact but rather appears in the form of what Hegel calls 'concrete universals.' Rather than cramming students with details, a university education should yield a construction and comprehension of basic principles together with a thorough grounding in the way they apply to a variety of concrete details. The principles will be remembered while the details are forgotten. Whitehead emphasises that these stages are not simply successive; rather they are interwoven at each stage, with one or another predominating but with the others also present. Thus at the stage of generalisation it is necessary to revisit elements of precision and romance at higher levels of intellectual maturation.

Whitehead's rhythmic theory is both confirmed and modified in an interesting way by the empirical research of William Perry on the intellectual and ethical development of college students. Perry discovered that American university students (even at the élite

[53] Alfred North Whitehead, *The Aims of Education and Other Essays*, New York: Free Press, 1967, chap. 2. Mary Elizabeth Mullino Moore adopts a variation of the rhythm in *Teaching from the Heart: Theology and Educational Method*, Minneapolis: Fortress Press, 1991, ch. 3.

institution of Harvard) are not as far along in intellectual maturation as Whitehead had assumed. They are certainly not at the stage of 'generalisation' when they enter college. Or rather, the rhythm seems to repeat itself in its own way during the college years, moving from a simple dualism (absolute principles of right and wrong) through various phases of acknowledging diversity and contextual relativism, to the position of recognising the need for some sort of personal commitment in a relativistic world, which enables one to act on the basis of principles or values. Students move from the 'romance' of naive belief, through an incredible deconstruction and disciplining of their minds in a bewildering array of academic perspectives, to the possibility of something like a mature world view. Perry doubts that many college students actually arrive at the latter, and they may never arrive at it if they do not continue to grow intellectually.[54]

The rhythm of education can be understood theologically to reflect the rhythm of the cosmos as a whole (the interplay of unity, separation, and reunion), or of the divine life itself (God's initial identity, the creation of a world other than God, the reconciliation of God and the world); and through this rhythm human beings are drawn more and more deeply into the mystery of reality.

Constructive and interactive knowledge

Constructive and interactive knowledge is the element of precision, discipline, criticism, construction and reconstruction in Whitehead's rhythm. Postmodern pedagogies have stressed that all such criticism and construction are human projects: we live in a humanly constructed world. One of the most interesting treatments of this theme is found in a study of 'women's ways of knowing' that was undertaken in response to the work of William Perry.[55] Noting that Perry's study had been based almost entirely on men, the authors sought to duplicate it among women by using a different method. Instead of Perry's sequence of positions moving from dualism to commitment, they identified five roughly parallel epistemological perspectives exemplified by college women: si-

[54] William G. Perry, Jr., *Forms of Intellectual and Ethical Development in the College Years: A Scheme*, New York: Holt, Rinehart and Winston, 1968, 1970, esp. chaps, 1, 5, 6.

[55] Mary Field Belenky, Blythe McVicker Clincy, Nancy Rule Goldberger, and Jill Mattuck Tarule, *Women's Ways of Knowing: The Development of Self, Voice, and Mind*, New York: Basic Books, 1986.

lence, received knowledge, subjective knowledge, procedural knowledge, and constructed knowledge.[56]

The authors named the final perspective 'constructed knowledge' (not in opposition to 'commitment' but embracing it) because the women they found at this position were intensely self-conscious, aware of their own judgements and desires, concerned about exclusion and inclusion, separation and connection, and wanting their voices and actions to make a difference in the world. They had a high tolerance for contradiction and ambiguity, had abandoned either/or thinking, had learned to live with conflict, and wanted 'to embrace all the pieces of the self in some ultimate sense of the whole', avoiding the male tendency to compartmentalise. In brief, these women had come 'to the basic insights of constructivist thought: *All knowledge is constructed,* and *the knower is an intimate part of the known.*'[57] Both of these insights deserve emphasis. On the one hand, to see that all knowledge is a construction and that truth is context-dependent greatly expands the possibilities of how to think about anything. It is a great liberation. Theories are models for approximating experience, and we are not only free to choose the models and systems we utilise but must also assume responsibility for them. True experts reveal an appreciation for complexity and a sense of humility about knowledge. They attend to experience with great care and are not threatened by ambiguity and complexity. They develop the freedom to move across systems and to make transdisciplinary connections. They know that truth becomes more elusive the older one grows, and that not the finding but the looking is wonderful.[58]

On the other hand, 'when truth is seen as a process of construction in which the knower participates, a passion for learning is unleashed. ... Constructivists become passionate knowers, knowers who enter into a union with that which is to be known.'[59] Knowing can no longer be abstract and detached but becomes connected and caring; domination is replaced by reciprocity and co-operation, readiness to doubt by readiness to believe, solitary scholarship by a desire for relationships.[60]

[56] Ibid., pp. 9-15.

[57] Ibid., pp. 133, 137.

[58] Ibid., pp. 138-140.

[59] Ibid., 140-41. The authors quote scientist-philosopher Michael Polanyi to this effect in his description of 'personal knowledge'. See *Personal Knowledge: Towards a Post-Critical Philosophy*, Chicago: University of Chicago Press, 1958, ch. 6.

[60] *Women's Ways of Knowing*, pp. 142-50.

The authors pursue the psychological and pragmatic overtones of constructivism more clearly than they do the epistemological and ontological ones. When knowers enter into union with what is to be known through a construction of it, what actually *is* known? Where and what is truth in this process? Is it the object under investigation (the *noema*) or is it the process of knowing itself (*noesis*)? Or are these somehow connected and is the truth in the connection? Is the process of constructing meaning in an interactive, intersubjective nexus in some way a mirror of an ultimate relationality that pervades all that is, including God? Is truth to be measured more in its pragmatic effects than in its disclosure of the being of things? These are questions about which postmodernity is genuinely puzzled and divided. We do not have to settle them to acknowledge the impact of viewing knowledge as constructive and interactive. Liberal theology as a critically constructive theology comes to a similar view.

Connected and imaginative teaching

Imagination both precedes and follows discipline in the pedagogical rhythm. Initial romance leads to disciplined learning, which in turn yields to a higher aesthetic imagination, an appreciation of beauty and harmony – not abstracted from but in the midst of a messy and conflictual world. Teachers evoke imagination in their students by getting them connected with the learning process, by engaging their bodies and stimulating their senses as well as their minds.[61]

Bernard Meland's identification of the 'appreciative consciousness' provides a helpful resource for understanding the place of imagination in education.[62] The appreciative consciousness is essentially imaginative and affective in character, and it, together with the rational conscious-

[61] This topic deserves more attention that I can give to it here. It is closely related to the themes of interactivity in knowledge and engagement in the practice of freedom. On connected teaching and interactive learning, see Belenky et al., *Women's Ways of Knowing*, pp. 194-227; Parker J. Palmer, *To Know as We Are Known: Education as a Spiritual Journey*, San Francisco: Harper, 1993; John C. Bean, *Engaging Ideas: The Professor's Guide to Integrating Writing, Critical Thinking, and Active Learning in the Classroom*, San Francisco: Jossey-Bass Publishers, 1996.

[62] Bernard Meland, *Higher Education and the Human Spirit*, Chicago: University of Chicago Press, 1953. On imagination see also Maria Harris, *Teaching and Religious Imagination: An Essay in the Theology of Teaching*, San Francisco: Harper, 1991.

ness and the moral consciousness, opens up the dimension of 'spirit'. The term 'spirit', while not entirely satisfactory, writes Meland, 'connotes a quality of human discernment which embraces the goods of the ethical, the intellectual, and the aesthetic life', and 'it holds these concerns together as inseparable facets of the human spirit'.[63]

Meland's theory has been developed out of resources provided by William James, Henry Nelson Wieman, and Alfred North Whitehead. The appreciative consciousness, as he defines it, is 'an orientation of the mind which makes for a maximum degree of receptivity to the datum under consideration on the principle that what is given may be more than what is immediately perceived, or more than one can think'. It can also be called intellectual humility, wonder, reverence, open awareness. It is evoked by the recognition that the actual is always pointing beyond itself to what is possible and hidden. There is an element of inexhaustibility in every experienced event, accompanied by a sense of expectancy, knowing that creativity is occurring. A second step beyond receptivity is the act of identification with what is given, sharing to some degree the feeling-content of an object: feeling is 'the wisdom of the body'. A third step is discrimination, the act of noting the vivifying contrasts that differentiate the datum and set it apart as distinctive. These three aspects of receptivity, identification, and discrimination are often associated with an aesthetic and poetic temperament, but they must, Meland believes, be incorporated into the educational project as a whole. Appreciation nurtures capacities such as empathy and sensitivity, and it helps people turn from self-centredness to reality-centredness. Religion without the appreciative consciousness can 'degenerate into a pathological concern for salvation from sin,' losing 'the envisagement of a good not our own, the beauty of holiness, the glory of God'.[64] Here, in sum, is a point of contact with the visionary mark of liberal theology.

Education as the practice of freedom

Education as the practice of freedom is the element of fruition, synthesis, freedom – the goal of the whole of liberal education. The African American literary scholar, bell hooks, establishes a connection between engaged pedagogy, the practice of freedom, and spiritual formation: 'To educate as the practice of freedom', she writes, 'comes easiest to those of us who teach who also believe that there is an aspect

[63] Meland, *Higher Education and the Human Spirit*, p. 13.

[64] Ibid., ch. 5.

of our vocation that is sacred; who believe that our work is not merely to share information but to share in the intellectual and spiritual growth of our students'.[65] Such teaching requires an engaged pedagogy, that is, one that approaches students with the desire to respond to them as unique beings, that creates relationships based on mutual recognition, and that is also concerned to bring about fundamental changes in the way things are done in the traditional 'banking system' of education.

A holistic, engaged pedagogy is more demanding, she believes, than even a critical or a feminist pedagogy, for it emphasises well-being, self-actualisation, happiness. 'If the helper is unhappy, he or she cannot help many people.' These very categories are heretical in most higher education. 'Indeed, the objectification of the teacher within bourgeois educational structures ... denigrate[s] notions of wholeness and uphold[s] the idea of a mind/body split, one that promotes and supports compartmentalisation.' The self is emptied out, leaving only an objective mind, and as a consequence many professors are not interested in spiritual and intellectual guidance but only in the exercise of power and authority. Such teachers cannot practise freedom. If teachers are not themselves engaged in and transformed by the teaching process, they cannot hope to transform their students.[66]

At the heart of engaged pedagogy is a critical thinking practised in conditions of radical openness and mutuality. Under such conditions, remarks bell hooks, she has been 'brought closer ... to the ecstatic than by most of life's experiences'. Somehow discipline and ecstasy come together in practices of freedom, which open up new possibilities and enable students and teachers alike to transgress established boundaries.[67]

One of bell hooks's acknowledged mentors is Paulo Freire, whose work on 'conscientisation' or 'consciousness-raising' has influenced a whole generation of educators.[68] The Portuguese term *conscientização* means both learning to perceive social, political, economic contradictions and taking action against them. By making it possible for human beings 'to enter the historical process as responsible subjects', conscientisation 'enrolls them in the search for self-affirmation and thus avoids

[65] bell hooks, *Teaching to Transgress: Education as the Practice of Freedom*, New York: Routledge, 1994, ch. 1.

[66] Ibid., pp. 15-21.

[67] Ibid., pp. 202-7.

[68] Paulo Freire, *Pedagogy of the Oppressed*, tr. Myra Bergman Ramos, New York: Herder and Herder, 1972. See also his *Education for Critical Consciousness*, New York: Seabury Press, 1973.

fanaticism'. It is rooted in concrete situations of oppression, and its principal method is dialogical, which serves as the 'midwifery' of a 'liberating pedagogy', since by means of it the oppressed bring to conscious awareness the reality of oppression and find for themselves the themes and resources for changing it. The objective is not to reverse the oppressor-oppressed relationship but to overcome it entirely: this is a pedagogy for the 'emergence of a new humanity'.[69]

Freire's contrast between the 'banking model' of education, in accord with which the teacher simply deposits information in the student, and the dialogical method of conscientisation seems to be transferable to almost any teaching situation. What Freire writes here is of great interest. Liberation is not a deposit to be made in humans; rather it is a praxis, 'the action and reflection of human beings upon their world in order to transform it'.

> Liberating education consists in acts of cognition, not transferals of information. It is a learning situation in which the cognisable object ... intermediates the cognitive actors. ... The teacher is no longer merely the-one-who-teaches, but one who is himself taught in dialogue with the students, who in turn while being taught also teach. They become jointly responsible for a process in which all grow. ... Authority must be *on the side of* freedom, not *against* it. Here, no one teaches another, nor is anyone self-taught. Humans teach each other, mediated by the world, by the cognisable objects.[70]

What Freire is saying is that the subject matter teaches itself, gives itself, and this subject matter is in some ultimate sense always freedom or associated with freedom. Teachers and students are caught up in it. Their dialogical relationship is the medium in which it appears, but they are not the source of it; rather they encounter in their thinking something that transcends both of them. Thus what is to be taught is thinking itself, not simply specific contents. In the process of thinking something happens that almost has the quality of 'inspiration'.

The connection of the practice of freedom with the free, open, and culturally transformative marks of liberal theology should be evident.

[69] *Pedagogy of the Oppressed,* ch. 1. See esp. pp. 19-20, 32-3, 52-4.
[70] Ibid., pp. 66-7; see the whole of chap. 2.

Conclusion

At least two claims are implicit in the correlations I have attempted to establish between the marks of a liberal theology and the elements of a transformative pedagogy.

1. *Liberal theology demands a transformative pedagogy.* Theology as such and as a whole generates an educational process. But liberal theology in particular requires a distinctive kind of pedagogy precisely because of its definitive marks: freedom, openness, criticism, construction, vision, experience, transformative praxis. According to this theology there is no canonical authority, sacred text, or supernatural revelation to which one can appeal in coming to know God or thinking about religious belief. There can be no theology, no *logos* of *theos,* without the lifelong formative process that we call education, without critical thinking and imaginative teaching, without turning to the *realia* of everyday experience, without the practice of freedom that concretises the very subject of theology, the gracious liberality of God. Calvin once remarked that God 'forbade his people to devote themselves to auguries, divinations, magic arts, necromancy, and other superstitions'[71] – all shortcuts to saving knowledge, attempts to bypass the lengthy pedagogical process. 'The Lord's way of education' (Horace Bushnell's reflection on Ephesians 6:4)[72] is a long-term nurturing, a *paideia.* Education, so long as it is truly liberal education and not indoctrination or catechesis, checks the constant temptation of religion to take the shortcuts. Beyond this, I am contending that liberal theology demands a particular kind of pedagogy, one that is transformative. This is because the goal of liberal theology is the praxis of freedom engendered by God's gift of freedom—or, expressed differently, the fullest possible flourishing of human beings, which calls for a pedagogy concerned not only with ignorance but also with evil, with all the things that bind, oppress, distort, and destroy life—thus a pedagogy that is not only formative but transformative.

2. *Transformative pedagogy requires an acknowledgment of its religious or theological dimension.* The second claim appears very difficult to sustain in the postmodern era, marked as it is by fragmentation, pluralism,

[71] John Calvin, *Institutes of the Christian Religion,* ed. John T. McNeill, tr. Ford Lewis Battles, 2 vols., Philadelphia: Westminster Press, 1960, 4.3.4.

[72] Horace Bushnell, *Christian Nurture* (1861), New York: Charles Scribner's Sons, 1886, p. 9.

relativism, historicism, scepticism, ultimately nihilism. But one of the things I have become increasingly convinced of is that precisely in such a time theology must have the courage to think boldly, to make audacious claims. We are in danger of letting theology die the death of a thousand qualifications, of stripping it down to the point that nobody will be offended by it or even notice it. If we really believe in God, we know that this belief touches every aspect of human existence, is concerned with the depth-dimension of all that is. Of no domain is this truer than that of education, for education entails the educing or leading forth of the human spirit into the widest range of its potentialities, which are not bounded by any natural or social environment. Implicit in this claim is an anthropology that argues for the transcendental openness of human beings. Such an argument could be developed along lines suggested by Karl Rahner,[73] but in this chapter it appears as a presupposition. Thus education from my point of view is already implicitly a religious activity, and those who are most deeply engaged in it are aware, I believe, of its sacral quality, its life-changing character. The *power* (or means) of education and the *object* (or end) of education are ultimately one and the same: truth, goodness, love, beauty, wisdom. Dare we say the truth, goodness, love, beauty, and wisdom of God? Perhaps it *is* possible for this to be said and heard more openly in the age of postmodernity insofar as the epistemological, cultural, and scientific closures of modernity have been reopened.

What liberal theology contributes to transformative pedagogy is an awareness of the religious dimension of its practices, an acknowledgment that the power of transformation is ultimately the power of God. Is it necessary to accept this claim in order to be a good teacher? No, of course not. But the best teachers seem to be aware of the presence of mystery in what they are doing, and toward it they assume an attitude of reverence. With bell hooks they know that there is an aspect of their vocation that is sacred. They in turn demonstrate that the transformation of human beings is not something restricted to the domain of religion.

The shared goal of liberal theology and liberal education is to nurture wisdom and love, enhance appreciation, encourage practices of freedom and justice – in a word, to promote the flourishing of human beings, to make them fully alive. Liberal theology, like all of theology, affirms Irenaeus's double axiom: 'the glory of God is human beings made fully alive – the aliveness of human beings is in beholding God'

[73] See *God's Wisdom*, pp. 108-10.

(*gloria Dei vivens homo, vita autem hominis visio Dei*).[74] Theologically speaking, it is for the sake of God and the glory of God that we do all that we do. This theological axiom is not explicitly affirmed by postmodern education, even if the religious mystery at the heart of education is recognised. The theological axiom is important, for it reminds us of the finality towards which all creaturely activity is oriented; yet God is glorified and beheld not directly but by letting the glorious light of freedom shine upon the whole of creation. In this light all is transformed, made fully alive. Just what this means in our own time and place is both a theological and a pedagogical challenge.[75]

Drawing these two claims together, I conclude that Christian theology has not communicated its deepest insights and values effectively under the conditions of modernity and postmodernity because of a massive pedagogical failure. This is why I regard the linkage of theology and education to be so critical. A theology for our time must be pedagogically effective. It can no longer rely on social coercion, cultural uniformity, and traditional authority. Its only weapon is the persuasive power of its words and practices. A tremendous hunger exists among our fellow citizens for the very things that Christian theology has to offer if they can be offered in such a way as to touch deep feelings, inspire the heart and mind, speak to the actual conditions under which human beings live today. This hunger is not being met because religious insti-

[74] Irenaeus, *Against Heresies* 4.20.7. For this reference and the free translation of it, I am indebted to Elizabeth A. Johnson, *She Who Is: The Mystery of God in Feminist Theological Discourse*, New York: Crossroad, 1992, pp. 14, 278 n. 32. The idea of 'human flourishing' is from Rebecca Chopp, *Saving Work: Feminist Practices of Theological Education*, Louisville: Westminster/John Knox, 1995.

[75] I do not intend to claim that only theology in the liberal traditions is concerned with good educational practices and the place of religion in such practices. I merely claim that there is an especially interesting fit between liberal theology and liberal education, and that the goal of cultural and pedagogical transformation is one shared by a revisionary theological liberalism. Other theological traditions will view the relationship between religion and education in a different light and will have distinctive insights of their own to offer. I should also note that in this essay I am unable to do justice to the complex distinctions and connections between 'theology' and 'religious studies', and especially to the question whether there is a place at all for theology in the world of religious studies. I make a case for an affirmative answer to this question (and to the corresponding question whether there is a place for religious studies in theology) in ch. 5 of *God's Wisdom*.

tutions, lacking theological insight and resources, have mounted ineffective educational programmes; and secular institutions, lacking any sense of a reorientation from self-centredness to reality-centredness, have lost contact with the sacred. What I hope for, precisely in a time when conventional religious beliefs and practices have declined dramatically, and education is controlled by an instrumentalist ethos, is a revitalised theology that is intellectually and ethically persuasive, and a pedagogy that is genuinely transformative.

Chapter 8

Liberal Theology and Transformative Pedagogy

A Response to Peter Hodgson

Elaine Graham

To debate the *future* of liberal theology invites certain value-judgements about its *past*. Those aspects of its legacy that are most valued, the essential visions which it embodies, carry with them the seeds of reconstruction and renewal. But this is not the place to rehearse such a history; merely to state a few working premises from which I derive the key principles on which I want to move forward. As a practical theologian, the development of my own discipline within the modern era was integrally linked with a tradition represented by Schleiermacher and others in which Christian theology and practice sought to understand, analyse and engage with scientific and social-scientific bodies of knowledge that had emerged independent of theology as 'queen of sciences'. Liberalism, like modernity, of course, has taken something of a battering at the hands of various critics; and liberal theology, too, has fallen into disrepute. Yet I have never understood liberal theology to be uncritical of the contexts within which it found itself called to articulate its claims; merely summoned to give an account of itself that was accessible and credible to its audience.[1] Liberal theology, as I understand it, thus recognises the autonomy of other intellectual positions and scholarly disciplines, and seeks to engage with them in order to gain ever more authentic accounts of God, the natural world and human experience. As one who has been deeply influenced by Marxism and feminism, I would find it impossible to

[1] See E. L. Graham, *Transforming Practice: Pastoral Theology in an age of uncertainty*, London: Mowbray, 1996, esp. ch. 3.

remain within an institution – academic or ecclesial – that rejected such powerful indictments of, and potential correctives to, its own ideological blank-spots and shortcomings.

This affirmation of the world in all its complexity, a wish to claim the world as both fallen and redeemed, would rank as an essential characteristic of such a future theology, a theology that is incarnational and sacramental (because contextual), transformative (because engaged), dialogical and self-critical (because respectful of others' insights). In Duncan Forrester's terms, such a theology is also, crucially, a *public* theology, insofar as it is not sectarian, obscurantist, self-justifying or blinkered.[2] Of course, there are other contemporary opponents of liberal theology who would equally claim that they were proclaiming an alternative and far more authoritative public theology, in so far as it 'out-narrated' the world-views of secularism.[3] But we cannot disinvent modernity, for all its shortcomings. If liberal theology survives, by that name or any other, it will do so by continuing to affirm that harsh reality whilst finding new and creative ways to respond.

Nevertheless, the doubtful fortunes of liberal theology, and of liberalism, are also a symptom of a crisis in modernity itself, a condition which some term *postmodern*. I share Peter Hodgson's broad position (and incidentally, share his high regard for Paul Lakeland's book),[4] that postmodernity is best understood as a critical *coda* to modernity, exposing the contradictions at the heart of modernity's optimism and expansionism, and articulating the voices of difference and exclusion at the margins of modernity's (and especially liberal humanism's) appeal to universalism, objectivity and progress. I would certainly want to say that there are good reasons for not dismissing the values of modernity as an entirely spent force. However, I am concerned that the project of reinvigorating these values, especially in relation to liberal pedagogy, is rather more problematic than Hodgson seems to believe. In particular, I want to suggest that a 'revisionary postmodern liberalism' must recognise the changing economic, political and cultural context in which we find ourselves. The shift in Western industrial economies from

[2] Duncan B. Forrester, *Truthful Action: Explorations in Practical Theology*, Edinburgh: T. & T. Clark, 2000, pp. 127-8.

[3] J. Milbank, *Theology and Social Theory: Beyond Secular Reason*, Oxford: Blackwell, 1990. For a critique of Milbank, see Robert Gascoigne, *The Public Forum and Christian Ethics*, Cambridge University Press, 2000.

[4] *Postmodernity: Christian Identity in a Fragmented Age*, Minneapolis: Fortress Press, 1997.

manufacturing and mass production towards information-based, global economies has wrought a transformation in the way we live and work; and thus in the nature of education – in my case, with that of Higher Education in the UK. I think a reconstituted liberal pedagogy for the twenty-first century will have to be prepared to defend itself against some powerful rivals – and meet them with a robust vision of the kind of society we want and with a compelling model of the aims and goals of education.

Principles of liberal theology

However, I want to return in more detail to the core convictions of liberal theology, partly because Hodgson sees that as a vital source for the reconstruction of pedagogy. He mentions Ernst Troeltsch as an exemplar of liberal theological tradition: Troeltsch's theology was characterised by a doctrine of God that stressed the providential nature of human experience and autonomy – an understanding that revelation was necessarily mediated through the realities of what Hodgson terms 'nature, culture and history'. God's presence in human history is still unfolding, and constitutes 'an invitation to a more consummate human-divine partnership'.[5]

Whatever its critics may say, therefore, I understand this kind of perspective as deriving from a profoundly theological apprehension of the world. Far from being some kind of loss of theological nerve, or merely a capitulation to secularism, it is born of a thoroughly incarnational understanding of the nature of God and the Gospel. Such an openness to the world as it is (for the sake of the world to come) constitutes the heart of an assent to the God of 'nature, culture and history'. Fundamentally, I would begin by affirming that the ethical, political and pedagogical practices of liberal theology require that we take contemporary experience seriously, and that this conviction derives from robust theological sources: specifically, the doctrines of creation and incarnation. However, the problem for liberalism is that in affirming the particularity of its own truth-claims, it is vulnerable to charges that it simply baptises the status quo; and consequently changing times and circumstances can leave it looking anachronistic. Poised as we are between modernity and postmodernity, I think we are

[5] See my article, 'Travelling Hopefully: History and Theology in the Work of A. O. Dyson', in *Modern Believing* 40 (1999), pp. 20-8, here p. 22.

in a position of having to ask how comprehensive, how reliable, our understandings of experience and culture can ever be; yet, at the same time, resisting the view that all knowledge and value is merely contingent or a function of self-interest. In practical terms, at a time when the activities of teaching and learning are as likely to be governed by market forces, consumer demand or external direction, what right does the liberal tradition have to claim a superior or more liberatory understanding of education?

Liberalism, pedagogy and the academy

Hodgson makes a great deal of Martha Nussbaum's inspirational manifesto for liberal pedagogy.[6] She offers a compelling vision of education as something which, emerging from the classical vision of the noble republic of citizens, is dedicated to the nurture of the life of the individual and, by implication, the health of the body politic. Nussbaum takes Westerners back to their educational roots by exploring Socrates' method, which was in many ways a reaction to the dogmatic education of his time. Through rigorous questioning that forces people to engage systematically with their basic assumptions, Socrates exemplified a model of free enquiry that was, and is, vital to a thriving democracy. Nussbaum concludes from this that open debate is fundamental to the process of education, and lays the foundations for students to learn habits of critical and open thought – skills fundamental to their future role as guardians of a free society.

With the help of the Roman Stoics (Cicero, Seneca and Marcus Aurelius), Nussbaum goes on to argue that a democratic society based on human dignity needs a constant commitment to open enquiry. Education must widen our horizons beyond the boundaries of immediate group, faction or nation in order to embrace the welfare of humanity as a whole. This links to a perennial commitment of liberalism, namely the universalism of human nature: a notion which has come under fire from philosophers of 'difference', of course, and rightly so. Yet I think Nussbaum, and others such as Jürgen Habermas and Seyla Benhabib, have attempted styles of communicative ethics that retain liberalism's commitment to emancipatory and progressive values without doing violence

[6] Martha Craven Nussbaum, *Cultivating Humanity: A Classical Defense of Reform in Liberal Education*, Cambridge, Mass: Harvard University Press, 1997.

to diversity. This points to a need for a *dialogical* perspective, one which is prepared to own the particularities of one's own values whilst always searching for points of contact with others. Yet it is still grounded in a profoundly humanistic conviction, that human communities prefer dialogue to isolation and collaboration to conflict.

Nussbaum also advocates the exercise of what she calls the narrative imagination: the practice of empathy, or placing ourselves in the shoes of others. In order to appreciate fully the perspectives and opinions of others, we must be able fully to identify with their position. Yet this is not to be confused with a woolly liberalism or some form of moral relativism; it merely advocates the importance of maintaining the conversation, the better to engage in systematic and rigorous debate which will enable students to come to an informed decision. Nussbaum's vision is inspirational, but it is – like liberalism in general – vulnerable to charges of historicism and particularity. In attempting to forge an inclusive, emancipatory and progressive agenda, it is required to admit to the contingency of its own foundations.

As an example of this we might look at the origins of liberalism itself: it is clear that we cannot separate liberalism and humanism, from which it sprang, from the particular circumstances of the emergence of modernity. Whilst the roots of liberal pedagogy lie in antiquity, as Nussbaum describes, they acquired a new currency in the period between about 1750 and 1848 amongst the emergent manufacturing and intellectual classes in North America and Europe. It was a time of economic, political and philosophical ferment in which the humanistic ideals of both classical antiquity and the Renaissance were well-suited to the ambitions of the leaders of the democratic revolutions in America and Europe. The ideals of the Enlightenment fitted their political aspirations perfectly, advocating a new social order in which the iniquities of ignorance, tyranny or poverty would be eradicated by the ideals of freedom of speech, religion and action; of the axioms of reward for effort; and the rejection of any limitations on human reason, such as tradition, superstition or autocracy. Liberalism was forged in the conflict between the economic, political and philosophical interests of a nascent industrial social order and the forces of tradition and conservatism.

The very rootedness of liberal values in such a context is, of course, why postmodern criticism is sceptical of them. The universal and supposedly self-evident axioms of individualism, progress, self-determination and reason were, the postmoderns would argue, no more than the vehicles by which American plantation owners, French intellectuals and British entrepreneurs could stake a claim to political and economic freedom against the (for them) retrogressive interests of Monarchy, Landowners and Church. Whilst proclaiming the values of reason, science and freedom as human universals, of course, these plantation owners, intellectuals and budding capitalists would never have dreamed of extending these privileges to their slaves, wives, daughters or factory hands. However, what is proclaimed as self-evident, universal and objective is open to the accusation of being no more than the rationalisation of the interests of a particular interest group. No knowledge is innocent or unmarked by its author's fingerprints; and claims to universal experience generally turn out to obscure important differences of perspective and material interest. It took later generations, and later political struggles, to widen that vision of human liberty; and to recognise that universal truth-claims are often simply rationalisations of self-interest.

This is something to which postmodern thinking has pointed, of course: for instance, Foucault's linking of knowledge and power, and Derrida's articulation of the way in which singular truth-claims always necessitate the suppression of alternative meanings. There is no going back, no return to a period of humanistic optimism before this loss of innocence. So all those who wish, like Hodgson, to articulate some form of a 'revisionary, postmodern liberal theology' are caught in a dilemma. They might say, like Martha Nussbaum, that these liberal values served us well and continue to do so, but there is clearly a question about how durable they can prove amidst a radically different social context. A vision of transformative knowledge as the goal of education and learning will have some fairly tough rivals for the hearts and minds of the next generation. Increasingly, the ideals of liberal pedagogy appear highly counter-cultural: and the principle of education for its own sake or education as an expression of the well-being of the civic realm has been superseded by an altogether more instrumentalist ethos.

Therefore, many of the values of which Hodgson speaks are extremely fragile, and under attack not just from postmodernists but neo-conservatives too, who are only too happy to adopt the postmodernists' clothing if it suits them. It comes as no surprise that Hodgson wishes to deploy Nussbaum for his task of reconstructing liberalism for a postmodern age, because her book in many ways is an attempt to reconstruct a liberal pedagogy in the face of opposition from those who interpreted the idea of a classical canon to reassert an exclusive and conservative notion of education. I am here thinking of Allan Bloom's *The Closing of the American Mind*[7] and Harold Bloom's *The Western Canon*,[8] both of which launched a swingeing attack on critics of Western education as exclusive, sexist, racist and Eurocentric. The two Blooms regarded themselves as counter-revolutionaries against what they saw as pernicious cultural relativism. Nussbaum is therefore trying to reinstate a more pluralistic pedagogy, albeit one rooted in the classical and Enlightenment tradition, but which can also stand up to its neo-conservative critics.

Citizens or consumers?

However, the values of liberal education may not be particularly compatible with the demands of mass education. I would like to identify two main ways in which the culture of pedagogical values has changed: firstly, education (especially higher education) is no longer an élitist phenomenon. For the past decade in Britain, there has been an attempt to widen the very narrow age participation rate. Accompanying this has been the voicing of concerns that higher education will experience 'dumbing-down' as a result.[9] Of course, the tradition to which Nussbaum points was always an élitist tradition – it was not a model for universal education. It means that we must not mistake a particular vision of education as the universal – but then again, what confidence do we have in the virtues they enshrine? Over the past few years higher education has expanded exponentially in Britain (unmatched, it has to be said, by anything like proportional increases in funding and resources. So if standards have slipped, it is just as likely due to chronic declines in real funding levels, and lack of investment). But as the debate shows, there is a real question about the implications of a move from an élite to a mass system of higher education: it is clear there is profound disagreement and ambivalence, even amongst liberal and progressive educators and policy-makers. The pessimists in the dumbing-down debate would tell us that standards in education have fallen so far that we are lucky to achieve basic literacy in our students, let alone political literacy for informed and sophisticated citizenship.

[7] New York: Simon and Schuster, 1987.

[8] London: Macmillan, 1995.

[9] Harriet Swain, 'Intellectuals fight "dumbing down"', in *Times Higher Education Supplement*, 12 March 1999.

Secondly, the changes in the labour market towards greater competitiveness and flexibility require different educational objectives – or so our political masters tell us. The practice of teaching and learning is increasingly market-driven. The job for life is rare: now, individuals are themselves a commodity, with the emphasis placed on self-improvement and adaptability. In the United Kingdom, the New Labour government places great stress on education as the key to social equity. But if one listens to and reads what is being said, it is easy to detect that the commitment to educational excellence and investment as a tool of opportunity, self-enhancement and the encouragement of talent is couched in overall terms of *economic efficiency*, and only secondarily or superficially in terms of *social justice*. Ideals of 'excellence', 'free enquiry', or 'education for citizenship' have been replaced by the language of employability, skills and flexibility. Gordon Brown, Chancellor of the Exchequer, manages to have his cake and eat it: in a speech in February 1997, he said that although education was an important means of achieving social equality, in a global economy economic efficiency and competitiveness superseded equality of outcome:

> what is right on ethical grounds is in the 1990s, good for the economy too. In our information-age economy, the most important resource of a firm or a country is not its raw materials, or a favourable geographical location, but the skills of the whole workforce. And so prosperity for a company or country can be delivered only if we get the best out of people, and that cannot happen without continuous and accessible equality of opportunity ... Today, in an economy where skills are the essential means of production, the denial of opportunity has become an unacceptable inefficiency, a barrier to prosperity.[10]

In this climate, what matters are measurable competences, learning outcomes and transferable skills. We might say that in education a cult of *fitness* has replaced that of *health*: that people are motivated not by the virtue of education for its own sake, but by a quite instrumental, often short-term approach. Nowhere is this more apparent in Britain, I think, than in the sad fate of adult education, or 'extra-mural', continuing education, which has found its principles of holistic, life-long learning undermined by the insistence that accreditation should determine funding. A letter in the *Times Higher Educational Supplement* of 19

[10] Gordon Brown, 'Equality – Then and Now', in Dick Leonard (ed.), *Crosland and New Labour*, London, Macmillan, 1999, pp. 35-48, p. 41.

March 1999 lamented the fact that universities had become so dominated by vocational training that this liberal tradition of education had become the province of the leisure industry.[11]

Given this rapidly changing, market-driven educational culture, it is not surprising that immediacy and instrumentalism are prized. Even church-related educational programmes are not immune from these preferences. One critic has recently decried what he terms the 'McDonaldization' of Christian education, reflecting a victory of style over content, highly programmed, directive, glossily packaged – and extremely successful.[12] Is this a sign of the commodification of pedagogy: its transformation into a branch of the service/leisure industry, its privatisation (no longer the public vocation of Hodgson and Martha Nussbaum), to be delivered as instant, easily digestible fast food, regardless of its nutritional or intellectual quality?

In the face of the fragmentation of Western culture, of religious and ethnic pluralism and the dissolution (for very good reasons) of a common (read androcentric, eurocentric) canon of excellence, a diversification of higher education may reflect a more welcome democratic, pluralist ethos, but it also means that we are left feeling uncertain about what has value, whether one form of truth is better than another, and whether there is any consensus about the kinds of qualities exemplified by an educated person. Thus, the issue here is: who is to decide what kind of future society we want our education system to be serving: and is it the role of education simply to *'service'* whatever is considered necessary, or is there a more prescriptive and visionary task of actively *'promoting'* values wider than whatever the market or the government might demand? Whilst I applaud Hodgson for giving a very vigorous defence of liberal pedagogy, I would argue that he may in fact be giving the right answers but to the wrong question. It is not simply a matter of restating liberal pedagogical values, but of recognising profound material and structural factors that leave them looking in many respects redundant. Have we reached a point where dominant models of pedagogy have more to do with 'training' than education; where liberal ideals of education for citizenship have been displaced by education for economic

[11] Stephen Rowland, 'No leisurely learning', in *Times Higher Education Supplement*, 19 March 1999, p. 15.

[12] Pete Ward, 'The Burgerisation of Religion', in *Church Times*, 8 January 1999. Cf. John Drane, *The McDonaldization of the Church. Spirituality, Creativity, and The Future of the Church*, London: Darton, Longman and Todd, 2000.

efficiency and consumership? Is this a situation where any notion of education as a shared journey, a mutual undertaking within an implicit canon of learning and excellence, has simply been replaced by a contract culture, in which 'freedom of choice' conceals a market-driven instrumentalism?

So is there anything that can be salvaged – indeed redeemed – from this situation? The challenge for the liberal theologian is to take a long hard look at what is happening to our culture. Far from being an impediment to transformative practice, the complexities of our situation are where liberal theology begins its work. So although I have concentrated on the instrumentalism and fragmentation of the postmodern/late capitalist context, I would hope that liberals would also look to the qualities of the postmodern condition that might be of value: its fluidity, its pluralism and questioning of authority, its resistance to exclusivism and its openness to religious sensibilities characteristic of the postmodern return of the sacred. And this latter area, namely a greater critical space for religion, and the possibility of some respite from the self-sufficiency of secular humanism, may enable theology to offer itself as a useful cultural resource for the debate. Because, it seems to me, at the heart of all this we have a basic question: what does it mean to be human? What kind of society do we want – and how do we realise that together? And at the heart of that – despite accusations that liberal theology is effectively void of the theological – is the question: what do we worship? What gods and idols – the State, the market, self-interest, progress – do we elevate as our ultimate values? Increasingly, we are confronted by choices concerning the future of employment, participation, human rights and justice – not to mention the technological and biomedical advances that will challenge taken-for-granted assumptions about what we mean by 'human nature' itself – and as these become more acute over the next generation, we are going to need all the resources we can muster to ensure that this dialogue is maintained and such ultimate values interrogated. And although the liberal theologian may only be able to contribute theological 'fragments',[13] these morsels will be grounded in a notion of God as revealed amidst 'nature, culture and history', with a vision of the fullness of humanity as rooted in divine grace, freedom and relationality. But above all, liberal theology must maintain its commitment to nourishing a public, open, democratic space in which the human conversation can take place.

[13] See Duncan B. Forrester, *Christian Justice and Public Policy*, Cambridge: Cambridge University Press, 1997.

Chapter 9

The Experience of Theological Education

Maintaining a 'Liberal' Agenda in a Post-Liberal Age

Clive Marsh

'... the complexities of our situation are where liberal theology begins its work.' (Elaine Graham)

Introduction

The exchange between Peter Hodgson and Elaine Graham is a rich one for those engaged in theological education in the present. Whether one is involved in formal or informal theological education, that is whether or not one's work is linked to the gaining of awards and qualifications by students, and whether it is in university, college, seminary, church-hall, living-room or elsewhere that this education takes place, the issues which the conversation raises are of the utmost importance. In this reflective response I want to do three things.

First, I want to broaden the scope of the debate about liberalism in theological education, by asking: which liberalism or liberalisms are we talking about here? Are we clear? What might the making of some important distinctions do to our debate? Secondly, I would like to re-examine a key aspect of theological education in which theological liberalism's impact is often assumed to have been especially influential. Thirdly, I wish to draw some conclusions for the contemporary public character of theology, and for theological education in particular. Here I shall reflect on some of the different contexts within which theology is being done, and where it might flourish most creatively.

Forms of liberalism

First, then, which liberalisms are we talking about here? In a response to the conference as a whole at which Hodgson's paper and Graham's response were delivered, Brent Sockness, of Stanford University, offered the suggestion that six liberalisms had been operative.[1] In this present chapter, I cannot do justice to Sockness's nuanced analysis. In speaking of five liberalisms, I take up only his distinction between political and theological liberalism, and add three more: ethical, economic and educational.[2]

It is clear that these five forms of liberalism interweave. Free-market economics, the believer's subjectivity, the cultivation of the free citizen, the freedom to choose one's behaviour pattern and a concern for the rights of the individual all appear to interlock neatly. It may be assumed that all of these are 'good things'. Even if not, however, it is not immediately clear that, when spelt out in this form, all those who tap into a 'liberal theological' heritage in Christian thought and practice necessarily support all such facets or forms of 'liberalism'. To a post-liberal critic, furthermore, whatever might be held to distinguish these forms is less significant than what binds them together: a persistent and pernicious prioritising of the human individual. For a postliberal, they are to be countered by the recognition that social stability and well-being require greater attention to the communal dimension of what it means to be human than such liberalisms permit.[3]

[1] Sockness identified two forms of political liberalism ('classical political liberalism' and 'progressivist social liberalism') and four forms of theological liberalism ('classical liberalism', 'socially-progressive or transformative liberal theology', 'philosophical liberalism' – usually taking 'the form of a philosophical defence of theism' and 'postmodern liberalism').

[2] I also acknowledge, however, that 'economic liberalism' is often inevitably tightly enmeshed in political liberalism.

[3] It should be stressed here, and will become clear later in the chapter, that post-liberalism has something to teach liberalism in theology. The extent of the 'recovery of community' which post-liberalism brings cannot, however, be taken to imply that liberalism had no interest in communal life. In the introduction to the translation of Schleiermacher's *On Religion: Speeches to Its Cultured Despisers* (Cambridge: Cambridge University Press, 1988), Richard Crouter lists as one of the 'critical issues' in the work 'The Classic Problem of Liberalism: The Free Individual Person in Human Communities' (pp. 51-3). It is profound and ironical that his discussion of Schleiermacher at this point could apply to where some post-liberal approaches to Christian communal practice have moved.

Some of these forms of liberalism naturally seem to have had greater impact than others in theology and theological education. The post-Kant 'turn to the subject' which gave rise to modern theology in the form of post-Schleiermacher theological liberalism is the most prominent. The immediate relevance of political and economic liberalism is less clear. Ethical liberalism was assumed more in the latter half of the twentieth-century to accompany theological liberalism than had earlier been the case. Theologies from the 1960s left many of theological liberalism's later critics making too many rather lazy equations. 'Educational' liberalism in the sense used by Hodgson, Nussbaum and others, with respect to the Greek tradition, has not, however, been what in recent decades has been meant when 'liberalism' has been referred to in the context of 'theological education'.

To make these distinctions is, however, vital in order to show how easy it has been, and is, for critics of tendencies in theology and theological education in the final decades of the twentieth century to characterise (negatively) as 'liberal' those features which they don't happen to like. More attention to the complexities involved would be welcome. Theology and theological education in the theological liberal tradition do not, and have not, inevitably shared in a slavish quest to idolise the individual subject. A glance at some of the varieties of theological liberalism since Schleiermacher, though it would not be a welcome tendency to Graf's reading of the history of theology, highlights this.

German liberalism since Schleiermacher has not been quite what the (theological) text-book accounts have suggested. Though Schleiermacher himself, for example, was keenly interested in the believing subject, he was a dogmatician for whom the community of faith was of crucial importance. Even more than this, the presence of God in Christ in the community of faith (the church!) was prior to all human receptivity of that presence. As has long been recognised, the second half of *The Christian Faith* should be seen as preceding the first half in terms of the 'order of knowing'.[4] In other words, Schleiermacher could only conclude what he did about the believing subject (and the sense of absolute dependence) because of the prior work of God in Christ in and through the Christian community. He might, in short, have been more of a post-liberal before his time than his post-liberal critics suggest.

[4] Schleiermacher himself discusses this in *On the Glaubenslehre: Two Letters to Dr. Lücke* (Chico: Scholars Press 1981), pp. 56-60, reminding his readers that he regards John 1:14 as 'the basic text for all dogmatics' (p. 59).

To take a later example: Ritschl is often regarded as the quintessential German liberal. However, if Joachim Weinhardt is right, and the fact that Ritschl was not regarded as a liberal in his own time is taken seriously, then what constitutes a 'liberal theologian' in the history of Western Christian theology needs, at the very least, careful re-examination.[5] If Ritschl is not liberal enough (for being too interested in 'church'), and a purer, more individualistically-focused, version of liberalism is envisaged, then this admittedly reinforces the post-liberal case. But it is not this refined form of this debate about definitions which has been influencing jobbing theological educators in recent times. The fact that assumptions about theological liberalism's inevitable individualism, made without adequate recourse to theological liberalism's more nuanced (and creative?) history, are slavishly repeated, should be a cause for concern.

Two more examples take us in different directions again. English liberalism in the Anglican tradition (in so many forms) has scarcely been detached from worshipping communities. The extent to which the experience of worship has truly been informing the theological exploration undertaken (in the 'other world' of the academy), is admittedly a crucial question. But the desire for a freedom to explore critically the credibility of Christianity—in the sense of what is worth believing in, as opposed to what is actually believed—has scarcely been wholly detached from ongoing commitment to the corporate, liturgical practice entailed in what it means to be church. The critical examination of worship itself is not likely either to appear or be central to any movement which looks at the interplay between a worshipping community and a wider world which chooses not to worship at all, worships in different forms, or worships in a truncated or distorted manner. But it is wrong to conclude that theological liberalism's apparent preoccupations with church/world and theology/culture questions mean that it has lost the theological plot.

In some ways the easiest target of critics of theological liberalism is a clutch of theologies of the 1960s and 1970s (e.g. 'Death of God' theologies, secular theologies), the final example I shall consider. Whether these are rightly to be considered as continuous with Schleiermacher and the German liberal tradition is itself a moot point. Even the ease with which they are to be lumped together in a kind of 'Honest to God

[5] See Joachim Weinhardt, *Wilhelm Herrmanns Stellung in der Ritschlschen Schule* (Tübingen: J.C.B. Mohr (Paul Siebeck), 1997), esp. p. 18: 'Ritschl was first characterised as a liberal by the dialectical theologians.'

phase' of British (or Western) theology should be questioned. A variety of distinct currents merits disentangling here. First, the close alliance between a new-found ethical freedom and theological liberalism led to the suspicion from liberalism's critics that 'anything went' during the 1960s. Certainly, one form of the 'turn to the subject' seemed to bear fruit here: the freedom to experiment reached a peak, in both positive and negative ways. Ethically speaking it became more and more acceptable to try out new lifestyles; theologically, the authority of churches was radically questioned at the most local of levels – it was no longer something which university lecturers and radical clergy alone would do; educationally, the life-experience of an individual pupil or student was to be taken wholly seriously.

If it proves easy to point to a rampant individualism, or be critical of what self-absorption a cultural turn to the subject could entail, in religious terms it also sharpened the observation that whilst theology is always about God, it is certainly also about what human beings make of God. The former shouldn't be reduced to the latter, but nor can it do without it. In terms of the micro-history of the late twentieth-century history of theology (as opposed to the macro-history of the 'post-Enlightenment period'), then, the postwar Barthian surge was opposed by the beginnings of an exploration of 'religion' beyond its more orthodox forms, an exploration the full impact of which is only now being felt. This took religious individualism to a new dimension, at the same time as pressing the questions of just whether and how such exploration could or should be normed, and, if so, by whom. Christian theology struggled to hold its own, and has needed to critique much of the results of that exploration. But if it turned religion even more inward, within the unchecked private spiritualities of its proponents, it also fuelled the counter-argument to the ardent secularists who predicted religion's demise. If Christian theology, and theological education, is still reeling from this inward turn, it is also now celebrating the re-emergence of religion into the public realm.

A third feature of 1960s and 1970s Christianity should, though, be mentioned, in addition to the ethical freedom, and to the final twist of inwardness in religion's journey through the twentieth-century. The 'experience-oriented' 1960s and 1970s also saw considerable concern for the social and political impact of Christian faith. That such a concern did not always see political, ethical and economic liberalisms all interweaving straightforwardly with theological liberalism should give pause for thought. In a further uncomfortable, unexpected and problematic twist, these socio-political concerns (even if seemingly carried by individuals throughout the 1960s and 1970s) fed into the exploration and reception and exploration of political and liberation theologies in the 1970s and 1980s. Liberals and liberationists hardly sit comfortably together, and the latter critiques the former at many points, sometimes without specifying which liberalisms are being opposed. But this aspect of the recent history of Christian theology in the West should not go unnoticed, as it is part of the counter evidence to the over-simplified picture which is often painted.

What is to be gained from this process of teasing out multiple liberalisms, and from this brief sketch of some of the anomalies of the histories of these liberalisms? My main points are these: first, there is more than one form of liberalism, and to fail to recognise this will confuse matters whenever the term is used. Secondly, even theological liberalism has many forms. We can refer, by the term 'liberal' at the most basic to the spirit of free and open enquiry. But we must also recognise a variety of forms of Christian theology's history in the West since the late eighteenth century which may carry the label 'liberal'. Thirdly, to adopt an open and free spirit of enquiry and to attend to the 'turn to the subject' does not necessarily entail idolising the individual. Such enquiry does, however, open up attention to the role of experience and the human dimension of religion in a new way. It need not, though, be a reductionistic exercise. Schleiermacher does not inevitably lead to Cupitt.

To speak of liberalism's impact in theology and theological education, therefore, means being somewhat clearer than many debates prove to be about which 'liberalism' one is talking about, and which aspects of the legacy of theological liberalism's recent (200-year) history one is tapping into, as a positive recipient or negative critic.

Experience: the pastoral cycle as a case-study in theological education

When I began as a tutor in Christian doctrine, I was struck by the tension between my desire to adopt a teaching method which enabled students to examine the theologies they began with (all students in my class were Christians), and the fact that the majority wanted to be 'taught' doctrine. There was a frustration that I was unwilling to spell out what they 'needed to know', but wanted them, rather, to disclose to each other what they already believed, and to find ways of expanding, adjusting, even correcting these beliefs. They would thereby be learning how to do theology in relation to available traditions.

With hindsight, I can see that I needed to do more upfront, and to make clearer the metacognitive aspects of what I was up to, something I sought to correct in later courses. I can also see that the kind of 'liberal' I thought I was being was always more 'post-liberal' than I realised.[6] But the experience of teaching, perhaps more than anything, has exposed me to the questions of what theology as a discipline is, how it is done, where 'experience' fits in, and how the shadow of theological liberalism has been cast over so much of the way that theology has been taught and learned in the West over the last three or four decades.

In this second part of the chapter, I shall re-examine just one aspect of theological education—the use of 'the pastoral cycle'—in which theological liberalism's impact is often assumed to have been especially influential. In so doing, I shall be examining the way in which theological liberalism's clothes have been stolen by educators working within a wide range of different theological frameworks. I shall, however, also be exploring a case-study which proves illustrative of so many of the issues as to what theology is, and how it is understood to work.

The 'pastoral' (or 'practical theology', 'hermeneutical' or 'action and reflection') cycle (or circle, or spiral) appears in many forms of theological education. Sometimes confined to the 'pastoralia' section of a theological curriculum, or activated by tutors or supervisors/mentors engaged in the organisation of placements, the pastoral cycle is in active use by theological educators of a wide variety of persuasions and in a broad range of contexts.[7] I have found it used by evangelicals who

[6] Or, of course, I was just plain orthodox, traditionalist, or evangelical all along. But I'd known from John Habgood (*Confessions of a Conservative Liberal*, London: SPCK, 1988) that being a liberal means being a critical traditionalist.

[7] To cite a selection of examples fairly randomly, from different types of publication and 'levels' of theological education: Juan Luis Segundo *The Liberation of Theology*, Dublin: Gill and Macmillan 1977, ch. 1: 'The Hermeneutic Circle'; Michael Williams, *Learning Through Experience*, Bramcote: Grove Books, 1981; Laurie Green, *Let's Do Theology*, London: Mowbray, 1990; Stephen Pattison *Pastoral Care and Liberation Theology*, Cambridge: Cambridge University Press, 1994, esp. pp. 60-4; Paul Ballard and John Pritchard, *Practical Theology in Action: Christian Thinking in the Service of Church and Society*, London SPCK 1996, esp. pp. 74-9; Emmanuel Lartey, 'Practical Theology as a Theological Form' in James Woodward and Stephen Pattison (eds), *The Blackwell Reader in Pastoral and Practical Theology*, Oxford: Blackwell, 2000, pp. 128-34.

would often be assumed to adopt a more propositional approach to faith, and politically-inclined Christians concerned to identify at all points which actions Christians are to undertake. It is used by a range of theological educators who might be prepared to own the label 'liberal', whose emphasis rests upon the methods and processes of theological education from the perspective of using the learner's experience. It even exists in a post-liberal form, in which the 'experience' with which the learner works is always identified as an 'interpreted experience' from the first. The cycle is used implicitly or explicitly in theological college and course training, in industrial mission, in much local church training and in university settings. Where it is used, however, a particular form of education is required. *If the cycle is to be used well, then it is presupposed that those who use it ('students' or 'learners', in the widest sense of the terms) will be able directly to take the opportunity to articulate and critically reflect upon their own experience, within a process which provides adequate time for this.* It can safely be assumed that it will not be best used within a lecture course *about* experiential learning or practical theology, and the 'experience' being reflected upon will be the first-hand experience of the learner him- or herself. But the variety of uses of the cycle renders complex the 'experience' being referred to, and generates profound questions about:

—the way that 'experience' is taken up within theology,
—the ease with which the cycle is adopted, and
—the diverse understandings of theological education which result.

Given that the construal of the pastoral cycle in these terms is a clear legacy of the 'turn to the subject' in modern theology, it is imperative that these questions be addressed in any enquiry into liberalism's impact upon theological education.

What does the pastoral cycle assume? What sort of 'experience' is being worked with? It depends, of course, which particular version is in view. In the context of political and liberationist versions, it assumes an action. The learner must be able to identify an action one has undertaken (individually, or, more appropriately, as part of a group) which can then become the focus of attention. Within pastoral studies (or in a placement/internship context), the experience might either be an action undertaken, or something which 'happened' to the learner (a 'critical incident' or a powerfully-charged moment). In the context of spiritual formation (a support or tutor group), then the basic experience might be a long-past conversion, a memorable peak-experience, or a point of crucial insight which was not merely the result of personal, rational enquiry. All of these examples share common features: they are 'experiences' which move beyond identifying the content and focus of theology as merely 'thought'. In affirming some form of 'experiential' approach to theology, then, they seek to ensure that theology's focal point be distanced from books or 'mere rationality'. But they may differ as to where the focus of theological enquiry is shifted. God may, of course, have been lost sight of by all such approaches (a post-liberal critique of all such experiential approaches). More charitably, God remains in the details, though precisely where can differ substantially between different uses of the pastoral cycle. A most basic distinction occurs between uses of the pastoral cycle which focus upon outer expressions of faith or human activity (e.g. in political or liberationist emphasis upon action) and those which focus upon the inner life (personal growth or spiritual formation uses). The two should not, of course, be polarised, even whilst the distinction is noted as important. A mind/body dualism is not being proposed here. But the identification of what kind of experience is being brought to the pastoral cycle to be 'processed' through it inevitably informs (and/or is controlled by) the version of Christian faith and theology which makes use of it. And it shapes the version of faith and theology which will result.

A feature common to most uses of the pastoral cycle does, however, raise major questions about its use in relation to 'experiential learning'. This is the fact that the sheer immediacy of the experience being reflected upon in most, if not all, of the suggested examples is at some stage removed from the educational task of processing the experience's significance and import. For this to be seen as a *disadvantage* perhaps already prejudges in favour of a decisive role for the *affective* dimension of faith and theology. In other words: if it is assumed better to keep 'experience' and 'use of the pastoral cycle' close together (in temporal terms), then it is also being assumed that the emotional components of human experience are an especially rich seam of enquiry for Christian faith and theology. Alternatively, it can be argued that because the pastoral cycle is, *in actual practice*, very rarely used in close conjunction with the experiences being processed by it, then the post-liberal case begins to carry great weight; so-called 'experiences' are not as value-neutral or raw as is often supposed, but are already 'reflected-upon experiences'. Experiential-expressivism is not only mistaken in theory but deceitful (and perhaps even unworkable) in practice.[8]

Educationally-speaking, however, we are being confronted with the possibility that though there is widespread use of the term 'experiential theology', and though there are many and varied references to the role of 'experience' in theology (especially via the uses of the pastoral cycle), 'experiential theology' and 'experiential learning' may not be quite as close in practice as is often assumed. None of the examples of the use of the pastoral cycle I have referred to may, in the strict sense of the term, be 'experiential learning' at all![9]

The cycle, I have suggested, is in widespread use in a variety of forms of theological education. It does not tend to impinge directly upon the teaching of systematic theology and doctrine courses, nor in the teaching of biblical studies and church history. Even in these areas of theological study, however, 'experiential approaches' cannot be ruled out. For those sympathetic to experiential methods in teaching and learning, ways can always be found to render one's subject-matter conducive to an experiential approach. It would be true to say, though, that it is more common for doctrine, biblical studies and church history to enter the picture at the reflective stage of the pastoral cycle, when the 'reservoir' of Christian resources is being drawn upon, in relation to

[8] The extent of the complexity of the pastoral cycle's use of experience is illustrated by a comparison between Segundo and Pattison (works cited in previous note). Segundo's hermeneutical circle undergoes what may be called a 'cerebral twist' in Pattison's appropriation and adaptation of it, in that Pattison's cycle begins with the 'insights and methods of liberation theology'. He thus does not appear to begin with experience at all (nor, in his defence, is he claiming in any simple way that he does!). Segundo's circle had begun with 'our way of experiencing reality' (*The Liberation of Theology*, p. 9). One could claim that neither in fact begins with 'experience' in any uninterpreted sense, and even that neither claims to. Segundo's 'way of experiencing reality' may not be an unadorned experience. Without venturing any further into this debate here it is, however, important to note that Segundo and Pattison differ, and that both in turn may well be different from the way in which the pastoral cycle is often in practice used (e.g. following Ballard and Pritchard's model) in pastoral theology.

[9] Relevant here, from the educational side of the argument, is Mike Wallace's essay 'When is Experiential Learning not Experiential Learning?' in Patricia Murphy (ed.), *Learners, Learning and Assessment*, London: Paul Chapman Publishing, 1999, pp. 231-44.

which a new action, or a new insight (for the next example of Christian practice) is being decided upon.[10]

But that the pastoral cycle is nevertheless used so broadly should be a cause of concern, not because it may be mistaken or not helpful, which would be difficult to argue on either count. It is problematic because it can be adopted so easily by those of so many different theological persuasions, in so many different settings. For the pastoral cycle is a method which implies a content. It is a method which suggests a particular valuing of 'experience' in Christian theology. It does not *necessarily* imply that the experience is somehow raw, and uninterpreted. But it does suggest that the experience being worked with, within the pastoral cycle, carries authority. How it does so would depend on how the cycle is then to be worked. (Will the reservoir provide resources which will counter or correct the experience? Must the 'right' resources always be located for the cycle to work properly? Will the experience or action being considered, or the future action being decided upon, always carry more weight than what is drawn from the reservoir?) We are, though, I think, dealing here with a way of doing theology which is, on the one hand, prone to the understandable post-liberal critique of implying that theology comprises what believers 'express', and on the other with an approach which is in widespread use because it seems to work. The former might well accuse the latter of being duped into experiential-expressivism. The diverse users of the cycle may, in turn, furnish evidence that post-liberal position is rather incomplete in its handling of the *de facto* role of 'experience' in theological reflection.

What, though, of the net result of all this for theological education? A number of consequences arise. First, approaches to the pastoral cycle from different theological persuasions and in different settings end up placing the emphasis on a different 'moment' of the cycle for a whole

[10] Educators use a variety of images for what happens at the 'reflection' stage of any version of the pastoral cycle. At this stage, one is using some kind of body of 'traditional' material (theological, psychological, sociological or whatever) to inform one's critical reading of the 'experience' being processed. I tend to use the image of 'reservoir' because it reminds people that reservoirs can run dry, and that the cycle cannot be used effectively without a practitioner keeping it topped up, that is, by 'keeping up' in a given field of study or two. Use of the cycle would be ineffective if operated with a dry reservoir. Concrete forms of a 'dry reservoir' include: old, dated research; ideas and beliefs based on books still on the shelf from training days – and never properly digested even then; untested hypotheses or working ideas never subjected to critical examination.

variety of reasons. Those inclined towards a more propositional or even cultural-grammatical view of theology (the point at which some evangelicals and post-liberals, for example, are close together) may, in fact, be paying lip-service to the effectiveness of the pastoral cycle through their highlighting the importance of *what* is put into the reservoir out of which the theological reflection occurs. The action or experience with which a run of the cycle begins or ends may then prove less important. By contrast, to a variety of liberals and liberationists, what one draws upon in order to reflect theologically, sociologically or politically, or economically may be less significant than the fact that one has acted and will act again. If a liberationist were to object to this charge, then this may merely indicate the extent to which there is a much clearer dogmatic component to liberation theologies (it matters *what* theology and *what* politics is being used) than liberals have wanted to admit.[11] The point of pressing this diversity is a simple one: what appears at first glance to be a case of similarity of method ('Do you make use of the pastoral cycle in your course? Yes? So do we ...') proves in many respects to be nothing of the sort. And at this point, more thought about method and process would prove useful.

A second consequence for theological education concerns the extent to which so-called 'religious experience' is to be tapped. The term 'experience', when used with reference to the pastoral cycle, does not usually, of course, refer to 'religious experience' at all. The very success and widespread applicability of the pastoral cycle in theological education and ministerial training relies heavily on the fact that 'experience' means 'life experience', 'everyday events', concrete occurrences within the sheer humdrum of life. Even if discussions about 'experience' in theology can too easily become discussions about

[11] This lies behind the point made about Segundo above (see above, n. 8). The question whether liberation theology 'starts from' concrete praxis is not as easily answered as may be assumed. The theoretical complexity of liberation theology is evidenced in Clodovis Boff's 'Methodology of the Theology of Liberation', in Jon Sobrino and Ignacio Ellacuria (eds), *Systematic Theology: Perspectives from Liberation Theology*, London: SCM, 1996, pp. 1-21. 'At the root of the method of the theology of liberation is the nexus with concrete praxis' (p. 10), yet the 'primary basic viewpoint of the theology of liberation, as of any theology, is the givenness of faith...' (p. 2). Commitment in practice to liberating actions is undoubtedly intended to be the point of entry to any reflective process. But somehow a given theology already exists into which liberating actions feed, and from which they draw.

'religious experience', it is not such religious experience to which the pastoral cycle appeals. On the contrary, daily life becomes the stuff of theological reflection. If such an approach runs the risk of producing 'theologies of running for the bus' (as one of my former students so disparagingly put it) then so be it. The counter argument is easy to locate: if theological reflection cannot be undertaken in relation to everyday life, then our question is not merely 'what is theology then for?', but 'what, then, has God been up to?'

Whether 'life experience' then becomes 'religious experience' as a result of the theological reflection process, and what the value of such a transformation might be, are, though, questions worth asking. Liberals who have been using the pastoral cycle over the past three or four decades have hopefully been chastened by criticism that their use of 'experience' in theology has been prone merely to baptise everyday occurrences rather uncritically. But the value of not looking for, or beginning from, identifiably 'religious experience' is that it avoids prejudging in every respect what religion is and how God can be said to be present and active in the world. The pastoral cycle opens up the possibility of new discoveries of God by those who claim to have glimpsed or encountered God in some way, and wholly fresh discoveries of God by those who lay no, or only slight, claim to any form of religiosity or spirituality. In this way *theological* education, and not only religious studies, becomes a practical possibility in a variety of settings for a diverse group of people. Anyone can do theology in some form, if they are willing to put themselves on the line, open their minds up, and be willing to see what religious traditions might be able to offer them.

Liberation theologies have, however, added a third and telling twist to the discussion of the role of experience in theological education. Here the question to be posed to the pastoral cycle concerns whose experience is to be best used. In the context of the legacy of theological liberalism's (and other persuasions') use of the cycle throughout the West it is clear that the cycle must make use of the participant's own experience. The doer, the agent, must act him- or herself, must reflect (and feel, as well as think) and then do or act again, having reflected. No-one can do this for you. But consciously perspectival theologies (be they Black, feminist, womanist, queer, urban, or whatever) raise fresh challenges. Without the notion that one group might actually learn from another (and that the hidden white, male, middle-class theologies which still dominate so much theological thought in the West might actually be challenged in some way), the pastoral cycle can be used in the reinforcement of all sorts of hidden drives and unexamined prejudices. This insight takes us in two directions. If the doer actually gets into new situations (if the wealthy Black student undertakes a placement in a poor white neighbourhood; if a seeing ministerial trainee works alongside blind staff), then a form of first-hand experience can be gained. Alternatively, and in addition, the question arises whose experiences have informed the material to be drawn upon from the reservoir. Whose work is being used normatively in the reflective process and why? It is a question posed less often than many others in the use of the pastoral cycle.

All of this should not lead the reader to assume that I am proposing the abandonment of the pastoral cycle's use in theological education. On the contrary, it has proved its immense value in ensuring that theology is understood as a profoundly practical discipline. In examining its use, my purpose has been to note how what has often been viewed as a lynchpin of liberal theological educational method has now achieved widespread (and accepted) use, but that its use is not unproblematic. Important too, though, is the observation that the problems associated with the cycle's use are not merely to do with its association with liberal theological traditions.

Liberal theology could thus be said to have contributed profoundly to the keeping alive of a sense of theology's practical character. That it has needed correctives is clear: the post-liberal reaction to liberalism has asserted the important role of believing communities in the process of maintaining traditions and fostering the theological reflection process. A variety of forms of neo-orthodoxy and confessionalism, alongside the post-liberal recovery of traditions, have provided a corrective to liberal traditions' tendency towards sheer pragmatism in the handling of concrete questions and issues. In the light, however, both of the first part of this chapter and the exploration of the role of 'experience' in theology just conducted, it is clear that it is much too simple, and far too damaging, to the recent history of theology and the task of theological education in the West, to squeeze out the liberal theological contribution, as if it has been superseded. Liberalism will play its role in accentuating the diversity of human experiences upon which theology must draw, and in relation to which theology must do its work. It will continue to assert the importance of such experience—via such educational methods as the pastoral cycle—in the face of those who may once again turn theology first and foremost into a mind game (as if systematic theology, or church history, mattered most). It will be critiqued and chastened on many fronts. But it will continue to resist being grouped lazily (by those who should know better) with modernity, and the Enlightenment, as if all three were now dead and buried.[12] They are not: they are part of who we all are. They are part of Western experience, upon which those in and influenced by the West must critically reflect.

Where, how and by whom should theology be done?

I have sought to help people do theology in some odd places. I resist saying 'taught' simply because I have 'taught' so little theology. This is not false modesty, though it is somewhat deceptive, for I have, of course, tried to pass on information to others in the context of structuring learning situations in a variety of settings (so in that sense I have 'taught'). But for 15 years, in formal and informal settings, in paid and unpaid contexts, I have been attempting to encourage people to do theology for themselves (via biblical study, Bible Study, reflection on experience, wrestling with doctrinal texts or themes, through asking questions of films, or in preparing to be preachers). And this is what I have taken to be 'teaching' at its best.

As a result of this, I have come to a simple conclusion: practical theology is the pinnacle of all theology. I say this as (technically-speaking) a biblical scholar turned systematic theologian who has been an active church-member for the duration of my teaching career, and who has struggled—because of diverse teaching locations and a desire to make conversations happen which usually don't—on a number of fronts. To name a few battles, I have fought with certain kinds of traditionalist and propositionalist who don't want to face the importance of concrete experience or of contemporary film and media; with educationalists who dislike theology; and with pragmatists (in theology and education) who dislike theory. I have been charged with élitism for being interested in traditional systematics and with not being serious enough for being interested in the theological significance of film. The variety of settings in which I have actually 'taught', however, has left me asking where the task of theological education might be best undertaken, given what it seems to have to do.

[12] On this see e.g. Colin Crowder, 'Liberalism in Theology and Religious Education', in Jeff Astley and Leslie J. Francis (eds), *Christian Theology and Religious Education: Connections and Contradictions*, London: SPCK, 1996, pp. 105-113, esp. pp. 106-7.

It would be useful to recall, first, where theology *is* actually being done (and by 'theology' in the context of this enquiry I mean conscious, critical reflection upon Christian traditions in relation to contemporary experience of God and world). On the British scene the formal contexts can easily be listed: old and new universities, colleges of higher education (often with church foundations), theological colleges and seminaries, on theological courses (gathered and dispersed, and as distance learning courses). Less obvious are the many contexts within which 'informal' theological education occurs, often overlapping with 'Christian education'. It is 'informal' because it is often not structured in relation to validated educational awards. But whilst some of it may be too *ad hoc* to be as useful as it could be, some is equally as rigorous, and is often more engaged than much of the formal theological education which is undertaken. I refer here to the worlds of 'study days' for clergy and laity, of reading groups, of refresher courses, of locally-run courses, of well-structured house-groups, of study breakfasts, of 'fraternals' (now even including women!). Some representatives of the formal sector get rather sniffy about this theological underworld. Some of this haughtiness is rather surprising and veils a rather thinly-disguised assumption that churches cannot do anything very professionally. Yet whilst educational institutions often provide the church with an excellent validation service, this situation says little of the spirit of partnership when the assumption lurks that no good, educationally-speaking, can come from the church when not blessed formally by one who is greater.

This netherworld is, though, in undoubted need of a colossal confidence boost on the British scene. The more that courses seek formal validation from educational bodies, the more the informal, unvalidated educational experience seems of little worth. In terms of recognised professional training, the validation process is essential. But the business of living, and of theologically reflecting upon living, needs no validation for it to happen, and to happen well. And it is here that the confidence-boost is needed. It is here that the rationales need recovering as a result of which ministers, priests, preachers, counsellors, community development workers—any lay person, in fact—would find time for explicit and informed theological reflection as an active and integral part of their lives. The 'I've no time for study' and 'I'm not a theologian' approaches are understandable when the former relates to ill-thought out job-structures in over-demanding roles, and the latter to a society in which there are, in fact, very few professional theologians. But they are tragic confessions when they indicate the extent to which churches, their representatives and their leaders abnegate their responsibilities as 'learning communities' and as learners. For churches have to be 'learning communities' whether or not their work is validated by educational bodies. 'Learning' is not their prime function (except in the widest sense of churches enabling people to learn to love God and others). Their main purpose is worship. But people learn through worship. And the faith which results in worship and grows within and outside worship clamours to be of an informed kind.

One of the profoundest ironies of the way that theological education has developed over the past three or four decades in Britain is that liberal theology's best interests may be served as much in the church as in the academy. To make such a bald statement is admittedly to polarise the issue unnecessarily. Neither church (mosque, synagogue, temple) nor academy can do without each other if religion is to continue to have a social and political function in British society (as is highly likely to happen, given the evident inadequacy of the secularisation thesis). And people who see just how important religion is will continue to take religious studies courses, and end up encountering theology through nursing, medical ethics, counselling and a variety of other avenues. But if postliberalism's challenge to theology will, on the one hand, leave the heirs of theological liberalism cautious about the ever-present tendency of Christianity towards ghettoisation, on the other hand, it has been to reinforce the recognition that both religion and society need bodies of people (in both sense of 'bodies') in order to work. The open, critically constructive, experiential, visionary and culturally transformative theology for which Peter Hodgson calls needs converts to it. Steve Bruce makes his point well about what has often been the case about theological liberalism (it hasn't made many converts).[13] This suggests, though, that it would be misguided to assume that it will remain sufficient in the long-term for those who wish to become theologically-informed to undertake all their theological exploration under the auspices of the academy. Even universities and colleges with religious foundations (e.g. on the British scene, Church Higher Education Colleges) may not wholly fit the bill. Even granted that many of the most ecumenical theological exploration groups that exist are formed in the context of university course-groups, the question of how such exploration then connects with real, living (awkward, struggling or growing) concrete religious

[13] See below, chap. 14.

communities is of the profoundest importance. Religion does not live on the strength of the explorations of individuals alone.[14]

So what, in short, is the liberal 'take' on all of this? In closing, I offer five proposals. First, liberalism's concern to foster openness in theological exploration is about resisting the temptation to consider theology as largely a matter of learning an insider's language. It is recognised that this will never be enough *theologically* to do justice to a God who is said to be incarnate in the world. The openness espoused by liberalism has in recent history too easily become mere critique of the church. Though this is always necessary, it is not enough and needs re-thinking. Openness has also stimulated, and been stimulated, by individualism. But this, too, has been found wanting. So the legacy of theological liberalism must try and respect the 'turn to the subject' without idolising either interiority or the isolated self, in grasping the crucial importance of concrete experience within theological exploration. And the resistance to turning theology solely into an insider's discipline entails recognising the respect which the 'other' (the religious other, the disciplinary other, the non-believing other) commands in her or his otherness.[15] Theological education in such a climate will always be even harder than it is already seen to be, for it will require its participants to learn more than a single language.

Secondly, theological liberalism will be able and willing to embrace the re-discovered sense of theology as *habitus*.[16] Doing theology is a way of life, not in the sense that anything one does counts as theology. Rather, theological reflection is part of what it means to live as a

[14] A point which relates to Crouter commenting on Schleiermacher: 'A reader may...wish to ask what keeps Schleiermacher's "voluntaristic" understanding of the church from drifting into a religious enclave and thus approximating those closed groups that he identifies as "sects". If all people must be seekers and find their own spiritual community for it to reflect their interests and adequately minister to them, this places a heavy burden of choice on the individual and will very possibly not be a program that can readily be maintained over time' (*On Religion: Speeches to Its Cultured Despisers*, p. 53).

[15] A point developed extensively, in dialogue with Critical Theory, by Elaine Graham in *Transforming Practice: Pastoral Theology in an Age of Uncertainty*, London: Mowbray, 1996, ch. 7.

[16] The term *habitus* has been in regular use in discussions about what kind of discipline theology is since Edward Farley's reference to it in *Theologia*, Philadelphia: Fortress Press, 1983. For a critique of Farley's understanding of *theologia* as too romantically pre-modern, see Graham, *Transforming Practice*, pp. 94-5.

Christian. Unlike post-liberalism, however, which insists on recovering the importance of the church for theology, theological liberalism seeks to respect the church within the context of a wider more complex web of communal contexts within which, and in relation to which, the Christian undertakes theological reflection. Admittedly, viewing the theological task in this way runs the risk of re-asserting the primacy of the individual – as individual theologian. The challenge for a chastened theological liberalism, however, is to explore how the individual theologian now best operates in a world of many inter-locking and sometimes competing communities, a post-modern world more complex than the modern world with which liberalism easily associated itself. In theological education, this will mean that theology's task will entail enabling Christians to operate as theological reflectors (reflective practitioners) in the context of whichever walks of life they move within.

Thirdly, whilst welcoming the many and complex ways in which communities now form, liberalism will, perhaps surprisingly, be somewhat resistant to the notion that theology can be done equally as well in 'virtual communities' as in embodied communities. In educational terms, this will not result in some lazy argument in favour of old-style residential theological training for clergy, as the only real way in which 'proper theology' can be taught and learned. But the emphasis upon concreteness of experience, and its place within the task of developing theological reflection as a crucial aspect of Christian living, will be mirrored in the importance of embodied communities of learning. There is a profound irony here, best illustrated by an example. I heard of a British theological course which was known to be outrageously 'liberal' (and received criticism accordingly). Its main educational focus, however, was its group-work. This example reveals an intriguing tension: between the supposed individualism of liberalism (which ostensibly leads nowhere doctrinally, and leaves everyone believing what they want), and its commitment to group-process, in which real, embodied encounter with others (in all their otherness) is both a risk and a challenge. The irony is sharpened when it is recognised that real encounter with others (in concrete, embodied form, week in and week out in the context of a learning group) is often what can sharpen the realisation that it is not possible to 'believe what one wants'. 'God' has never been the property of individuals, and no-one has really believed that everyone can have their own god, however individualised life-experience inevitably is. Openness really will have to extend to letting people say what they need to say. But the interplay—clash, even—of differing experiences will ensure that God is found between, rather than only in, people.[17]

Fourthly, liberalism will be unashamedly committed to enabling as many as want it, to undertake theological education formally and informally. It will not be alone in this, of course. But liberalism will even want to try and persuade people who might not want it, that it will be good for them. For informed worship and living will surely be all the better for it. In this, liberalism will risk the charge of élitism because of its commitment to education.[18] Liberalism is itself often associated with an élite. Those who have espoused theologically liberal views have often been those who have benefited from more education than most receive. When spoken of in global cultural terms, liberalism is a cultural phase of the affluent West. Can such a set of associations now be in alliance with a sense that theological education should be for anyone who wants it? Perhaps not. But here, theological liberalism should sit rather uneasily with economic liberalism where the latter enables those to seek theological education only if they have the means to pay. Things do cost money, and the managing of scarce resources (including people's time and skills), is in part a theological challenge in itself, in theological education too. But the widespread accessibility of the pastoral cycle, and its success as a way in which people can get inside the habit of theology, invites the thought that theological liberals should be at the forefront of promoting that access.

Fifthly, liberals must carry on being prepared to risk the charge of reducing theology to anthropology or ethics. It will ever be thus for any movement which seeks to locate theological reflection firmly in the messiness of daily life. Even liberals know that theology is about God. They didn't need Barth to remind them. But because theology is about God it is therefore also about human beings. Christian theology has a particular 'take' on the way in which theology is about human beings

[17] It is also worth noting that worshipping communities, at their best, bring the strangest mix of people together at one time. Their diversity constitutes an educational nightmare, yet invites consideration of how such diversity might be educationally used more profitably by the church as itself a (virtual) community of (embodied) learning communities.

[18] Whether this is a peculiarly British, or even English, difficulty is not easy to determine, but too much British Christianity is deeply suspicious of theological education. When coupled with social class reservations about what education can 'do' to people, then the religion/education alliance can prove potently negative.

because of the way it speaks of God in Jesus Christ. 'Incarnation' can be construed in a variety of ways, but must always both link Christian theological reflection with Jesus of Nazareth, and state how continuing concrete human experience embodies and expresses the presence and work of God in the world. Liberals are always likely to be at the forefront of grappling with that particular aspect of Christian understanding of God. Post- post-liberalism, this need not be seen as a problem. Chastened theological liberalism can be grateful for post-liberal critiques. But in playing its role in theological education inside and outside of the church, its experience will always be that of promoting a close relationship between theological exploration and human life as it is lived. This cannot, surely, be a bad thing.[19]

[19] I am grateful to Mark Chapman and Vaughan Roberts for their comments on an earlier draft of this chapter.

Part Three

Addressing the Critics

Chapter 10

Karl Barth and Liberal Theology

Timothy Gorringe

There is a rumour which has been current for some time that Karl Barth was vehemently opposed to liberal theology. I would like to say that the rumour was baseless, but that would be an exaggeration. In circular letters to friends in 1923 and 1924, after all, Barth described Schleiermacher's theology as 'one great swindle' which made one want to cry out in wrath, and talked of 'wanting to seize him by the throat!'[1] 1923 saw the open correspondence between Barth and that doyen of liberal theology, Adolf von Harnack, in which he repudiated the views of his old teacher in the sharpest possible way.[2] Were not the twelve completed volumes of the Church Dogmatics an attempt to reconstruct theology on a different footing from that which it had been given in the nineteenth century, effectively a liberal footing? They were. And yet the picture of Barth as a sour 'neo-orthodox' opponent of liberal theology was always mistaken, as we can see both from the 'Afterword' he contributed to the publication of his Schleiermacher lectures in the last year of his life, and from the eirenic, affectionate and warm hearted article he contributed to the *Schweizerische Theologische Umschau* in 1960 on the subject of 'the future of liberal theology'.[3] Barth's road allowed him, he said, to keep liberal theology in view as it travelled its own road ('Welcome to you from afar!'), to accompany it in sympathetic comradeship. Not just that, but Barth began by describing himself as 'a

[1] *Karl Barth-Eduard Thurneysen Briefwechsel*, vol. 2, Zurich: Theologischer Verlag, 1974, pp. 207, 223.

[2] On this see H. M. Rumscheidt (ed.), *Revelation and Theology: An analysis of the Barth-Harnack correspondence of 1923*, Cambridge: Cambridge University Press, 1972.

[3] Translated in slightly abbreviated form by L. A. Garrard in *Hibbert Journal* 59 (1960-61), pp. 213-9 under the somewhat misleading heading 'Liberal Theology Some Alternatives'. I follow this translation.

truly liberal theologian'. He does not defend the claim, but one can point above all to his concern with the 'humanity of God', which governed his theology from start to finish, and which explains his passion for the poetry of Goethe and the music of Mozart, his lifelong enthusiasm for Plato and Kant amongst the philosophers, his championing of the poor, not just in his early days in Safenwil, but throughout his life, and the variety and openness of his friendships. As an adjective 'liberal' is a great human, but especially Enlightenment, word which points to broad sympathies as opposed to narrow sectarianism and the damning of those with whom you do not agree. In this sense Barth was always a liberal, and his liberalism is reflected in the geniality of his theology, what Bonhoeffer called his *hilaritas*, and in the generosity of his judgements. *Nein!* was not characteristic, and has to be understood in its context. Barth damned remarkably few theologians: only Ritschl was never admitted to grace, because Barth identified him with the bourgeois Germany of Bismarck's era, which he still encountered in Göttingen in the 1920s. The other theological movement he could never stomach was Moral Rearmament. He concluded the article on liberal theology by warning his liberal friends not to touch it 'even with their little finger'.[4]

I propose in the first instance to summarise Barth's article on liberal theology, which is not as well known as it should be. Barth defined liberal theology as

> a theology in the succession of Descartes, primarily and definitely interested in human, and particularly the Christian, religion within the framework of our modern outlook on the world, considering God, his work and his word from this point of view, and adopting the critical attitude towards the message of the Bible and ecclesiastical tradition – to this extent an anthropocentric theology.[5]

The emphasis on modernity and on the critical attitude can, it seems to me, be accepted as characteristic of liberal theology. What it owes to

[4] This was a prominent bone of contention with Brunner in the 1930s, and he never saw the point. Invited to comment on Barth's article Brunner first praised it but then said that he thought Moral Rearmament had much of value to offer. This difference is an essential clue to understanding *Nein!*. Brunner also felt that Barth was far too pacifist, and far too soft on communism 'which is an even more dangerous foe to Christianity and real Humanity than Hitler ever was'. This judgement, which was only too common in the fifties, also marks out the gulf between them. See 'Karl Barth's Alternatives For Liberal Theology: a Comment', in *Hibbert Journal* 59 (1960-61), p. 319.

[5] Barth, 'Liberal Theology', p. 213.

Descartes, if anything, and the extent to which it is anthropocentric are matters to which we shall have to return.

The editors of the paper asked Barth not to consider existentialist philosophy and theology, at that time at its apogee in Switzerland, where Karl Jaspers had attracted huge crowds to his lectures for the past decade. Nevertheless, Barth recommended that anyone attracted to liberal theology should begin with a close look at Kierkegaard, 'possibly the last word of anthropocentric theology'. He believed that such a theology would certainly end up in disaster, but nevertheless felt it would be difficult to avoid the temptation to begin there. If, however, that was ruled out, he suggested three main possibilities. The first was to return to Biedermann, a disciple of Hegel, whose 'confidence in the human, finite, spirit ... reverence for the dignity and authority of man's powers of thought, were unbounded'.[6] This would put sonship of God at the centre of theology, revealed and incarnated in Jesus of Nazareth. Put thus, it sounds uncomfortably close to Strauss, but Barth found in Biedermann (who, to the best of my knowledge, never crossed either the Channel or the Atlantic) a dedication to studying Christian doctrine, understood as the study of the self-realisation of the Absolute, 'in accordance with its inner necessity' and to seek to raise it from the level of intuition to pure concept.[7]

A second, and much more important suggestion, repeated in his 'Afterword', which was effectively his last major theological statement, was to return to Schleiermacher. No one who studies the *Dogmatics* can fail to be struck by the extent to which Barth continues to engage in dialogue with Schleiermacher, and it is true that, whilst the revolution he and Thurneysen initiated began with a rejection of Schleiermacher and all his works, Barth never turned his back on him. When Brunner's attack on Schleiermacher appeared in *Das Mystik und das Wort* in 1924, Barth was sympathetic to much in it, but felt that Brunner had gone too far. Quoting the libretto of the *Marriage of Figaro* he wrote that 'An inner voice always spoke to his advantage'.[8] The truth is that Barth loved Schleiermacher, and 'old love never fades'. This was because what he said of Schleiermacher, in his eighty-second year, was true of himself: 'Schleiermacher was an open, expansive, and truly comprehensive spirit ... in all the branches of his life's work, he had

[6] Ibid., p. 214.

[7] Ibid., pp. 214-15.

[8] K. Barth, *The Theology of Schleiermacher*, Edinburgh: T&T Clark, 1982, p. 267.

something positive to say.'[9] Barth found in Schleiermacher, 'real thought, courageous and free'. He had, of course, major questions to put to him: was Schleiermacher's theology intrinsically a Christian theology, orientated towards worship, preaching and pastoral care? Or was it primarily a philosophy? Do people in his theology relate to an uncolonisable Other, or are they essentially united to everything which might confront them? Do people relate to a reality which is particular and concrete, or to a general reality? Relatedly, is the Spirit absolutely particular and specific or universally effective? But then he asked, are these questions posed correctly, in terms of Schleiermacher's intentions? Famously he asked whether anyone building on Schleiermacher might not produce a theology of the Holy Spirit – certainly one of the key questions in Barth's reading of liberal theology, and one to which I shall return.[10]

A third possibility, which might cause more astonishment, is the suggestion that people might turn to Martin Buber – a person to whom Barth had not responded warmly in the twenties in Germany. Buber had recognised that 'Unless we have heard and applied to ourselves from the very outset (a priori) the question, "Where is thy brother Abel?", we shall have to face the wretched question, "Is there a God?".'[11] Along the same lines he commended the person against whom he directed some of the sharpest salvos of the first *Romans*, Leonhard Ragaz. 'I couple him with Martin Buber because he, too, was concerned, passionately and impressively concerned, with the problem of the solidarity of God and my neighbour, my neighbour and God, and in this sense with the Kingdom of God, in contrast to all religious and ethical Solipsism'.[12] Why, he asked pointedly, are liberal theologians as much on the side of the powers that be, as militarist (even to the point of accepting the atom bomb) and as conventionally Western as the mass of the orthodox?

Other possibilities might be to think of Gandhi;[13] Albert Schweitzer; even Tillich or Reinhold Niebuhr. Whichever way they took, it was as

[9] Ibid., p. 272.

[10] Ibid., pp. 275-9.

[11] 'Liberal theology', p. 218.

[12] Ibid. This change of mind gives us some idea how Barth might have viewed the liberation theology which was to emerge at Medellin in the year of his death.

[13] It is interesting to note that ten years earlier he had said that he never understood Bonhoeffer's interest in going to India.

true for them as it was for him that 'Theology can be based on nothing but on daring'. There is no cheap grace for liberal theology either.[14]

As this summary makes clear, the word 'liberal', like the word 'evangelical', does not cross the Channel quite unchanged. In the same volume of the *Hibbert Journal* in which Barth's article on liberal theology appeared, H. A. Turner contributed an article on 'The Relevance of Liberal Theology' which found the challenge to liberalism to emanate entirely from New Testament studies, indeed from Loisy, Schweitzer and Bultmann, all of whom were, in Barth's view, prominent liberals.[15] Barth played no role in it at all! For Turner the return to liberalism involved dethroning the ascendancy of eschatology (four years before the appearance of Moltmann's *Theology of Hope*) and a return to the emphasis on the moral teaching of the New Testament which had been the heart of Harnack's theology. Had Barth ever seen it he would have been mystified.

In the list of possibilities Harnack is conspicuous by his absence. Turner takes *The Essence of Christianity* as the quintessential expression of the liberal position, but I suspect Barth would have argued that that was to short-change it. Harnack was first and foremost a historian of doctrine, and the public lectures which constituted the Essence were addressed to a lay audience, and have nothing like the weight of Biedermann or Schleiermacher. Barth's project, as he developed it in the 1920s, was to develop a theology which was equal in weight and seriousness to Schleiermacher's. 'Liberal' for Barth did not mean light weight.

Equally conspicuous by its absence is any argument on the foundation of Christian doctrine, which occupied the first two and a half volumes of the *Church Dogmatics*. Barth refers to a critical position on Scripture as characteristic of liberalism. What he put in its place, of course, was an immensely sophisticated hermeneutic, a dialectic of freedom and authority, which sought a third way between biblicism on the one hand and an undisciplined appeal to all sorts of 'classical' authorities and experiences on the other, between allegory and literalism, between the 'tradition' of Trent and the Bible of Wittenberg. It was an argument for an understanding of tradition as that which grounds and nurtures our imagination to which we are all, willy-nilly, heirs. In this respect Barth's claim to be 'truly liberal' is also vindicated.

[14] 'Liberal Theology', p. 219.

[15] H. A. Turner, 'The Relevance of Liberal Theology', in *Hibbert Journal* 59 (1960-61), pp. 320-30.

At the heart of Barth's disagreement with liberal theology as it appears in these two articles is the accusation that it is 'anthropocentric', a characteristic which Barth traces to the 'turn to the subject' in Descartes. Are either of these accusations fair? Barth, of course, writes as a convert, a Saul who became a Paul under the impact of the First World War and the peculiar religious socialism of Christoph Blumhardt. Prior to that he had been a Pharisee of the Pharisees, a card-carrying liberal. This meant that Barth knew liberalism from the inside, but he also needed to live it down. In his analysis of the catastrophe of 1914, as we see very clearly from the lectures and addresses of the next two years, Barth came to believe that Christianity had become culturally imprisoned, that it had lost any sense of an 'other', or as he preferred to say, following Rudolf Otto, a 'Wholly Other', to challenge it. This is doubtless true, but is it a phenomenon peculiar to liberalism? To ask the question is to answer it, for it is clearly equally true of thirteenth-century Christianity, or for that matter of the Reformed Christianity of the 1540s and 1550s. It is an illustration of the perils of success. But what of anthropocentrism, something Barth discerned not only in Kierkegaard but also in the great analysis of Reformed hymnology of the seventeenth- and eighteenth-centuries, part and parcel of Protestantism from a very early stage.[16] But is the first person pronoun really more pronounced here than in fourteenth-century mysticism? And in any case, what do the seventeenth-century hymn writers owe to Descartes? In terms of the history of ideas, tracing the centrality of subjectivity to Descartes is dubious, and we need to push back at least to the fifteenth century, and the re-discovery of 'man the measure of all things'.

Another frequent accusation levelled at theological liberalism is that it is reductive – that it submits the mysteries of faith to what is ultimately a rather trivial rationalism. This accusation surfaces in some of the letters of the 1920s (for example, Schleiermacher's treatment of the resurrection as the resuscitation of a corpse) but it is not a prominent theme of Barth's polemic. He is more concerned with the allied concern to explain the faith in 'modern' terms. Apologetic was something he always remained hostile to, believing that there was virtue in speaking the language of Canaan. In this respect the continuing interest in narrative and symbol in contemporary theology owes much to Barth, but of course he too recognised perfectly clearly that part of the task of theology was to engage with whatever contemporary challenges

[16] *Church Dogmatics*, vol. 1/2, Edinburgh: T&T Clark, 1956, pp. 252-7.

presented themselves, which is why he devoted such care to Sartre, de Beauvoir and Karl Jaspers, amongst others, in the *Dogmatics*. Barth did not win the Sigmund Freud prize for the excellence of his literary prose for nothing, and he did not write in the language of a Christian ghetto. His difference from a great liberal like Schleiermacher is that he does not seek to find new ways to convey the same truths, but seeks rather to explore ways in which the truths of ancient formulations, such as the anhypostasia, can speak to the present. His use of these ancient categories can make his work seem far less radical—perhaps less liberal—than it really is.

Both in the article on the future of liberal theology, and much more fully in the *Afterword* on Schleiermacher, Barth explores the possibility that a liberal theology would really be a theology of the Third Article. This is surely the nub of the issue. Barth adopted the Trinitarian scheme he did, speaking of the Trinity as Creator, Reconciler and Redeemer, because of his early conviction that theology had to embody a thoroughgoing commitment to eschatology. One of the problems with it, however, was that it functioned to block his exploring the work of the Holy Spirit here and now. Barth praises many of the positives of liberal theology – courage, openness, exploration. But at the heart of liberal theology as I understand it is neither anthropocentrism, nor apologetic, but the conviction that the Spirit is abroad in the whole of God's world, to be discerned both in 'other religions' but also in the 'secular' sphere. An absolutely characteristic liberal position was that of the great Anglican priest Alan Ecclestone who read Shakespeare as he read the psalms, sharing William Blake's view that 'the lover of art is the lover of Jesus'. Barth was in no position to make this move, and ended up instead with the 'lights of creation' in *Church Dogmatics*, vol. 4/3, failing sufficiently to put his Christology in pneumatological perspective. He was right (in my view) to believe that Schleiermacher collapsed the Spirit into anthropology, but wrong to believe that this is what liberal theology automatically does. In this respect the description of Schleiermacher as 'the great ripe classic of modernism' is misleading. The warning that this can fatally easily happen—a warning issued with raised finger in the *Afterword*—is well taken, but it is a danger we have no option but to take if we believe in a God who acts in God's world, who is active, and not asleep. Liberal theology is a theology of daring in the sense that it takes this risk. The challenge from Barth is to take the incarnation as our principle of discernment.

Chapter 11

Shape-shifting Disturbances as Divine Presence

Rita Nakashima Brock

'For a long time ... "mystified" doctrines have taken away the power from women, the poor, and the powerless, for they help to sustain the notion that 'divine presence' is located somewhere else and not in ourselves' (Kwok Pui Lan).[1]

Introduction—the US context

This chapter stands in the legacy of American liberal theology: its commitment to justice and the social good, its openness to human knowledge as informing theology, its relativising of exclusive Christian claims to truth, and its support of democracy. This chapter also challenges some of the Eurocentric and androcentric assumptions of liberal theology, especially its commitment to theory and its over-emphasis on the individual. The final challenge is to the liberal attachment to a form of atonement theology, which rejects the Anselmian version, but perpetuates the Abelardian moral influence theory of the model of love found in Jesus' sacrifice on the cross.

North American religions reflect four centuries of global immigration. Muslims now outnumber Episcopalians, as well as Presbyterians. European Americans participate in Lakota sweat lodge ceremonies, practice yoga and tai chi, and meditate at Buddhist centres. Asian immigrant Buddhist temples dot the landscape from Florida to California. Rabbis and Imams teach in Christian seminaries. Mosques, temples, and churches are built side by side.[2]

[1] *Discovering the Bible in the Non-Biblical World*, Maryknoll, NY: Orbis Books, 1995, p. 18.

[2] Diana Eck's Pluralism Project at Harvard University, 'On Common Ground: World Religions in America', CD Rom, New York: Columbia University Press, 1997, explores this heterodox mix.

The 'mainline' Protestant churches originating in Europe have seen nearly three decades of decline in numbers and public influence, while a variety of other forms of Christianity have proliferated. If the numbers demonstrate anything, mainline white Christianity in America continues to fade. Without the imperial apparatus of government, militia, and money behind it, Christian orthodoxy has lost its hegemony. Many theological options have emerged.

Despite this growing religious pluralism, Northern European Enlightenment Protestantism casts the shadow of a long legacy in law and government practice, as well as in social attitudes about race, class, and gender. Dissident groups have developed and sustained alternative, and largely hidden, forms of culture and values in the face of that hegemony. The current religious array illustrates how much has been happening below the public surface. Recently, a variety of voices heretofore marginalised within Christianity have erupted with new theologies through 'hidden transcripts',[3] as they seek ways to affirm life with God in an increasingly diverse world.

Much is at stake in these eruptions. North Atlantic, white Christianity is implicated in an array of atrocities and injustices. Colonialism and conquest, intertwined with religious missions and theologies, resulted in the genocide of indigenous peoples, in the enslavement of African peoples, and in the forced servitude of poor Europeans and Asians. A legal system of 'democracy', established by a white, male, land-owning minority, allowed that minority to inflict its will on the vast majority of human beings under the guise of protecting 'liberty'. Religious ideologies of subordination and paternalism have maintained brutal and often fatal forms of violence against women and children. These religious ideologies, in secular form, reappear in law, most notably in marriage legislation, when clergy act as agents of the state despite the so-called Constitutional separation of church and state. Christian notions of orthodoxy and sexuality have supported murderous attitudes and practices toward anyone deemed religiously or sexually deviant. Indigenous peoples in the United States still live under colonial occupation.

Christian leaders constructed and continue to reinforce an economic empire that has resulted in a permanent global underclass. That many economically privileged people, including those of us with advanced

[3] See James C. Scott, *Domination and the Arts of Resistance: Hidden Transcripts*, New Haven, CN: Yale University Press, 1990. Scott uses this term to suggest the well-rehearsed nature of discourses that erupt from marginalised groups. The well-formed nature of the discourses indicates long periods of formation within dissident groups, hidden from the public sphere and their oppressors. Such transcripts, often enduring through generations, rehearse histories of suffering and ridicule the hegemony and pretensions of those in power.

educations and comfortable lives, have benefited from this hegemony should not blind us to the way such privilege has been created and the coercive means by which it is maintained on a global scale, even in first world countries. Rich and poor are not separate categories of human beings. They are intertwined, interdependent parts of the same economic system, and Christians, in democracies where they are the majority, are the main supporters and enforcers of that system.

Christian voices and practices resisting forces of injustice have existed alongside this hegemonic system, creating social movements, such as abolition, women's suffrage, the Social Gospel movement, the Civil Rights Movement, and the sanctuary movement. While marginalised by the hegemony of white, male supremacy, these movements have long sustained a commitment to fairness, peace, and democracy violated by that hegemony.[4] From such movements, a variety of theological voices have emerged. Hybridised forms of Christian theology have emerged from the struggle for justice, from cross-cutting dialogues among religions living side by side, and from the diversity of Christianities in North America. This chapter explores the theological implications of two such forms: the women's movement and the Asian American movement.[5]

American theologians are engaged in disputes about whether or not claims to universalism repeat the legacy of Euro-hegemony.[6] The deconstruction of such claims is partly a response to the intellectual and political power of modern androcentric and Eurocentric thought, which is associated with colonialism, sexism, racism, and imperialism. This debate about universalism has predominated among Euro-American theologians, including feminist theologians, and reflects their training in European-based intellectual schools of thought. The proliferation of varieties of postmodernism is a function of European modernism and can be seen as a form of hyper-modernism – to be 'post' something is to be a

[4] Gary Okihiro (in *Margins and Mainstreams: Asian Americans in American History and Culture*, Seattle: University of Washington Press, 1994) argues that 'minority' movements in United States, while marginalised by racism and sexism, belong at the centre of history and culture because they have been more committed to democratic principles and have struggled to enact them in the face of their denial by the dominant system.

[5] See William Wei, *The Asian American Movement*, Philadelphia: Temple University Press, 1993 for a summary of its formation in the 1960s.

[6] For an analysis of this tension in feminist Christian theology, see Serene Jones, 'Between a Rock and a Hard Place: Feminist, Womanist and *Mujerista* Theologies in North America,' in *Religious Studies Review* 21 (July 1995), pp. 171-8.

function of it.[7] Peoples of colour in North America, including feminists, womanists, and mujeristas, have tended to construct our theologies within our own distinctive historical and cultural resources, placing them at the centre of our work, arguing against the hegemony of North Atlantic traditions while using whatever is useful from them.

My own work inclines uneasily toward this latter option and its postmodern liberal allies. I say uneasily because I have found my own liberal intellectual training valuable, and it continues to influence my thinking. While I am aware of some of the limits of Western liberal theology, I find the nihilistic tendencies of much postmodernism disquieting. If claims to human subjectivity are hegemonic social constructions, how does one create a basis for solidarity in the work for justice? Regardless of what specific forms they take, state terrorism, genocide, intimate violence and murder, war, rape, hate crimes, and economic destitution are real forms of evil in our world today. The demand for justice and the ethical call to create the conditions for right relationships should be no less compelling, if perhaps socially constructed.[8] We must, however, be aware that the imposition of one culturally hegemonic solution to evil always risks aggravating the problems it attempts to solve and creates new ones.

The indigenisation of Christianity in various Native American communities and non-Western societies has revealed some of the many hybridised forms Christianity can take and reminds us of its original history of spreading and surviving through syncretism. Christian heterodoxies and diversities are aspects of its character as an historical movement, from the very beginning. There is no pure, superior, or original form of Christianity – it was heterodox from the start. Traditional arguments for the superiority of Christianity, based on a reductionistic, nostalgic view of the past, have become untenable in the context of dialogues with other religions, post-colonial theories, post-Holocaust theologies, and analyses of sexism, racism, and heterosexism

[7] Postmodern thought suggests that it lies in the trajectories of modern movements in theology, including the responses that reject modernism, such as fundamentalism, and those which mostly embrace it, such as liberalism.

[8] African philosopher Anthony Appiah notes: 'We will only solve our problems if we see them as human problems arising out of a special situation, and we shall not solve them if we see them as African problems, generated by our being somehow not like others' (*In My Father's House: African in Philosophies of Culture*, New York: Oxford University Press, 1992, p. 136). For both philosophical and policy-based discussions about creating universal norms based in capabilities, drawn from work by economics Nobel laureate Amartya Sen, see Martha Nussbaum and Jonathan Glover (eds.), *Women, Culture, and Development: A Study of Human Capabilities*, New York: Oxford University Press, 1995.

in Christian traditions. Christian theology cannot survive credibly by arguing for the exclusivity, superiority, or uniqueness of Christianity. Its limits and its value lie with Christianity's historical particularities and specificities, and with what it shares in common with other religious traditions. In exploring this approach of specificity and commonality, I will firstly, outline a theological method based in witness; secondly, I will use this method to explore theologically a site of cultural specificity in feminist and Asian-American work on the self; thirdly, I will suggest how such understandings bring new insights to our understandings of human sin and suffering; and finally, I will examine the implications of these insights on theologies of the atonement.

Witness as a theological method

The deconstruction of white, North Atlantic Christian hegemony is an important moral response to profound human suffering. Rebecca Chopp suggests we use Elie Wiesel's concept of literatures of testimony as a theological method.[9] Testimonies seek to describe the extremities of human experience as forms of resistance and affirmations of survival. Such experiences rupture the reliance on reason as the court of judgement. Testimony attunes itself to a particular kind of specificity – that of the profound suffering of a group of people disclosed in the verbal representations of its members. Testimony, thus, refers to collective or social experiences, not only to personal (and possibly idiosyncratic) anguish.

Testimony calls us to 'otherness, a reality greater than even the basic rules of individual and public life'. All reason and theory are called into question for the sake of moral responsibility and of service to those who suffer and hope. Chopp asserts:

> Theology itself has to be understood as a responsiveness to the moral summons of testimony ... outside the court of modern reason and colonial politics. ... Theology, in this contemporary view, is more a combination of calling and obedience to the need for justice and salvation, than it is a rational discourse of what correctly describes humanity and Christian tradition.[10]

Chopp's work focuses especially on the eruption of holocaust testimonies, which have made painfully clear, as nothing else, a long history

[9] See 'Theology and the Poetics of Testimony', in *Criterion*, winter 1998, pp. 3-11.

[10] Ibid, pp. 8-9.

of Christian anti-semitism. Other forms of witness to genocide and oppression have become more public in the second half of the twentieth century as the 'hidden transcripts' of oppressed groups have emerged. Continual attunement to and dialogues with 'the other,' with complex and varied forms of human life and experience, are moral imperatives. These imperatives call on Christians to learn specific ways to demystify our own hegemonies and to sustain, redeem, and enliven our intertwined destinies. In engaging in dialogues as a consequence of testimony, we search for ways to create right relationships; we learn to speak within the limits and possibilities of our own historical traditions and to challenge injustice. We seek to liberate, heal, and make whole what is threatened or already broken.

Edward Said notes, in relation to the modernist tendency to privilege theory, when theory travels it does so successfully as 'intransigent practice'.[11] Chopp argues that the same is true of modern theology as it uses critical reflection under the lens of theory to determine which experiences and witnesses are faithful and true. Such faith in theory belies the roots of thinking in feeling. Many theories make sense of reality, while often being at odds with each other logically. The choice to favour one over another is not rational, but is based in interest, which is a feeling.[12] To put it another way, theory is always reductive, constructing a picture of reality that focuses on certain aspects of it. When theory illuminates with intellectual insight, it masks other realities – both revealing and masking simultaneously. Hence, theory is provisionally true and untrue at the same time.

Testimony is the act of bearing witness to what has been hidden, and does not rely for its veracity on theory. Rather, it moves in the ethical spheres of right relationship. Those who hear testimony become witnesses by their willingness to listen. This interactive and emotionally complex transaction is the basis of theologies which are constructed through dialogical and praxis-based methods. Chopp's analysis, in highlighting the moral demands of testimony, focuses on justice for those violated by human evil. This emphasis on justice has a long history in both Judaism and Christianity, beginning with the Pentateuch. The Bible is itself a collection of testimonies.

In conceptualising testimony as a theological method, Chopp relies on the Western priority given to word and language, a philosophical emphasis especially prominent in the second half of the twentieth century, and also used by postmodernists to create theories of social construction. Testimony begins to fail when we examine intimate violence.

[11] Cited in ibid, p. 4.

[12] See Alfred North Whitehead, *The Function of Reason*, Boston: Beacon Press, 1986, for an analysis of reason.

Women who have been raped in war, for example, most recently in Kosovo, will often deny experiencing such crimes and refuse to testify.[13] To admit to being raped is to risk being shamed, losing their families and marriages, or being prosecuted.[14]

Testimony is constricted by the failures of words. The majority of human communication does not happen verbally or linguistically, but in deeper intimacies of knowing. We know bodily, moving in the rhythms and choreography passed to us in a culture. We learn and know through embodied signals. Our bodies recall deeply, beyond words.[15]

Intimate violence happens to the body and the psyche. Christian language has sanctioned it.[16] We know tacitly from being in another's presence and sensing what can rarely be put into words. Silence teaches before we have language; the body remembers attempts to murder the soul. The mute presence of the dead also communicate. In attuning ourselves to another's testimony, we must also be aware of the limits of testimony as a form of witness. In cross-cultural contexts language often fails.

Testimony as a theological method is also limited by its focus on moral imperatives. As important as testimony of atrocity is—and it is of crucial importance—survivors of atrocities are not simply victims. Our commitments to each other are rarely just moral, when they are full and satisfying relationships. Our relationships are also driven by aesthetic imperatives and the relational demands of encountering others, both similar and strange, as agents of their own lives. To use theological language, the fullness of the presence of God in the world is known in the fullness of our relationships. And the fullness of relationships includes anguish as well as blessing, horror as well as beauty, silence as well as poetry.

[13] Elizabeth Bumiller, 'Deny Rape or Be Hated: Kosovo Victim's Choice', in *New York Times*, June 22, 1999.

[14] In some Latin American countries, such as Brazil, men who rape are given the option to avoid prosecution by marrying their victims. Women have no choice in the matter, much as they do not in the Deuteronomic codes on rape. Needless to say, many women keep silent about being raped.

[15] On this see Margaret M. Keene, John D. E. Gabriel, et al., 'Double dissociation of memory capacities after bilateral occipital-lobe or medial temporal-lobe lesions', in *Brain* 118 (1995), pp. 1129-48, and Vaidya, C. J., Gabrieli, et al., 'Evidence for multiple mechanisms of conceptual priming on implicit memory tests', in *Journal of Experimental Psychology: Learning, Memory, and Cognition* 23 (1997), pp. 1324-43.

[16] Renita Weems (in *Battered Love: Marriage, Sex, and Violence in the Hebrew Prophets*, Minneapolis: Fortress Press, 1995) analyses the classical prophets' use of domestic violence as a paradigm for God's punishment of Israel, sanctioning it as divine activity.

Mute presence can witness, through the bodies of the dead and the living, and through noncognitive, embodied acts. We bear and are witnesses to a variety of transforming realities – the more embodied, the more transformative. Through many forms of witness we encounter new ways to understand. In the imaginative attempt to encounter another and to examine our own frameworks of power and meaning, our ways of behaving and knowing are transformed.

We consent to believe in order to understand, not to be certain or to verify empirically or theoretically, but to experience the possibility of change through right relationships. This possibility is what it means to be attuned to the presence of God in the world and to be transformed by it. Provisionally, and with the hope of transformation, we take on multiple orientations, examining how and what we know, how we care and what we do in our relationships. Through acts of imagination, of the suspension of disbelief, we enter into the experience of another and are transformed. We explore our ways of being in relation to God incarnate as spirit, as shape-shifting disturber and sustainer of life.[17]

We consent to provisional forms of knowing God. Witness is one way to explore what it means to be a human being in relation to God as spirit. We know the divine presence in the world in its unfolding through our capacities for imagination, empathy, care, and transformation. Witness embraces human sorrows and joys and is attuned to how we construct a life in a complex, ever-changing world. The self in relation to God incarnate is a witness.

The human self

In a previous work, I discussed ways of thinking about selves as shaped profoundly by the accidents of family, environment, language, and culture, an inclination that has its roots in my own cross-cultural life experiences.[18] The practical, moral issues that led me to core theological questions about the self and its relationships emerged through my work in the 1970s with diverse groups of adolescent survivors of sexual and domestic violence. I have also participated throughout my adult life in feminist movements against such forms of violence and in movements for racial justice. More recently my writing has become explicitly cross-

[17] Michael Welker (in *God the Spirit*, Minneapolis: Fortress Press, 1994) notes that the biblical spirit is never self-referential. He describes the spirit as sometimes conveying confidence, not certainty. More often, the spirit is disruptive.

[18] This relational anthropology is found in my book, *Journeys By Heart: A Christology of Erotic Power*, New York: Crossroads Press, 1988.

cultural through my work on prostitution in five Asian countries and the United States.[19]

Since the 1980s in America, feminists and post-modernists have proposed ways of thinking about the human self that argue for its radically social nature. For example, feminists using psychoanalytic object-relations theory discuss the false, individualistic, and androcentric ego in the Western tradition and propose relational understandings from which polarised forms of gender identity arise. Gender is understood to be socially-constructed and only loosely attached to biological sex, which is itself an unstable category.[20] Deconstructive theories, also based in Western psychological theory, have argued against essentialist theorising and assert the socially- and historically-constructed nature of gender, the self, and language. This critique of 'essentialism' targets the universalising and hegemonic tendencies of Eurocentric theory, for example in its interlocking constructions of race, gender, nationality, and class.[21]

The East Asian view of human beings has, perhaps, an even more radically social understanding of the self, understandings found in Asian American communities. One aspect of East Asian Buddhism and Taoism is the implicit assumption of the fluid, nonsubstantial nature of all things, including the human self. Ego is understood as illusory. The examples and behaviours of many people shape individuals, and this shaping is important to the well-being of the whole and how it functions. The nonessentialist metaphysical claims of Buddhism deconstruct power for the sake of alleviating suffering, that is, for soteriological reasons.[22] Because communities, clans, kinship, ancestors, and other social units, roles, and relationships tend to be relatively well-defined in East Asian societies, the individual is expected to be adaptive. It is better not to exhibit a clear, self-possessed ego. The emphasis is not on the critical

[19] See Brock and Susan Thistlethwaite, *Casting Stones: Prostitution and Liberation in Asia and the United States*, Minneapolis: Fortress Press, 1996. The Asian countries are Japan, Korea, Thailand, Taiwan, and the Philippines.

[20] See, for example, Catherine Keller, *From a Broken Web: Separation, Sexism, and Self*, Boston: Beacon Press, 1986; and Nancy Chodorow, *The Reproduction of Mothering: Psychoanalysis and the Sociology of Gender*, Los Angeles: University of California Press, 1978.

[21] For an analysis of their interlocking and intractable qualities, see Anne McClintock's *Imperial Leather: Race, Gender and Sexuality in the Colonial Conquest*, New York: Routledge Press, 1995. See also Judith P. Butler, *Gender Trouble: Feminism and the Subversion of Identity*, New York: Routledge, 1992.

[22] Both Western theories of deconstruction and Buddhist metaphysics are concerned with wrong uses of power. However, Western deconstructive ways of performing theories that claim the self is socially-constructed feel stubbornly egoistic in comparison with Buddhist practices.

capacities of a free individual, but on the capacities for responsibility and relationship of persons-in-relationships.

Such an orientation to self creates tensions in North America between Asian subcultures and the dominant European one – Asians exist in subcultures embedded in societies of exaggerated individualism and racism. Maxine Hong Kingston's powerful Chinese-American memoir bears witness to this tension.[23] She struggles with conflicting Asian and American sensibilities and values in relation to being a gendered and racialised person. In East Asian societies, calling attention to a single person or to oneself is regarded as an antisocial act. The Western 'I', the rational Cartesian individual is rarely spoken except for extreme emphasis. This 'I' self is virtually absent in Kingston's work, which she explicitly notes with some ambiguity and frustration, since her reticence to say and experience 'I' leaves her feeling invisible and marginal. Kingston implicitly discloses herself via her witness to relationships with the living and the dead. Such relationships constitute her framework of personal meaning. To explore these relationships in constructing her memoir, her imagination crosses oceans.

When it appeared in 1976, Kingston's work was regarded as a new form of memoir, a vivid blend of folktales, imagination, speculation, self-examination, and family stories. Kingston explores her life by creatively reconstructing the lives of women in her family in China and in the United States, both living and dead. Her moral, aesthetic, and political commitments emerge through the indirect, subtle implications of the stories she tells.

The moral core of Kingston's work—its concern with the oppression of women, its exposure of internalised self-hatred fostered by racism, and its fierce commitment to justice—is revealed through what she calls 'talk-story.' Story-telling is a common East Asian mode of conveying moral lessons. Chinese philosophical and religious traditions tend to be relatively disinterested in metaphysical and epistemological questions and more interested in moral and ethical questions, according to Chinese feminist theologian Kwok, Pui Lan.

> Truth is not merely something to be grasped cognitively; it must be practiced and acted out in the self-cultivation of moral beings .... At the time of foreign encroachment in the early twentieth century, Chinese students set forth many burning questions: 'Can Christianity save China?' 'Why does not God restrain the stronger nations from oppress-

[23] *The Woman Warrior: Memoirs of a Girlhood Among Ghosts*, New York: Alfred A. Knopf, 1976.

> ing the weaker ones?' 'Why are the Christian nations of the West so aggressive and cruel?'[24]

Cries of anguish against injustice occur in East Asia. Moral distinctions are made between good and evil, but the ontological status of these distinctions and strategies for obtaining justice and for creating moral societies differ from Western models. The struggle to find balance and harmony in the midst of multiplicity shifts emphasis toward aesthetic and relational or communitarian values. Values are assumed to be universal in their observable, lived manifestations. Within life's ambiguities, the human task is to be discerning and responsible through the capacity to become wise and to maintain relationships that sustain life and harmony.[25] What is religious is an orientation not unlike many indigenous traditions, such as those found in North America.[26] 'Religion' is more how one lives, and less what one believes. One struggles to live in right relationship to all of life, materially, interpersonally, spiritually.

Sin

Christian ideas of sin have tended toward the personal and individualistic. While sin is understood ontologically to be an essential aspect of the entire human condition, its articulation has been largely in terms of its corruption of the individual soul and the loss of relationship between God and the soul. Liberation theologies, along with early twentieth-century Social Gospel theologians such as Walter Rauschenbusch, have challenged orthodox and neo-orthodox theologies of sin as individual and inherited and have upended the progressive optimism of liberal theology. Against older orthodoxies, liberation theologians assert that sin is a social phenomenon; it has a structured, social, historical character that can be identified and that can be fought in history. In other words, oppressive systems are manifestations of sin that must be resisted, and these larger forms of sin should be the focus of our struggle.

Parallels can be found between the liberation emphasis on social and systemic sin and feminist discussions of patriarchy and systems of

[24] Kwok, *Discovering the Bible in the Non-Biblical World*, p. 11.

[25] For a more extensive discussion of this aesthetic dimension, see my essay 'Interstitial Integrity' in Roger Badham (ed.), *Introduction to Christian Theology: Contemporary North American Perspectives*, Louisville: Westminster/John Knox Press, 1998, pp. 183-96.

[26] Vine Deloria, Jr., *God Is Red: A Native View of Religion*, Golden, CO: Fulcrum, 1992.

male dominance. However, some feminist theologians have suggested new individual dimensions of sin within a thoroughgoing gender analysis because so much of the gendered life of women concerns intimate relationships outside public view. From this reinterpretation, our understanding of the limits of the traditional understandings of sin is deepened, and individual sin is interpreted contextually and socially.

Feminist theologians such as Valerie Saiving, Judith Plaskow, and Dorothee Soelle have argued that the identification of sin with 'pride' or 'concupiscence' is predicated on the experience of élite men, who should be wary of the misuses of their own power. For many women, feminists argue, the constraints and expectations of stereotypical gender roles lead to women's struggle to define a self at all outside the demands of relationships in which women's self-abnegation is expected. When sin is named pride, attempts by women to assert our own dignity and worth in the face of sexism are regarded as sinful.[27]

Sin cannot simply be pride. Sin is the abuse of power, which has both social/political and interpersonal dimensions. Mary Potter Engel, in examining sin from the experiences of women, suggests a nuanced distinction between sin as interpersonal and evil as social/political. She begins from the perspective of survivors of sexual and domestic abuse and forms her work on their lives as witnesses. The liberation analysis of sin as structured into the many institutions and relations of an oppressive society, she suggests, is systemically-organised evil. She defines sin as what individuals do to reinforce evil.

> Evil and sin together may be called 'wickedness,' the complex condition of the lack of right relations in the world in which we live naturally, socially and individually. Though they are inseparable, it is important to distinguish the two. Evil, as Latin American liberation theology has taught us, is systemic. It is not superpersonal forces but structures of oppression; patterns larger than individuals and groups with a life of their own that tempt us toward injustice and impiety – social, political, economic arrangements that distort our perceptions or restrain our abilities to such an extent that we find it difficult to choose or do good. By contrast, sin refers to those free, discrete acts of responsible indi-

[27] On this see Judith Plaskow, *Sex, Sin, and Grace: Women's Experience and the Theologies of Reinhold Niebuhr and Paul Tillich*, Washington: University Press of America, 1980; Valerie Saiving, 'The Human Situation, A Feminine View', in Carol Christ and Judith Plaskow (eds), *Womanspirit Rising*, New York: Harper & Row, 1979; and Dorothee Soelle, *Political Theology*, tr. John Shelley, Philadelphia: Fortress Press, 1990.

viduals that create or reinforce these structures of oppression. Neither causes the other; evil and sin are mutually reinforcing.[28]

Individual violations of other persons disrupt life-sustaining relationships and create oppressive relationships that destroy community and undermine systems of justice and care.[29] With this social understanding of human beings, what Christians call sin is defined as what destroys our capacities for right relationships. The destruction of relationships, of love, is the violation of the spirit of God.

Potter Engel identifies four understandings of sin that more accurately describe its interpersonal dimensions. These are: sin as distortion of feeling, sin as betrayal of trust, sin as lack of care, and sin as lack of consent to vulnerability. Systems, such as male dominance, militarism, multinational capitalism, racism, and colonialism, are evil because they 'distort our perceptions or restrain our abilities to such an extent that we find it difficult to choose or to do good'.[30]

This interpersonal understanding of sin assumes that it is a function of both the particular contingencies of our lives and the larger social forces that shape human behaviour. As Potter Engel points out, the dimensions of sin for victims of abuse are complex. Sinful acts by one person can produce a reaction that mirrors the sins of those acts. Some mechanisms, such as lack of trust, develop as necessary survival mechanisms for those abused and exploited by others at formative moments in their development. In their dimensions as protective reactions to conditions akin to brutal, captive torture, we must understand such 'sinful' acts as psychological mechanisms of survival. These mechanisms allow for self-protection at the time of the violation. They have the power, however, to reproduce themselves as pathologies for generations in the absence of intervention.[31]

Near the end of her memoir, Kingston describes a moment when she torments a quiet, soft-spoken Chinese-American girl in the bathroom of

[28] Engel, 'Evil, Sin, and the Violation of the Vulnerable', in Susan Thistlethwaite and Mary Potter Engel (eds), *Lift Every Voice: Theologies from the Underside*, San Francisco: Harper & Row, 1990, p. 155.

[29] The feminist work on intimate violence has exposed an almost entirely hidden and socially sanctioned system of evil by giving it language. Terms such as domestic violence, sexual harassment, clergy sexual misconduct, marital rape, and child sexual abuse were non-existent twenty years ago. The first feminist study of rape in the United States to examine it from the perspective of survivors of it was published in 1975 by Susan Brownmiller, *Against Our Will: Men, Women, and Rape*, New York: Simon and Schuster.

[30] Engel, 'Evil, Sin, and the Violation of the Vulnerable', p. 157.

[31] See Judith Lewis Herman, *Trauma and Recovery*, New York: Basic Books, 1992, for a nuanced description of these mechanisms.

their Chinese language school. She is furious at the girl for being too much like everything Kingston hates in herself: self-effacing, soft, compliant, obedient. Years of pent-up anger, internalised contempt, and frustration spill out in a moment of violence. Kingston knows she should stop. She cannot. She is so ashamed of her act that she is bedridden and silent for a year. Lateral violence erupts when the downward pressures of oppressive power have nowhere else to go. For Kingston to understand what she had done, she had to understand her struggle to claim her dignity, voice, and self-respect while living as an Asian American female in a racist and sexist society.

In the Western Christian tradition, we have had no religious language to describe these complex nuances of response to abuse, violation, oppression, and deliberately inflicted pain. Responses to abuse and oppression such as suspicion, anger, bitterness, despair, grief, outrage, and self-destructiveness are categorised as sin, for which there is no answer except repentance and forgiveness of the perpetrators of evil. That answer revictimises survivors of intimate violence in the church. Intimate violence involves complex emotions in which personal boundaries are violated and love is confused with hostility and aggression. Survivors are counselled to forgive their abusers and to subject themselves to further violation.[32] They are preached the example of Jesus' silent, suffering servanthood, which is upheld as a supreme moral example of self-sacrifice to emulate. Abelard's moral influence theory describes Jesus' saving significance in this altruistic way.

While liberals have, by and large, rejected most ideas of the atonement, the moral influence theory, its valorisation of sacrificing love and altruism, continues to hold great sway. This theology denies the moral responses of resistance and outrage to those victimised by intimate violence. This idealisation of sacrifice silences victims of intimate violence and attenuates the struggle against such evils because responses to violation, such as anger, self-preservation, and wilful disobedience to authority, are called sinful. Hence, the only means to be moral is to acquiesce to evil.[33] My first book[34] attempted to address this lack by using the

[32] Forgiveness has its place in a healing process, but the decision to forgive and the point at which to forgive must come from the internal processes of survivors, after their lives are no longer in danger. To counsel forgiveness without resistance to evil is to provide means for the perpetuation of evil and to protect its perpetrators. Such counsel confuses love with abuse, and they are not the same thing.

[33] There are countless examples from domestic violence shelters of the life-threatening implications of this theological idea of redemptive suffering and forgiveness.

[34] *Journeys by Heart: A Christology of Erotic Power*, New York: Crossroads Press, 1988.

term brokenheartedness, which I suggested as an alternative to original sin. However, Korean Minjung theology has developed a more adequate term.[35]

Human suffering and *han*

To explain the human response to being oppressed, violated, or abused over long periods of time, Korean culture uses the term *han*. In *The Wounded Heart of God*, Andrew Sung Park notes that Christian theology has focused far too extensively on sins that are committed and far too little on the woundedness and pain that sin creates.[36] In suggesting *han* as a corrective to that lack, Park notes that 'Han is the abysmal experience of pain. It has two aspects: active and inactive. Active *han* is closer to aggressive emotion, while inactive *han* is similar to a quiescent spirit'.[37] *Han*, in its many dimensions, is understood to haunt the dead as well as the living, such that *han*-ridden spirits roam the earth full of anger, bitterness, and grief.[38]

Han has complex structures because the psychological consequences of violence have complex structures. These structures are created by powers that frustrate hope, that violate human beings at the core of their sense of self, that squeeze the powers of life and struggle from human caring. Park describes such structures as a wounded heart – a collapsing feeling of pain, a fall into despair, and resentful bitterness. Hyun Younghak says *han* is 'a sense of unresolved resentment against injustices suffered, a sense of helplessness because of the overwhelming odds against oneself, a feeling of total abandonment (why hast thou for-

[35] Minjung theology is a form of liberation theology that addresses the struggles of the poor, outcast, and common people of Korea.

[36] *The Wounded Heart of God: the Asian Concept of Han and the Christian Doctrine of Sin*, Nashville: Abingdon Press, 1993. See also Kang Nam-Soon, 'Han' in Letty M. Russell and J. Shannon Clarkson (eds), *Dictionary of Feminist Theologies*, Louisville: Westminster/John Knox Press, 1996, pp. 134-5, David Suh *The Korean Minjung in Christ*, Maryknoll, NY: Orbis Press, 1985, and Chung Hyun Kyung, *Struggle to be the Sun Again*, Maryknoll, NY: Orbis Press, 1990.

[37] Park, *The Wounded Heart of God*, p. 15.

[38] At the World Council of Churches Seventh International Assembly held in Canberra, Australia in 1991, Chung opened her plenary address 'Come Holy Spirit' by reading a long list of those who had died unjustly, the spirits of *han*.

saken me?), ... an obstinate urge to take "revenge" and to right the wrong – all these combined'.[39]

Chinese culture shares this dimension of resistance to injustice, though it uses different ways to refer to the same phenomenon, referring to those who have died unjustly as hungry or angry ghosts. The core of Kingston's work is resistance to evil. Rather than choosing a suffering servant image as the centre of her life story, she selects the legendary and imaginary woman warrior who fights oppression. The warrior organises her people to resist their oppressors. Her warrior undergoes the discipline of intensive spiritual training. She has the names of all who have been killed carved in the flesh on her back. The names are her revenge and help her remember the ghosts of all who died unjustly. Kingston compares herself to this warrior image. Her life fails to measure up. At the same time, she knows her pen is her sword, her resistance to the silencing and pain that is her American destiny.

Christian theology has confused sin and *han* and has profoundly distorted our ability to understand the complexities of human resistance to evil and the suffering injustice causes. In the face of life-threatening domestic violence and other forms of violation and abuse, the church has counselled silent suffering and forgiveness, using the moral example of Jesus' self-sacrifice. The political brutality of the Roman empire is confused with the love of God; the pathologies of perpetrators of violence are confused with the human capacity to love. This latter confusion is particularly dangerous because victims of intimate violence often love their abusers and want to be loved in return.

When we make self-sacrifice the primary virtuous response to violence, we persuade victims to become obedient to the power of others to perpetuate evil. If a victim resists or flees evil, she is seen as lacking moral virtue. Acts to guard one's own well-being are called selfish, disobedient, or prideful. To be perfect, like Jesus, is to be a worthy victim by demonstrating obedient love.[40] One avoids sinning by accepting violence and forgiving it. In fact, this theological model accepts in victims the passive, defeated, or acquiescent side of *han*.

Such acquiescence, however, leads to further victimisation. To survive dire circumstances requires deep internal emotional resistance. Outrage is one healthy response to violation. Those who are sexually or physically abused or tortured must develop psychological mechanisms such as dissociation or anger to survive. Struggles for liberation often

[39] In 'Minjung, the Suffering Servant and Hope', paper presented at Union Theological Seminary, New York City, 13 April 1982, cited in Park, *The Wounded Heart of God*, p. 19.

[40] This theological interpretation is not, however, accurate to the picture of Jesus one finds in the Gospels, especially in the Gospel of John.

begin with outrage. The absence in Christian theology of a concept like *han* disempowers those most victimised by oppression because we lack a theological way to understand the ambiguities within which people survive destructive and life-threatening circumstances.

The attribution of sin rightly belongs to those who misuse power; *han* belongs to those hurt by such acts and systems of evil. For many of us, both sin and *han* are dimensions of our lives as we sit in the complex interstices of relationships of power and as we struggle to live within systems of power both malign and benign.

Living into the presence of God[41]

Liberal theologies long ago challenged the atonement in its expiatory, substitutionary, and Christus Victor forms. These forms, liberals argue, make God unworthy of worship and violate the loving, tolerant father image favoured by such theologies. Liberals have, however, tended to retain some form of the moral influence theory of the atonement. As I have noted above, this theory in particular has had devastating consequences for trapping victims in cycles of violence. The moral influence theory reinscribes *han* as a spiritual and moral necessity. The perpetrators of evil are masked and protected, and victims are presented with a model that endures evil silently. Truths about violence and oppression remain untold.

When we turn the theological lens toward victims of violence, it becomes evident that any attempt to make the execution of Jesus theologically necessary participates in evil and denies the life-giving presence of God. Making Jesus' execution necessary for human salvation, or for the restoration of human relationships to God, perpetuates and masks evil. Atonement theologies prevent us from facing the truth about Jesus' murder. His execution was an act of human evil.

A Palestinian Jew from rural Galilee, Jesus lived in a brutal political time.[42] He was likely a social revolutionary, a prophet resisting the

[41] Much of this discussion of atonement is from my *Proverbs of Ashes: Violence, Religion, and a Witness for Life*, Boston: Beacon Press, 2001 (co-authored with Rebecca Ann Parker). See our previous discussions of this topic in Joanne Carlson Brown and Carole R. Bohn (eds), *Christianity, Patriarchy, and Abuse: A Feminist Critique*, New York: Pilgrim Press, 1989; and *Journeys By Heart*.

[42] Richard A. Horsley (in *Jesus and the Spiral of Violence: Popular Jewish Resistance in Roman Palestine*, San Francisco: Harper & Row, 1987) describes the downward, oppressive pressures of Rome on the peasantry of Palestine. The Roman imperial system overburdened people with taxes and tributes and forced them into debt and loss of land. The empire co-opted cultural systems, especially religious/economic/political systems, to make them serve the needs and

Roman imperial system of oppression. His movement appears to have received widespread support among a variety of Galileans, Samaritans, and Judeans.[43]

To organise such a movement was dangerous. It carried the death penalty. The Romans executed him, in the most brutal way. As a warning to others, they made crucifixion a gruesome and wrenching public spectacle. A bloody human being was hung on a cross, his body flogged until he appeared to have been forced through a meat grinder. The torture was intended not only to kill the individual, but to threaten the populace. It was a deliberate instrument of social control for an empire whose success depended on obedient participation by the oppressed in conscription, slavery, cultural accommodation to Rome, and taxation.[44]

Such human violence damages in ways that are never repaired. It creates losses that can only be mourned, destroys lives that are never restored. Jesus' life was one of these. He was murdered by an organised system of human violence. The Gospels testify to this atrocity committed against Jesus, even as they attempt to absolve Rome. His death redeems no one.

The harm done to Jesus was irreparable. He did not recover from the violence. He did not heal. He did not awaken from death as if it were merely sleep. Human beings who benefited from a system of violence deliberately tortured and murdered him. It was not the will of God to do this or have it done to any human being. Jesus died a horrible death at human hands, for political and religious reasons. Violence does not redeem, it destroys.[45]

It would have been better if Jesus had lived a long life. His murder did not advance the kingdom of God – it cut short his work to organise a movement. It did not defeat evil or expiate for sin. It did not save anyone else from being brutalised. It did not win anyone's freedom from the clutches of the devil, and it did not counteract the powers of hell.

> Crucifixion is ... a manifestation of trans-subjective evil, a form of execution which manifests the demonic character of human cruelty.[46]

wants of the ruling minority and their friends and collaborators. Furthermore, the military and judicial branches of the empire suppressed resistance with violence, including mass killings of the people, and killings of individual leaders who expressed opposition or resistance to Rome.

[43] John Dominic Crossan, *The Historical Jesus: The Life of a Mediterranean Jewish Peasant*, San Francisco: Harper, 1991.

[44] On this see Martin Hengel, *Crucifixion: In the Ancient World and the Folly of the Message of the Cross*, Philadelphia: Fortress Press, 1977, p. 25, cf. pp. 30-1.

[45] Cf. Hengel, *Crucifixion*, p. 90.

[46] Ibid., p. 87.

The anguishing history of the twentieth century is the clearest evidence that such hell thrives in our midst.

The Christian tradition has claimed that Jesus' brutal execution was necessary for human salvation, that God had foreordained this act, and that through the torture and murder of God himself in human form, the world was saved. Nothing has been saved by this claim, but state violence has been sanctioned as divine will. And rage—unacknowledged and unexorcised *han*—has been turned on Jews for something that was claimed to be foreordained by God.[47]

Doctrines of the atonement take an historical act of state terrorism, subsume it into a spiritualised intimate transaction between a parent and child (the Father and Son), and use this model of loving acquiescence to intimate violence as a solution to state murder. The atonement says that state violence has been solved—saved—by the virtuous endurance of intimate violence. The church has persuaded people to believe this by claiming that they will lose their lives and be separated from God if they do not believe it. By creating an image of love as obedient submission to intimate violence as a revelatory—and necessary—event, theology has sanctioned the endangerment of women and children in their own homes.

Is it any wonder that state terrorism has been perpetrated by Christian empires and by governments of Christian citizens, and that Christian theology has never fully addressed the evil of intimate violence? This theological legacy of violence has encouraged ignorance of evil, rather than the knowing and resisting of it. We cannot come to terms with what we refuse to understand.

We need move only briefly outside the surface spheres of first-world comforts to realise that the story of Jesus and his execution is repeated over and over in our world, unrelentingly. This century has seen the worst atrocities human beings can commit, on an unprecedented scale by 'civilised' Christian nations. For the first time, human beings have confronted the possibility of the annihilation of our entire species, a capacity created first by Christian leaders of a country who used nuclear weapons for no justifiable reason, either militarily or ethically, against innocent civilians, who were killed by the blasts in Hiroshima and Nagasaki. Justifications for this atrocity were invented after the deeds were done, and they were government lies.

Good people are often sacrificed for the wrong reasons. We are told white-washed national histories of noble causes to justify or hide con-

[47] John Dominic Crossan discusses the devastating lie that has led to the Holocaust in *Who Killed Jesus? Exposing the Roots of Anti-Semitism in the Gospel Story of the Death of Jesus*, San Francisco: Harper, 1995.

tinuing legacies of colonialism, white supremacy, and imperialism that mark us still. We pretend our leaders do not sanction and conduct state violence, and we believe we are basically good people. There are many good people in every country. But we live inside systems far larger than our individual choices can control, systems that benefit a few at the cost of many.[48]

Human beings can inflict great evil, while appearing good. They can commit violence against their own families and loved ones in the unlit corners of their private homes while appearing as good Christians in the light of day. Torture and murder are repeated in the privacy of homes of affluence and privilege, as well as among the destitute.

Because we tend to think of individual morality and goodness, we do not to see how larger political and economic forces make an impact on our personal lives. We are not supposed to draw these links, just as we are not supposed to notice that Christian theology subsumed state terror into an act of intimate violence, masking the dynamics of state sponsored terrorism and constructing a model of personal sacrifice to evil as redemptive. Individual self-sacrifice does not forestall state terrorism. They feed off each other, interlinked to larger systems of human violence.

In his farewell speech to his community in the Gospel of John, Jesus tacks between two winds, the power of God who gives knowledge and peace and the destructive forces of the empire, 'the world'. He claims the empire has no power over him. In other words, the empire has not made him afraid to do the work of justice that God has called him to do. He knows they will kill him, brutally, but he goes knowing he is doing the work that shows he is truly the son of God. He is truly in the divine presence because he practises truth, love, and justice. Not to do so is to let the empire win. Jesus ultimately does not lose, for he has not been cowed. His courage remains steadfast and so his relationship to God remains, regardless.

We must not confuse this picture of Jesus' commitments to justice with self-sacrifice. He is not returning to an abuser whom he loves, and he is not succumbing to abusive violence to prove the power of his love to overcome the evil of his murders. He does not walk into the jaws of death confused about the nature of evil and love. He does not believe Pilate cares about him or his people. He is clearly contemptuous of Pilate's power. The gospel witness consistently makes clear that Jesus holds fast in faithfulness to his knowledge of God and refuses to back down on the demands of resistance to oppression. To the end, he contin-

[48] On this see Juliet Schor, *The Overworked American: The Unexpected Decline of Leisure*, New York: Basic Books, 1993; and *Beyond an Economy of Work and Spend*, Tilburg, Netherlands: Tilburg University Press, 1997.

ues to face evil for the sake of the people he loves. Those who kill him want to kill that knowledge in him. In the farewell discourses, he gives his community reasons to live beyond what evil can do. 'Righteous Father, the world does not know you, but I know you; and these know that you have sent me. I made your name known to them, and I will make it known, so that the love with which you have loved me may be in them and I in them.' (John 17:25) Nothing positive or theologically revelatory is added to the message of the Johannine Gospel by Jesus' death.[49]

The Gospel tries to absolve Pilate of responsibility, but Jesus defies his enemies to the end (John 19:11). Pilate is doing evil, which, according to Jesus, is Pilate's responsibility. The Gospel writer tries to show Jesus' power over Pilate by having Pilate respond to Jesus' challenge by wanting to release him. This is a fatal lie, for it led to blame falling on the Judeans instead of where it belonged, with Rome. The consequences of this horrible lie have been genocide. The history of Christian anti-semitism has been another consequence of not telling the truth about Jesus' execution.

Jesus' execution served the cause of an oppressive system. But that system did not have the last word. The presence of God in the world was not destroyed. Life endured. Commitments to justice were not erased. Jesus' community attempted to continue his work. His death did not save; the endurance and courage of his community carried forward the possibility of life, of a future beyond death.

Knowledge of divine presence is inextricably bound to ethical practice and right relationships – to living what we know to be true as best we can. Ethical practice, covenanted living, derives from acting as if we believed the presence of God is in the world. We encounter that presence through our attunement to its many forms. When we are separated from the presence of God, we are separated from each other as well. The spirit of God endures in many forms, as shape-shifting disturber and sustainer of life.

The perpetrators of violence and injustice do what they will. They are responsible for the evil they commit. We are responsible for seeing it and finding ways to resist it, to practise justice, and to make space for love to flourish. This is what Jesus tells his friends to do. This is the way to keep the divine presence in human life. This is the future of Christianity in North America, of Christian theology in this new century. Life with God is that simple and that difficult.

[49] Ernst Käsemann long ago suggested the dispensability of John's passion narrative in *The Testament of Jesus*, Philadelphia: Fortress Press, 1968.

Chapter 12

Postmodern Theology

The Apotheosis or Scourge of Liberalism?

Gavin Hyman

In recent years, liberal theology has witnessed a sea-change on the theological horizon. For centuries, this horizon was one where Enlightenment assumptions were unquestioningly taken for granted. In the words of Leslie Houlden, the prevailing orthodoxy was that 'we must accept our lot, bequeathed to us by the Enlightenment, and make the most of it'.[1] Recently, however, this orthodoxy has increasingly been called into question, particularly by those theologians who would call themselves 'postmodern'. Theological disputes have therefore been transposed from being merely disputes *within* a framework to being more complex disputes *between* frameworks. Liberal theology is now faced with the task of transposing itself accordingly, and has not always been successful in doing so.[2]

In this chapter I propose to clarify the precise nature of postmodern theology's relationship to liberal theology. I shall distinguish between two distinct forms of postmodern theology – the nihilistic postmodern

[1] Leslie Houlden, 'The Creed of Experience', in John Hick (ed.), *The Myth of God Incarnate*, London: SCM Press, 1977, p. 125.

[2] John Hick, for instance, conducts his dispute with Gerard Loughlin as though it were a dispute within his own framework, rather than one between two different (namely, modern and postmodern) frameworks. The result is that Hick distorts and misrepresents Loughlin's criticisms as well as his theological position. See John Hick, 'A Response to Gerard Loughlin', in *Modern Theology* 7 (1990), pp. 57-66, and John Hick, 'Reply', in Harold Hewitt Jr. (ed.), *Problems in the Philosophy of Religion: Critical Studies in the Work of John Hick*, Basingstoke: Macmillan, 1991, pp. 206-9. For a discussion of these replies, see my article, 'Hick and Loughlin on Disputes and Frameworks', in *New Blackfriars* 79 (1998), pp. 391-405.

textualism of Don Cupitt and Mark C. Taylor and the theologically conservative postmodern theology or 'Radical Orthodoxy' of John Milbank, Graham Ward and Gerard Loughlin. I shall argue that they are each related to liberal theology in quite antithetical ways. Nihilistic postmodernism initially *accepts* modern liberal assumptions, and then presses them so thoroughly and consistently that they eventually subvert themselves. To illustrate this, I look in particular at the work of Don Cupitt to show how Cupitt's move from realism to non-realism, and subsequently from modernism to postmodernism was prompted by his prior acceptance of the modern liberal framework and, in particular, a Kantian-inspired epistemology and a distinctively modernist understanding of the *via negativa* and divine ineffability. So I argue that Cupitt's postmodernism emerged organically and logically out of the liberal theology that he had formerly professed.[3] In contrast, I shall show how the 'Radical Orthodoxy' of John Milbank and Gerard Loughlin confrontationally reacts against liberal theology by questioning and rejecting many of the premises upon which it is founded. To this end, I shall look in particular at Gerard Loughlin's criticisms of John Hick's philosophy of religion which he regards as being both incorrigibly secular and philosophically untenable. In this sense, therefore, I argue that whereas nihilistic postmodernism is the *apotheosis* of liberalism, conservative postmodern theology is the *scourge* of liberalism. Thus, there are *two* postmodern challenges to liberal theology which the latter will have to address in two quite distinct ways.

[3] In this chapter, I concentrate on Cupitt's transition, but one could also trace a similar transition in the work of Mark C. Taylor from *Journeys to Selfhood: Hegel and Kierkegaard* (Berkeley: University of California Press, 1980), through *Deconstructing Theology*, Atlanta: Scholars Press, 1982 to *Erring: A Postmodern A/Theology* (Chicago: University of Chicago Press, 1984). In Taylor's case, however, the modernist pressures that tipped him into postmodernism are more Hegelian than Kantian. For a discussion of this transition, see Mark C. Taylor, 'Retracings', in John R. Stone (ed.), *The Craft of Religious Studies*, Basingstoke: Macmillan, 1998, pp. 258-76.

Don Cupitt

I begin by examining the way in which Don Cupitt's non-realism (and subsequently postmodernism) emerged out of the modern liberal theology that previously engaged him.[4] I shall show how this version of postmodern theology explicates what is implicit in modern liberal theology, emerging organically out of it, rather than confrontationally reacting against it.

Let us therefore turn to this liberal modern theology that Cupitt formerly espoused. He subsequently described it as 'a moderate version of British Empiricism'.[5] which was firmly rooted in the same modernist liberal tradition as that of John Hick. Thus, he was at one with Hick in his insistence upon the cognitive nature of religious statements, and in rejecting the sort of non-realism he was later to profess. He said that 'Faith may enable a man to apprehend an object which otherwise he could not have apprehended, but it does not create that which it apprehends. On the contrary, it is in the last analysis receptive.'[6] If religious language is receptive, however, one is led to enquire into the nature of this reception. How does religious language 'connect' with that about which it purports to speak? Cupitt addresses this question in *The Leap of Reason* (1976),[7] and answers it by presenting us with a programme of five stages. In the first stage, the mere *possibility* of a transcendent realm is established. This idea is elaborated in Cupitt's 'prison metaphor' which is, in turn, a version of Plato's allegory of the cave. The parable differs from Plato's, however, in that 'there is most

[4] This raises the question of the way in which Cupitt's non-realism is related to his postmodernism. In this chapter, I present Cupitt's thought as a movement from modern liberalism (prior to 1980) through an intermediary 'non-realist' (1980-1986) stage before arriving at his later postmodernism (from 1986). Cupitt himself is ambiguous in his use of the term 'non-realism'. Sometimes he uses it in this intermediate sense, but at other times he uses it to refer to all of his writings subsequent to his taking leave of realism. Essentially, the difference between his intermediate non-realism and his later postmodernism is that in his 'non-realist' books, he had taken leave of objectivity, metaphysics and transcendence, but had not yet embraced the postmodern concerns of deconstruction, linguistic reflexivity and the crisis of representation. In this chapter, I concentrate on his move from liberal realism to non-realism.

[5] Don Cupitt, *Christ and the Hiddenness of God*, 2nd edition, London: SCM Press, 1985, p. 5.

[6] Ibid., p. 43.

[7] Don Cupitt, *The Leap of Reason* (1976). 2nd edition, London: SCM Press, 1985.

definitely no chink in the prison wall, and we do not postulate that our prisoner has any extraordinary faculties. So he has no direct knowledge of "outside": only his own heightened consciousness, the leap of reason'.[8] Thus, the possibility of a transcendent realm is first established on the basis of the subject's 'own heightened consciousness'. Cupitt's second stage is to consider the *objectivity* of this transcendent realm as an absolute perspective 'from which human world-views can be compared, and which provides the Archimedean point by which we can make the transition from one of them to another'.[9] This transcendent realm serves as Cupitt's bulwark against relativism.

In the third stage, a great communal effort 'projects human and this-worldly features upon the unknowable face of the transcendent'. This results in all the 'myth, doctrine, morals, rituals, symbols, and visible institutions'. Such a religion is true insofar as its fruits are intellectually, morally and aesthetically satisfying.[10] The fourth stage is an iconoclastic negation of the third stage, in recognition that 'I am obliged to recognise the limitations of even the noblest religious system that can be devised'.[11] But if all knowledge is relative to some conceptual scheme, the negation of this last stage is to take leave of all knowledge, leaving this fourth stage with an in-built agnosticism. In the fifth stage, there is a recognition that the fourth stage cannot be distinguished from agnosticism or scepticism, and that yet at the same time, silence is not sufficient to express the transcendent that was affirmed in the earlier stages. Therefore, the fifth stage advocates that religion live in 'a constant flux and reflux between stages 3 and 4. This spiritual dance is the central source of intellectual and artistic creativity in any culture'.[12] Thus, for Cupitt, it was this fifth stage that is central to any monotheistic religion: 'It is this fiery dance between the affirmation of images and their negation, between rapturous piety and the cry of dereliction, which is the heart of religion'.[13]

One implication of such a system is that it gives rise to a 'two Gods' idea, since there is what Scott Cowdell calls the 'working God' of religion that is part of the doctrine, symbols and stories affirmed in stage three, alongside the ineffable transcendent God that is affirmed in stage

[8] Ibid, p. 37.
[9] Ibid, p. 76.
[10] Ibid.
[11] Ibid.
[12] Ibid, p. 77.
[13] Ibid, p. 78.

two, and upon which the 'working God' of stage three is 'projected'.[14] We shall see that this 'two Gods' idea was an important component of both the Kantian-inspired epistemology and the *via negativa* idea, as I shall discuss below.

We may, therefore, say that the religious philosophy of the 'early Cupitt' embodied a number of quintessentially modern and liberal characteristics. He begins with the individual's 'heightened consciousness' and pre-linguistic religious experience, he regards religious traditions as local mythical expressions of a single underlying reality, and he exercises subjective rationality as a means of expressing a universal human condition. I shall now look at the philosophical processes by which Cupitt subverted this tradition.

Cupitt and Kant

Rowan Williams has observed that the foremost figures of influence in Cupitt's subversion of liberalism into non-realism were Kant and the Buddha. Whereas the Buddha is the authoritative precedent for Cupitt's religious vision, Kant provides that vision with much of its philosophical underpinning.[15] This is significant because it might be said that the essence of Kant's philosophy lies in its turn to the subject. As Kant himself puts it:

> Hitherto it has been assumed that all our knowledge must conform to objects. But all attempts to extend our knowledge of objects by establishing something in regard to them *a priori*, by means of concepts, have, on this assumption, ended in failure. We must therefore make trial whether we may not have more success in the truth of metaphysics, if we suppose that objects must conform to our knowledge.[16]

The 'early Cupitt' embraced this Kantian turn to the subject and its associated epistemology. He said that 'I do substantially accept the Kantian critique' (of what Cupitt calls the Platonic quest for absolute know-

[14] See Scott Cowdell, *Atheist Priest? Don Cupitt and Christianity*, London: SCM Press, 1988, p. 5.

[15] See Rowan Williams, '"Religious Realism": On not quite agreeing with Don Cupitt', in *Modern Theology* 1 (1984), pp. 3, 22 n. 3.

[16] Immanuel Kant, *Critique of Pure Reason*, tr. Norman Kemp Smith, London: Macmillan, 1933, p. 22.

ledge of an absolute object).[17] He did so, however, with certain qualifications. For Kant, the noumenal world, together with the human mind, produces the phenomenal world of our experience through the medium of concepts which Kant calls the *categories* of understanding (quantity, quality, relation, modality, and their subdivisions) – these are *a priori* and hence universal and invariable modes of human perception. Cupitt, however, rejected Kant's universal categories in favour of culturally-relative ones. Kant, he said,

> recognised that our empirical knowledge is relative to intellectual programming, but thought he could vindicate the objectivity of knowledge by proving *a priori* that there is and can be only one programme. But we know empirically that there is an endless variety of different programmes.[18]

So in addition to embracing Kant's 'turn to the subject', Cupitt intensified this subjectivist tendency by insisting on the relativity of Kant's categories. He thereby moved away from Kant's universalism towards a much more subjectivist relativism. At this point, however, he still resisted thoroughgoing relativism by invoking a transcendent realm 'which alone is able to relativise and so overcome relativism itself'.[19] This transcendent realm served much the same purpose, therefore, as the 'Real' in John Hick's pluralist philosophy of religion. Both concepts served as the final precarious barrier against the relativism that they had otherwise so wholeheartedly embraced. Indeed, so precarious was it that countless critics have since pointed out the emptiness and superfluity of Hick's 'Real',[20] and Cupitt himself was later to concur with these critics and abandon his own transcendent realm. This was perhaps an inevitable step, because once one has embraced neo-Kantian subjectivist relativism, Hick's 'Real' and Cupitt's 'transcendent realm' become philosophically difficult to justify, and also superfluous and unnecessary. As Paul Eddy has said of Hick's 'Real': 'there is *nothing* residual that *requires* the postulation of an unknowable (divine)

17 Don Cupitt, *The Leap of Reason*, p. 38.

18 Ibid., p. 55.

19 Ibid., p. 65.

20 Amongst the numerous assertions of the dispensability of Hick's 'Real' and its relationship to Kantian epistemology, see Gerard Loughlin, 'Noumenon and Phenomena' in *Religious Studies* 23 (1987), pp. 493-508; and Paul Eddy, 'Religious Pluralism and the Divine: Another look at John Hick's neo-Kantian proposal', in *Religious Studies* 30 (1994), pp. 467-78.

noumenon'.[21] As we shall see, Gerard Loughlin agrees, and says that the only possible justification for Hick's 'Real' is that of 'faith', akin to the faith by which Christianity is 'justified'. But whereas Christian faith is grounded in revelation, Hick's faith in the 'Real' has no such grounding, and is therefore infinitely more vulnerable.[22] Cupitt came increasingly to recognise the force of these considerations. Thus he was later to say that 'pluralism, relativism and scepticism may be kept at bay for a while but can never finally be overcome'.[23]

Cupitt therefore took leave of realism in favour of non-realism, and took leave of the noumenon in favour of nothing but phenomena. And it is evident that it is precisely Cupitt's appropriation and development of a Kantian epistemology that tended him towards this relativism and non-realism. Two conclusions may be drawn from this. First, it is clear that the movement from liberalism to non-realism and ultimately from modernism to postmodernism is provoked not by external pressures or criticism, but merely by an explication of that which is implicit within liberal modern theology itself. Thus, to take the Kantian example we have been considering, the concern of the non-realist is not to criticise Kantianism from outside the modern framework, but merely to point out internally that Kantianism has an implicit subjective idealism, which, if explicated fully, leads to something rather more radical than the liberal modernist will allow. Secondly, it is evident that this subversion is but a small step along the linear, progressive road from modernism to postmodernism. A step so small, in fact, that their similarity has often been remarked upon. As Colin Gunton has said: 'Postmodernism is the subjective side of Kantianism, beginning, as it does, with the structures of human experience, collapsed into an individualism which borders on solipsism'.[24] One may want to question this somewhat pejorative characterisation of postmodernism, but it does at least confirm my suggestion that Cupitt's postmodernism is indeed the end result of a linear, progressive movement along which modernity subverts itself from within. Gunton goes on to say that Cupitt's position is the extreme outcome of the modern turn *inwards* to experience and the individual experiencer: 'The contribution of postmodernism is to have spelled the

[21] Paul Eddy, 'Religious Pluralism and the Divine', p. 477.

[22] Gerard Loughlin, 'Noumenon and Phenomena', pp. 506-7.

[23] Don Cupitt, *The World to Come*, London: SCM Press, 1982, p. 89.

[24] Colin Gunton, 'Knowledge and culture: towards an epistemology of the concrete', in Hugh Montefiore (ed.), *The Gospel and Contemporary Culture*, London: Mowbray, 1992, p. 96.

logic and to have revealed the intellectual and moral decadence of the modernist tradition'.[25]

Let us now turn to the other decisive internal pressure that prompted the turn from liberalism to non-realism. Stephen Ross White asks what it was that prompted Cupitt to take this turn in 1980, and answers: 'It was, I believe, a fusion of his previous ideas about the *via negativa*—now worked out more fully and in a more organised fashion—with a new realisation of the implications of that negative way if followed to its own logical conclusion'.[26] The *via negativa* had always been an important concept for Cupitt, because of its importance for divine transcendence, which he had always striven to preserve. Indeed, it was this concern that gave rise to the 'two Gods' idea referred to earlier – the distinction between the transcendent God and the 'working God' of the religious programme. It was Cupitt's concern to protect divine transcendence that prevented him from equating the latter with the former. If God is indeed utterly transcendent, then he cannot be contained by, or equated with, the images of God found within the various religious traditions or programmes. But the harder the concept of transcendence is pressed, the less knowable, and therefore the less *real* God becomes. And if all the religious 'functions' of God are performed by the 'working God' of practical, everyday religion, then the transcendent God is left high and dry, serving no useful purpose whatsoever, and becoming increasingly superfluous. As Cupitt says: 'A high and orthodox emphasis on the divine transcendence forces me in the end to a non-cognitive or (as people say) "subjectivist" philosophy of religion'.[27]

In his liberal modernist phase, Cupitt had attempted to reconcile the *via negativa*—the ambiguous dance between affirmation and negation—on the one hand with the cognitive nature of religious language on the other. But this gave rise to such internal paradoxes, tensions and inconsistencies that the balance ultimately became untenable, and the non-realist turn inevitable. As he put it (in a mode that is more Spinozist than Kantian):

> [O]ver the years I have tried to combine belief in God with spiritual freedom by pressing the themes of the 'negative theology' and the di-

[25] Ibid. It should be noted, however, that as Cupitt's postmodernism progressed, his 'inward' turn was reversed into an 'outward' turn. See esp. *Solar Ethics*, London: SCM Press, 1995.

[26] Stephen Ross White, *Don Cupitt and the Future of Christian Doctrine*, London: SCM Press, 1994, p. 71.

[27] Don Cupitt, *Taking Leave of God*, London: SCM Press, 1980, p. 51.

> vine transcendence ever harder. Eventually I was saying that God does not determine and cannot be thought of as determining the spiritual life from outside, for God is altogether unspecifiable. God had to become objectively thinner and thinner in order to allow subjective religiousness to expand. It is only one step further to the objectively atheous position here propounded.[28]

The fact that Cupitt views his non-realist turn as 'one step further' again confirms our characterisation of Cupitt's movement from modernism to postmodernism as a linear and progressive one, each movement resulting from an explication of what was implicit in the previous position. White makes a similar point in his comment on the passage just quoted: 'The major development in *Taking Leave of God*, therefore, was not so much a new thought or idea on Cupitt's part, but rather a realisation of the implications of what he had thought for some time'.[29]

If the non-realist turn was partly prompted by the *via negativa* idea, which was so integral a part of Cupitt's liberal modern theological project, however, one is led to question the extent to which this idea is itself grounded in a modernist framework. The concept itself is, of course, an ancient one. But it has been suggested that Cupitt's appropriation of it is distinctively modern. Denys Turner, for instance, says:

> Cupitt's 'negative theology' contains little in common with classical mystical apophaticism. Cupitt derives from his account the impossibility of reconciling an objectively existing God with the divinity of Jesus: and what would one expect from a fundamentally anti-incarnational theology of God than that it would become 'thinner and thinner'?[30]

Turner goes on to contrast Cupitt's 'negative theology' with that of Aquinas, suggesting that the fundamental difference between them is that Aquinas' apophaticism is fully consistent with an incarnational Christianity, whereas Cupitt's is not. And this is because Cupitt's *via negativa* was locked into a distinctively post-Kantian framework. In fact, this was something that Cupitt freely admitted:

[28] Ibid., p. 13.

[29] Stephen Ross White, *Don Cupitt and the Future of Christian Doctrine*, p. 75.

[30] Denys Turner. 'Cupitt, the mystics and the "objectivity" of God', in Colin Crowder (ed.), *God and Reality: Essays on Christian Non-realism*, London: Mowbray, 1997, p. 121.

> The old negative way belonged with and was intelligible in terms of, a certain view of the universe which has now passed away. ... The modern negative theology, after Kant, has to endure objective uncertainty about the existence of God. There are many ways of trying to cope with this but, however one copes with it, it is a new situation.[31]

So Cupitt posits a clear distinction between the classical negative theology of Aquinas and his own 'modern' negative theology after Kant. His main objection to the former apophaticism was its vacuity, as for instance when Aquinas says: 'From divine effects we do not come to understand what the divine nature is in itself, so we do not know of God what he is'.[32] But, following in the tradition of the seventeenth century deist John Toland, Cupitt says: 'The affirmation that God exists has no content unless something can be said about what God is'.[33] Aquinas' apophaticism might have been intelligible in a universe that held to the doctrine of degrees of being, but in our universe, claims Cupitt, such formulas appear utterly vacuous. It is for this reason that Cupitt instead espoused a modern Kantian understanding of the *via negativa*, maintaining that Kant's fundamental innovation in this respect was to insist that it is God's *existence* rather than his *nature* that is unknowable. In other words, the transcendent God must give way to the 'working God' of practical religion, thereby making a move from realism to non-realism, which was Cupitt's first step towards postmodernism. Thus, we can see that Cupitt's postmodernism is an exacerbation of another distinctively modern pressure, and as such, is the apotheosis of liberalism.

To a certain extent, Cupitt concurs with such an analysis. This is clear when he says that '[p]ost-modern religion is *ecstatic liberalism* in that it insists upon letting go. It says: Nothing is sacrosanct, everything is revisable. There's nothing out there or in here, and we should be truly

[31] Don Cupitt, 'Kant and the Negative Theology' in Brian Hebblethwaite and Stewart Sutherland (eds), *The Philosophical Frontiers of Christian Theology*, Cambridge: Cambridge University Press, 1982, p. 60.

[32] Thomas Aquinas, *Summa Theologiae*, 1a, 13, 8. Quoted by Cupitt in 'Kant and the Negative Theology', p. 60.

[33] Don Cupitt, 'Kant and the Negative Theology', p. 58. In *Christianity Not Mysterious* (1696), John Toland asked 'Could that Person justly value himself upon being wiser than his Neighbours, who having infallible assurance that something called *Blictri* had a being Nature, in the mean time knew not what this Blictri was?', p. 133. See Don Cupitt, 'The Doctrine of Analogy in the Age of Locke', in *Journal of Theological Studies* 19 (1968), pp. 186-202.

beliefless.'[34] But for Cupitt, postmodernism is not only the culmination, but also the subversion of liberalism. Hence, he says that when one has made the postmodern turn, 'then Enlightenment *passes* completion and begins to turn back upon itself and devour itself'.[35] Radical Orthodox theologians agree that such nihilistic postmodernism is the culmination of liberalism, but deny that there is any real subversion of the tradition. Graham Ward, for instance, suggests that it 'is not the deconstruction of the liberal tradition (however much they employ the term "deconstruction"), it is the apotheosis of the liberal tradition'.[36] Thus, far from being a subversion of liberalism, Cupitt's postmodernism is viewed as a form of 'cosmic liberalism'.

'Radical Orthodoxy'

Let us therefore turn to this second version of postmodern theology, which has come to be known as 'Radical Orthodoxy'.[37] It claims to be not only more genuinely postmodern, but also more genuinely theological. The leading exponent of this form of postmodern theology is John Milbank. Its antithetical relationship to liberalism is perhaps most clearly evident if we return to the distinction between the negative theology of Kant and of Aquinas. Cupitt, we saw, invoked a form of negative theology that was indebted to a Kantian epistemology. It is precisely such a conflation that John Milbank wants to guard against. Like Cupitt, he says that there are two possible agnosticisms – the metaphysics of Kant on the one hand and of Aquinas on the other. He says that whereas Kant is totally agnostic concerning God-in-himself but dogmatic with regard to his relationship with finite beings, Aquinas is less agnostic concerning God-in-himself but more agnostic with regard to our relationship to God: 'It is only Aquinas's agnosticism which really exemplifies the principle that there is no *ratio* between finite and infinite, and

[34] Don Cupitt, 'After Liberalism', in D. W. Hardy & P. H. Sedgwick (eds), *The Weight of Glory*, Edinburgh: T & T Clark, 1991, p. 255.

[35] Ibid., p. 254. My emphasis.

[36] Graham Ward, 'Postmodern Theology', in David F. Ford (ed.), *The Modern Theologians*, 2nd edition, Oxford: Blackwell, 1997, p. 590.

[37] On this, see the manifesto: John Milbank, Catherine Pickstock and Graham Ward (eds.), *Radical Orthodoxy: A New Theology*, London: Routledge, 1999.

upholds the ontological difference.'[38] For Milbank, this ontological difference disappeared in modernity, though its disappearance may be traced back to Duns Scotus who conceived of a prior notion of 'being' which both God and humanity share in an infinitely differing degree.[39] He says that without the preservation of this ontological difference, the nihilistic and postmodern turn is inevitable: 'Once the notion of a pre-established harmony and a noumenal exceeding of the categories of the mere "understanding" are abandoned, one will realise that such categories simply belong to our linguistic being-in-the-world, and the question, "Can they be extrapolated?" pertains to the question "Is there a 'beyond', a transcendent at all?"'[40] In other words, a conflation of the *via negativa* with Kant's agnosticism inexorably leads one to abandon the transcendent (as indeed Cupitt did), and such abandonment is a distortion and rejection of Christianity. It is for this reason that Milbank maintains that modern Kantian metaphysics must itself be abandoned. In fact, this is the essence of the 'Radical Orthodox' challenge to modern liberalism.

The details of this challenge are perhaps made most explicit in the work of Gerard Loughlin who, in his doctoral dissertation and in a spray of articles, has clearly specified his objections to the modern liberal framework embodied in the work of John Hick. His objections are both philosophical and theological, although, for Loughlin, there can be no dualistic separation between them, for all philosophy takes place within the theological metanarrative and across the matrix of faith. That being said, his primary philosophical objection to Hick's theology is that it is 'speculative'; that is to say, it exercises universal rationality in order to determine 'the way the world is'. For Loughlin, the end of modernity has exposed the futility of this quest, as we have become aware of the particularity and tradition-constituted character of all rationalities. The idea of a universal truth that can be discovered through the exercise of reason has now collapsed. As Loughlin puts it: 'We can see things from our own point of view, try to see them from someone else's point of view; but we cannot see them from an absolute or universally agreed

[38] John Milbank, *The Word Made Strange: Theology, Language, Culture*, Oxford: Blackwell, 1997, p. 9.

[39] This is a common refrain amongst Radical Orthodox theologians. Fergus Kerr, however, has questioned this interpretation of Duns Scotus as a scapegoat for all the ills of modern theology. See his review of Phillip Blond (ed.), *Post-Secular Philosophy*; Catherine Pickstock, *After Writing*; and John Milbank, *The Word Made Strange* in *New Blackfriars* 79 (1998), pp. 352-8.

[40] John Milbank, *The Word Made Strange*, p. 11.

point of view.'[41] It is Hick's claim to a universal vantage point that is characteristic of modernist frameworks. As John V. Apczynski says of Hicks' system: 'Its modern origins include the Enlightenment rejection of all forms of tradition-constituted reason in favour of a universal conception of rationality appealing to methods and principles deemed unexceptionable by any reflective person.'[42] But it is just such a conception of universal reason that Radical Orthodox theologians claim to be untenable.

But this does not mean that we should abandon ourselves to the nihilistic flux, for they maintain that this is merely the culmination of modernity, in the same way that we have seen that Cupitt is the apotheosis of liberalism. It is another instance of the rational self observing 'the way the world is', namely, nihilistic and without truth. So they maintain that after modernity, a true postmodernism entails locating oneself groundlessly within a story, a narrative, a tradition, and that the best such narrative is the Christian narrative. This is also, therefore, a theological objection in that it maintains that Hick's methodology gives rise to a speculative hypothesis rather than a narrative of faith. The result is that Christian theology is subordinated to rational philosophy. Within Hick's framework, philosophy is the discourse that orders and positions all other discourses. It is the guardian of what can and cannot be said. Thus it is that theological statements can only be validated on philosophical grounds. If they cannot be so validated, then they must be rejected. Loughlin wants to reverse this analysis, so that it is theology, as a narrative of faith, which founds and embraces all other narratives. He says that the important point about theology is that 'it is fundamental and foundational. There is nothing more fundamental than it, nothing which founds it. ... It is its own foundation; or, which is the same thing, it is without foundation.'[43]

It is Loughlin's contention that when Christian theology is founded upon something external to it, whether philosophy or reason, it is inevitably distorted. He examines the place of central Christian doctrines within Hick's philosophical system, such as God, Christology and eternal life, to show how they are either discarded completely or reduced to

[41] Gerard Loughlin, 'Noumenon and Phenomena', p. 500.

[42] John V. Apczynski, 'John Hick's Theocentrism: Revolutionary or Implicitly Exclusivist?', in *Modern Theology* 8 (1992), p. 47.

[43] Gerard Loughlin, 'Mirroring God's World: A Critique of John Hick's Speculative Theology', unpublished dissertation: University of Cambridge, 1986, p. 58.

deformed shadows of their former selves. For instance, he points out that the triune God of Christianity is moved form the centre to the periphery and becomes merely a particular mythological representation of the empty 'Real'. A dualism is thus installed between the Christian God and the 'Real' that lies behind it. Furthermore, divine revelation is abandoned in favour of a theoretical postulate – the same noumenal Real.

Let us therefore consider these claims.[44] With regard to Hick's conception of God, we must first establish to which God we are referring. For there are essentially 'two Gods' in Hick's system. First, there is the Real that is the objective underpinning of all the major world religions and secondly, there is the triune God of Christianity, which is merely the Real as interpreted mythically by the Christian community. Now Loughlin claims that this distinction between God and the Real 'beyond' God, is itself a distortion of the Christian conception of God. For the object of Christian worship has never been conceived of as an expression or conception of some other more real and foundational entity. The Christian God himself has been conceived of as the ultimate reality and the foundation of all there is. Furthermore, Hick's respective conceptions of both the Real and the Christian God also severely distort the God of Christianity. The Real is both 'empty' and yet also has an ontological continuity with the world of 'things.' We can say nothing about it, other than through the various conceptualisations of it. At the same time, Loughlin says that the Real

> would appear to be not ontologically but epistemologically transcendent; beyond religious experience in the same way that all noumenal reality is beyond phenomenal experience. But ontologically the Real would appear to be of a piece with the rest of the world, for an ontological continuity between the world and the Real is required by Hick's long held avowal of an epistemological continuity between religious experience and sense experience.[45]

That Hick's Real should be both epistemologically empty and ontologically at one with the world is perhaps to be expected. For we saw in our discussion of the 'early Cupitt' that these two characteristics are

[44] It is not my intention here to discuss Hick's response to Loughlin's criticisms. But for Hick's replies and my subsequent discussion of these replies, see n. 2, above.

[45] Gerard Loughlin, 'Prefacing Pluralism: John Hick and the Mastery of Religion', in *Modern Theology* 7 (1990), p. 39.

closely linked. When God is conceived of as being ontologically continuous with the world, his transcendence can only be preserved by making him epistemologically transcendent to such an extent as to push him beyond the reach of any knowledge. But Loughlin claims that both of these characteristics of Hick's Real are distortions of the God spoken of and worshipped by Christians through the centuries. Thus, he says that Hick's system looks profoundly unsatisfactory as a Christian paradigm since the Christian God is moved from the centre to the periphery, with the centre being occupied by the empty Real. Loughlin asks what grounds Hick has for asserting that the centre is occupied by a noumenal Reality. How does Hick know that this is what underlies the various world religions? The 'raw data' of the world religions could be interpreted in any number of ways; they could all be equally false, they could each refer to a different reality, and so forth. Loughlin insists that the only answer Hick can give to this question is that of 'faith', and that, contrary to the faith of Christianity, which is grounded in revelation, it is difficult to see quite what Hick's act of faith is grounded in, given that its object is unknowable. 'Religious experience' would appear to be Hick's most likely answer, but the validity of this for Hick's act of faith is negated by his recognition that there is no religious experience without interpretation, and no part of the experience that can be isolated from the interpretative element. Thus Loughlin concludes that Hick's system is unacceptable as a Christian paradigm of the world religions: 'It simply is not credible to suppose that Christian theology could advocate abandoning divine revelation in favour of a theoretical postulate – Hick's noumenal Real.'[46] For Loughlin, this is a severe distortion of the Christian doctrine of God. Furthermore, he argues that other central Christian doctrines are similarly deformed by Hick's system. He says that Hick 'has to deny the central truth-claims of the religions and distort their self-descriptions. Consequently it is not so much the religions that appear in his texts as deformed simulacra.'[47]

For Radical Orthodox theologians, such deformations reach their culmination in nihilism. For they claim that modern liberalism must necessarily reach its apotheosis in nihilism, as is illustrated by the intellectual journeys of Don Cupitt and Mark C. Taylor. Modern liberalism, they claim, contains within itself the seeds for its own destruction. Thus, John Milbank claims that there can be no 'liberal enclave', and

[46] Loughlin, 'Mirroring God's World', p. 258.

[47] Loughlin, 'Prefacing Pluralism: John Hick and the Mastery of Religion', p. 48.

presents us with a choice of either nihilism or theology. He says that it is indeed an either/or: 'philosophy (Western or Eastern) as a purely autonomous discipline, or theology: Herod or the magi, Pilate or the God-man'.[48] So whereas Cupitt accepted Hick's philosophical framework and subverted it from within, conservative postmodernism attacks that very framework from without, and does so in the name of theology. Thus, far from being the apotheosis of liberalism, the postmodern challenge of radical orthodoxy stands as the *scourge* of liberalism.

Conclusion

In conclusion, we have seen that there is not one, but two postmodern challenges to liberal theology. Both versions agree that modern liberalism must ultimately culminate in nihilism, but whereas the postmodern a/theology of Don Cupitt embraces that nihilistic descent, the 'Radical Orthodoxy' of John Milbank and Gerard Loughlin attempts a theological out-narration of it and by implication, the liberalism that precedes it. Whereas nihilistic postmodernism initially embraced the philosophical framework of modern liberalism, and subsequently developed and intensified it until it eventually subverted itself, radical orthodoxy, by contrast, confronted, questioned and ultimately rejected that framework at the outset, primarily on theological grounds. If liberal theology is to rise to have a future, therefore, it will have to develop two quite distinct strategies to confront each of these two very different postmodern challenges. One such strategy is already highly developed. As Cupitt says:

> It remains possible (as Kant, Wittgenstein and Derrida all suspect) that Plato's ghost will never be finally exorcised, and people will always be tempted by the illusions of metaphysics. In which case the battle between nonrealists and realists over God will never end.[49]

This 'battle' is one that has been fought vigorously for some time. In contrast, however, liberals have been much more reluctant to engage with the other form of theological postmodernism we have been considering. This is a task they should at least confront because, as Grace

[48] John Milbank, 'Knowledge: The Theological Critique of Philosophy in Hamann and Jacobi', in John Milbank, Catherine Pickstock and Graham Ward (eds), *Radical Orthodoxy*, p. 32.

[49] Don Cupitt, *After God: The Future of Religion*, London: Weidenfeld & Nicolson, 1997, p. 62.

Jantzen has said of the postmodern challenge, 'whether in the end we agree or disagree, I believe that we are greatly impoverished if we refuse to engage at all. Epistemology, especially in the philosophy of religion, is inescapably about "knowing the difference"'.[50] In this chapter, I have endeavoured to contribute to the inauguration of such an engagement. It will be an engagement which 'knows the difference' between two antithetical postmodern challenges.[51]

[50] Grace M. Jantzen, 'What's the Difference? Knowledge and Gender in (Post) Modern Philosophy of Religion', in *Religious Studies* 32 (1996), p. 448.

[51] I am most grateful to Graham Ward, Don Cupitt and Ian Markham for their helpful comments and suggestions on earlier drafts of this chapter.

Chapter 13

A Liberal Helping of Postliberalism Please

Paul D. Murray

Writing in *The Legitimation of Modernity*, Hans Blumenberg helpfully distinguished between modernity defined in terms of the now widely questioned Cartesian search for an 'absolute beginning founded only on itself '—what in Richard Rorty's terms equates to the attempt to ground enquiry upon 'ahistorical criteria of rationality'—and modernity defined in terms of a looser but more enduring attitude or spirit of 'self-assertion'.[1] His point in making this distinction was to claim that whilst the rise of historicist criticism has served to undermine irrevocably modernity as construed in the former sense, it has in the process left modernity as 'self-assertion' well intact. Likewise, the deliberate ambiguity in the title of this essay trades upon the attempt to draw a related distinction between, on the one hand, the now largely discredited identification of theological liberalism as a loosely connected family of formal strategies and methods in modern Christian theology supposedly bound together by the shared assumption that there exists some prior, universally accessible standpoint outside of Christian faith and against which such faith is rightly to be measured and, on the other hand, theological liberalism understood as a less formal though for that matter perhaps more pervasive attitudinal disposition or spirit of rigorously self-critical questioning and searching enquiry in Christian theology.[2]

[1] Hans Blumenberg, *The Legitimacy of the Modern Age*, tr. Robert M. Wallace, Cambridge, Mass.: MIT Press, 1983, esp. pp. 145-6. For Rorty's comment on this, see 'Solidarity or Objectivity', in *Objectivity, Relativism, and Truth: Philosophical Papers*, vol. 1, Cambridge, Cambridge University Press, 1991, pp. 21-34, esp. p. 33.

[2] For a rejection of the first more formal construction of theological liberalism proffered here see John Habgood, 'Reflections on the Liberal Position', in D.

Now leaving aside for the moment any discussion of the significant philosophical and theological problems which theologians of a self-styled postliberal persuasion have claimed to find in the first more formal construction of theological liberalism outlined above, it must be acknowledged from the outset that important questions exist, as Friedrich Wilhelm Graf's fascinating chapter in the present volume bears eloquent witness, as to whether there really are any particular theologians whose work actually fits this construction.[3] Staying with postliberal writings for a moment one might think, for example, of Hans Frei's fascinating retrieval of the mature Schleiermacher as a profoundly ecclesial (in Frei's terms 'type 3')[4] theologian who was concerned—contrary to his standard depiction since Barth—not with the vain attempt *to establish Christian faith on the basis of* a methodologically prior analysis of human religious experience in general or *to demonstrate its correlation with* such an analysis (Frei's types 1 and 2 respectively) but rather with the large-scale but nevertheless—in terms of the primacy of Christian faith and discourse—*a posteriori* attempt to give fresh systematic articulation to the Christian community's own understanding in terms meaningful first and foremost to contemporary Christians and by so doing in terms meaningful also to other contemporaries. The more general

W. Hardy and P. H. Sedgwick (eds), *The Weight of Glory, A Vision and Practice for Christian Faith: The Future of Liberal Theology*, Edinburgh: T & T Clark, 1991, pp. 5-13. In the Epilogue to the same book ('Epilogue: The Strategy of Liberalism', pp. 299-304, here p. 299) Dan Hardy likewise describes the liberal position as having 'no sharp boundaries' and as being 'as broad in its interests as in the means by which it pursues them'. Further, what Habgood has to say is suggestive of the distinction drawn above between liberalism as a formal strategy and liberalism as a spirit of enquiry. With regard to the present volume, I would point to Peter Hodgson's call for a 'revisionary postmodern liberal theology' as seeking to continue in like fashion with a liberal spirit of enquiry in Christian theology whilst rejecting any claim to neutrality, universality or identity with prevailing secular thought forms. This agreement being noted, I would, however, distance myself from Hodgson's apparent acceptance of the 'decentering of Christ' as being part and parcel of the '*late modern*' or '*critical postmodern*' package with which he identifies himself.

[3] For the classic account of Christian theological postliberalism, see George A. Lindbeck, *The Nature of Doctrine: Religion and Theology in a Postliberal Age*, London: SPCK, 1984.

[4] Cf. Hans W. Frei, *Types of Christian Theology* (eds George Hunsinger & William C. Placher), New Haven & London: Yale University Press, 1992, esp. pp. 34-8.

salient lesson to take from Frei's creatively generous reading of Schleiermacher is that the more formal and typically postliberal construction of theological liberalism that is at issue here is itself, if pressed too vigorously, somewhat ironically in danger of appearing as the product of just the kind of ahistorical form of universalising which postliberalism claims to avoid.

That said, the burden of this chapter is to suggest that whilst the combined effects of the now widespread move beyond philosophical foundationalism to more historically, socially and linguistically situated accounts of human rationality[5] and of the theological recovery of a more full-blooded sense for the distinctiveness of the Christian tradition have rightly served to call the value and viability of liberalism as a family of formal theological strategies into serious question in recent years, there is nevertheless something of permanent value in liberalism construed as a theological attitude, disposition or ethic of enquiry. More specifically my argument is that postliberalism in the first or postfoundational sense relinquishes this liberal spirit of enquiry at its own peril and requires, indeed, to appropriate what is of lasting value here far more fully than is sometimes the case with theology which sails under the flag of postliberalism, precisely if it is truly to be as authentically and distinctively Christian in its mode of theologising as it characteristically lays claim to being. It is in this sense that the request expressed in the title of this chapter for a full and generous portion or 'liberal helping' of postliberalism is at once a request for a certain necessary theologically liberal helping of Christian postliberalism to be fully itself.

Alternatively stated, where Jean-François Lyotard suggests that the 'postmodern' is best taken as referring to a continuing moment of critique *within* the modern project rather than to a subsequent historical period which can be clearly demarcated off *from* it,[6] so

[5] Cf. Richard Rorty, *Philosophy and the Mirror of Nature*, Oxford: Blackwell, 1980.

[6] See Jean-François Lyotard, *The Postmodern Condition: A Report on Knowledge*, trs Geoff Bennington and Brian Massumi, Manchester: Manchester University Press, 1984, p. 79. For Lyotard the postmodern moment of critique within modernity is more precisely to be understood in terms of continuing with the modern values of creativity and critique whilst resisting what from a postmodern perspective is deemed to be the unsustainable concern for neutrality and universality within which these same values were typically set. He refers to this in a much cited phrase as an 'incredulity towards metanarratives' (p. xxiv; cf. p. 37).

likewise the dual concern of this chapter is, firstly, to argue for a postliberalism in theology which functions *not* as an unqualified rejection of theological liberalism, but rather as a self-conscious attempt to resituate and so to continue with the basic liberal values of rigorous questioning and self-critique within a more nuanced postfoundational account of human rationality and, secondly, to claim that it is precisely the typically postliberal emphasis upon the distinctive character of the central Christian narratives and of the identifying rules of Christian thought and practice which should itself promote the adoption of the kind of stance advocated here. As such I am in full sympathy with the line taken by Nancey Murphy in her recent work, *Beyond Liberalism and Fundamentalism*.[7] However, where Murphy pursues the route of philosophical analysis to this end by seeking to show that the move beyond foundationalism in contemporary philosophy has made possible a similar move beyond the bifurcation of Christian theology into conservative and liberal camps, I will pursue a more directly dogmatic route to this same goal. That is, where Murphy focuses on the first of the concerns noted above (i.e. to argue for a postliberalism in theology which functions as a self-conscious attempt to resituate basic liberal values within a more nuanced postfoundational account of human rationality), this chapter focuses in the main upon the second more explicitly dogmatic concern.[8] With this in view I turn now to a more detailed consideration of George Lindbeck's hugely influential work, *The Nature of Doctrine: Religion and Theology in a Postliberal Age* which upon its publication in 1984 rapidly established itself as the manifesto of theological postliberalism.[9]

The constructive thrust of Lindbeck's argument flows from a creative combination of, on the one hand, the Wittgensteinian emphasis upon the particularity of language and culture and the determining role

[7] Murphy, *Beyond Liberalism & Fundamentalism: How Modern and Postmodern Philosophy Set the Theological Agenda*, Valley Forge: Trinity Press International, 1996.

[8] For further on the relevant philosophical discussion at this point, see Paul D. Murray, 'Truth and Reason in Science and Theology: Points of Tension, Correlation and Compatibility', in Christopher Southgate, Celia Deane-Drummond, Paul D. Murray, Michael Robert Negus (eds), *God, Humanity and the Cosmos: A Textbook in Science and Religion*, Edinburgh: T & T Clark, 1999, pp. 49-91.

[9] An earlier and less developed form of some of what follows has previously been published in Paul D. Murray, 'Theology After The Demise of Foundationalism', in *The Way*, (April 1998), pp. 160-9. I acknowledge with thanks permission to reproduce the relevant material here.

which they together perform in the context-specific shaping of thought and practice with, on the other hand, a profound retrieval of the Barthian emphasis upon the need for Christian theology to be shaped throughout in accordance with the distinctive self-revelation of God in Christ.[10] The net effect is that Lindbeck, along with his other erstwhile Yale colleagues such as Hans Frei, takes the postfoundationalist emphasis upon locality and contextuality as justifying a welcome return to a situation in which Christian theology can once again be properly shaped by the particular narratives, practices and 'grammatical rules' (i.e. doctrines) of Christian faith after having for too long allowed the terms to be set by an alien and inhospitable discourse – that of modern secular humanism. Or as Hans Frei put it: 'the most fateful issue for Christian self-description is that of regaining its autonomous vocation as a religion, after its defeat in its secondary vocation of providing ideological coherence, foundation, and stability to Western culture'.[11] When expressed in these terms Hans Küng's designation of Karl Barth as the initiator of an appropriately postmodern paradigm in Christian theology begins to fall into place.[12]

In this perspective Christian communities simply do not need to expend their energies in self-defeating attempts to justify their discourse and practice against the supposedly neutral terms of prevailing secular reason, for no such neutrality exists; nor would it be desirable even were it to exist for it would only serve to mask that which is distinctive about the Christian tradition.[13] In short, it is both philosophically legitimate and theologically right for Christian communities to start with their own discourse and practice and to proceed to interpret the world in those terms rather than *vice versa*.[14] More precisely, while Lindbeck does not rule out any attempt to give an

[10] Cf. Lindbeck, *The Nature of Doctrine*, pp. 17-19, 23, 24, 32-41.

[11] Hans Frei, 'The "Literal Reading" of the Biblical Narrative in the Christian Tradition: Does it Stretch or Will it Break?', in Frank McConnell (ed.), *The Bible and the Narrative Tradition*, New York: Oxford University Press, 1986. See also William C. Placher, *Unapologetic Theology: A Christian Voice in a Pluralistic Conversation*, Louisville: Westminster/John Knox Press, 1989. For a helpful overview of Yale postliberalism, see John Thiel, *Nonfoundationalism*, Minneapolis: Fortress Press, 1994, pp. 38-78.

[12] Cf. Hans Küng, 'Karl Barth and the Postmodern Paradigm', in idem., *Theology for the Third Millennium: An Ecumenical View*, tr. Peter Heinegg, London: Harper Collins, 1991, pp. 257-84.

[13] Cf. Lindbeck, *The Nature of Doctrine*, pp. 23, 36, 40, 48, 57, 61.

[14] Ibid., pp. 117, 118.

account of Christian faith in terms deriving from 'other' spheres of discourse and practice, he very clearly relegates such attempts to a secondary level of concern that is to be pursued in a purely *ad hoc*, piecemeal fashion as and when occasion demands.[15] The primary task is to give an account of Christian faith in its own terms. The crucial question however is as to what precisely this means.

Whilst it is undoubtedly helpful to recover a sense of the Christian tradition as having a distinctive contribution to make to the task of interpreting the world—one, moreover, which may on occasion demand that it adopt a stance of implacable opposition to prevailing cultural norms—the somewhat unnuanced language about the primacy of the gospel narratives and the need to 'absorb the world' into the text of Scripture can tend somewhat less helpfully to suggest the image of the tradition as a fixed static entity which requires mere reception and faithful preservation rather than ever fresh articulation. Such a view is problematic, ironic though it may seem, first and foremost on dogmatic grounds as it runs counter to the more dynamic image of the tradition that is implied by its central belief in the risen Christ as a living personal reality who continues to make an impact on the particularities of new situations in ways which whilst always consistent with the scriptural witness to the ways of God in Christ and the Holy Spirit are also always genuinely new. From this perspective the continuity of Christian identity consists less in strict repetition or regulative observance than it does in the dynamic coherence of personal integrity.[16] Alternatively stated, Lindbeck's emphasis upon the need for the faithful observance of underlying grammatical rules, whilst helpful, could be held to do inadequate justice to the creative forwards-looking dimension of Christian

[15] Ibid., pp. 129, 131, 135. See also William Werpehowski, '*Ad Hoc* Apologetics', in *Journal of Religion*, 66 (1986), pp. 282-301.

[16] As the Roman Catholic Modernist, Alfred Loisy put it: 'The particular and varied forms of this development ... follow one another, as it were, in a framework whose general proportions, though not absolutely constant, never cease to be balanced, so that if the figure changes, its type does not vary, nor the law that governs its evolution. The essence of Christianity is constituted by the general features of this figure, the elements of this life and their characteristic properties, and this essence is unchangeable, like that of a living being, which remains the same while it lives, and to the extent to which it lives' ('Author's Introduction' in *The Gospel and the Church* (1902), Buffalo: Prometheus Books, 1988, p. 43. Cited in Sykes, *The Identity of Christianity: Theologians and the Essence of Christianity from Schleiermacher to Barth*, London: SPCK, 1984, p. 139.

living which goes some way beyond merely thinking the same underlying thoughts and doing the same basic things in a variety of changing contexts.[17] On the contrary, as a living within the Spirit's unfolding of God's truth in Christ, Christian living involves a continually fresh discerning of thoughts and actions which are at once congruent with the patterns remembered as having marked Jesus' own life and genuinely fitted to the contingencies of contemporary reality.[18] This combination of continuity and creativity is perhaps better captured with the musical image of dynamic improvisation within accepted forms than it is by Lindbeck's linguistic and grammatical comparisons.[19]

Further, this dogmatic question about the character of Christian tradition is redolent with significant ecclesiological implications. As any conversant with the debate about female ministry will recognise, an unqualified emphasis upon the need to absorb the world into the text of received tradition can all too easily serve to reinforce the status quo and that even in the case of issues hitherto not explicitly dealt with in the tradition. In fairness it must be acknowledged that Lindbeck is both

[17] For a related criticism of Lindbeck's work, see David F. Ford, 'System, Story, Performance: A Proposal about the Role of Narrative in Christian Systematic Theology', in Stanley Hauerwas and L. Gregory Jones (eds), *Why Narrative? Readings in Narrative Theology*, Grand Rapids, Michigan: Eerdmans, 1989, pp. 191-215, esp. p. 213.

[18] This description of Christian living fits with what Karl Rahner identifies (in 'Practical Theology Within the Totality of Theological Disciplines', in *Theological Investigations IX*, tr. Graham Harrison, London: Darton, Longman and Todd 1972, pp. 101-114, here p. 102) as the task of 'practical theology' which he believes to be an essential aspect of all Christian theology: 'Practical theology is that theological discipline which is concerned with the Church's self-actualisation here and now – both that which *is* and that which *ought to be* ... The Church is a historical quantity. Without endangering its abiding essence it is true to say that the Church not simply *is*, but must be continually "happening" anew. This "occurrence" of the Church, however, is not simply its being in essence perpetually present in a space-time always external to it, but the historical form of this essence—unique in each instance—to which the Spirit of the Church calls it through its particular and unique historical situation.'

[19] A fascinating exercise in this regard is Frances Young, *The Art of Performance: Towards a Theology of Holy Scripture*, London: Darton, Longman and Todd, 1990; significant also is the work of Jeremy Begbie. See 'Theology and Music', in *The Modern Theologians: An Introduction to Christian Theology in the Twentieth Century*, ed. by David F. Ford, 2nd edn, Oxford: Blackwell, 1997, pp. 686-99, esp. pp. 686, 693-7; and *Theology, Music and Time*, Cambridge: Cambridge University Press, 2000.

alert to the potentially conservative manner in which a postliberal agenda might be applied[20] and sensitive to the fact that the process of reading the particularities of life in the light of the tradition will itself lead to the tradition being given fresh voice on occasion.[21] At one point he even writes of the need for Christians to be open to the possibility of learning things from non-Christian religions and culture about which 'Christianity as yet knows nothing and by which it could be greatly enriched'.[22] Nevertheless, this remains, at the explicit level at least, very much a minor theme in *The Nature of Doctrine*. Pulling somewhat in the other direction, the dominant emphasis is, in contrast, upon the danger of allowing the tradition to be accommodated to the terms of prevailing culture[23] and it is this more cautious note which too frequently characterises the work of those who take the label 'postliberal' to themselves. Whilst valid in its own right, such caution can serve, particularly when pressed in unqualified form, to paralyse and so distort the living body of Christ[24] and, likewise, to promote a forgetfulness of the way in which ecclesial existence is itself always in danger of degenerating to the level of a lived lie in such a fashion as requires constant critical exposure to the various questions and concerns posed to it by contemporary culture.[25] At its most extreme it can justify an arrogance which presumes that the Christian tradition really has nothing to learn.

Related to this, the very notion that it is possible to draw a clear demarcation between ecclesial existence and Christian tradition on the one hand and prevailing culture on the other is again open to question. As a glance around the congregation in any large urban parish church reveals, questions as to whether the Church should be open to the world, and if so how, are made somewhat irrelevant by the realisation that the world in all its diversity is already present within the Church. Consequently, and as the likes of Karl Rahner and the mature

[20] See The Nature of Doctrine, p. 126.

[21] See ibid., e.g. pp. 33, 81, 84.

[22] Ibid., p. 61.

[23] See ibid., p. 133.

[24] On this, see Karl Rahner, 'Thoughts on the Possibility of Belief Today', in *Theological Investigations, V*, tr. Karl-H. Kruger, London: Darton, Longman and Todd, 1966, pp. 3-22, esp. p. 16.

[25] On this, see Karl Rahner, 'The Church of Sinners', in *Theological Investigations, VI*, tr. Karl-H. and Boniface Kruger, London: Darton, Longman and Todd, 1969, pp. 253-69. Cf. Ford, 'System, Story, Performance', pp. 213-4, esp. pp. 259, 260-61, 262-3.

Schleiermacher before him realised, the task of rearticulating the tradition in contemporary terms represents what is already an authentic, even 'internal' Christian concern rather than an illegitimate excursion into alien terrain. Again, the diversity of the New Testament writings itself attests to the fact that the Christian story does not exist in some pure, unalloyed form but rather that it subsists in the myriad different yet recognisably Christian tellings and performances which it supports. Indeed, in line with the fleshy materiality of orthodox Christian faith in the incarnation of the Word of God in the particular human being Jesus of Nazareth, there simply never has been an account of the tradition which was not shaped in part at least by the broader social, cultural and linguistic contexts in which it was enacted.

In summary then, whilst approving wholeheartedly of the postliberal emphasis upon the need to preserve that which is distinctive about the Christian voice, an adequate—by which I mean authentically Christian—account of theology in postliberal perspective will, I suggest, be one that marries this emphasis with a far more explicit appreciation both for the internally diverse and even contested nature of Christian tradition and for the way in which Christian identity is maintained precisely through a process of continual challenge, refreshment and renewal.[26] More precisely, I would claim that it is intrinsic to the particular commitments and cherished traditions assumed in an authentically Christian practice of theology that it be constantly exposed in an expansive, recursive and intensive fashion to the refreshing scrutiny of new questions, new problems and new situations. As has been noted, my further belief is that the preservation of what I have referred to as a liberal disposition or liberal spirit of enquiry in Christian theology has an essential continuing role to play in this regard.

In line with this I have suggested that the need to preserve such a spirit of enquiry is itself implied both by a sufficiently radical reading of the central Christian belief in the risen reality of Christ and, along with this, of the notion of Christian life as an ever fresh living within the Spirit. Such points can be pressed further. For example, it could be argued that the belief to which Barth himself gave such eloquent and lengthy rearticulation in volume 3 of the *Church Dogmatics* to the effect that the entire created order is brought into being through and so re-

[26] Of central importance here is Stephen Sykes account (in *The Identity of Christianity*) which views the church as 'a body with unavoidable and restless internal conflicts' (p. 8; cf. p. 11).

lates to the uttered Word of God in Christ does itself suggest the need for orthodox postliberal Christian theology to embrace a process of constant self-critical exposure to the challenge and refreshment of other traditions of thought and practice. The point here is that if the notion of the deepest significance of all things ultimately being Christological in orientation is thought through along the lines advocated by Aquinas with all of created reality in its myriad diversity and particularity being held to reflect something of the rationality and being of God,[27] then it comes to appear possible, perhaps even likely, that there are things to be learned about the reality of God in Christ which can only be learned by allowing the insights of other aspects of human understanding to refresh and to renew the perspective of Christian faith.[28] Reinforcing this, the belief that the entirety of created reality continues to be energised in its diverse particularity by the Transforming Power or Spirit of God again suggests the validity from an orthodox Christian perspective of viewing the full extent of such reality as being a genuine locus of the sustaining, revealing and transforming action of God in Christ and the Spirit.

Such a stance clearly entails within it a greater degree of preparedness to accept and to test for the presently limited and inadequate character of all Christian theology than some might feel comfortable in embracing. Again, however, it can be claimed that such an attitude belongs properly within an authentically Christian practice of theology. As both the *via negativa* and the *via analogia*—the latter when correctly understood at least—have each long maintained, it is the

[27] Cf. Aquinas, *Summa Theologiæ*, vol. 8: *Creation, Variety and Evil* (Ia.44-49), tr. T. Gilby OP, London: Eyre and Spottiswoode, 1967, p. 95; see also Janet Martin Soskice, 'Bad Language in Science and Religion', in *Explorations in Science & Theology*, London: RSA, 1993, pp. 69-78, esp. p. 71.

[28] On this see F. J. A. Hort, *The Way The Truth The Life*, 2nd edn, London: Macmillan, 1894, p. 85: '"I am the Truth"...marks every truth which seems alien to Christ as a sign that the time is come for better knowledge of Christ, since no truth can be alien to him who is the Truth' (cited in Habgood, 'Reflections on the Liberal Position', pp. 11-12); see also Stephen Sykes, '"Orthodoxy" and "Liberalism"' in David F. Ford and Dennis L. Stamps (eds), *Essentials of Christian Community: Essays for Daniel W. Hardy*, Edinburgh: T & T Clark, 1996, pp. 76-90, esp. pp. 76-7: 'To be orthodox is not a matter of lazily repeating the decisions and arguments of the past to meet each new critical proposal. The transformational dynamic of orthodoxy is only in evidence where theologians fully accept the contemporary task of uncovering presuppositions, analysing arguments and engaging in vigorous dialogue.'

very reality of the object that is at issue in faith (i.e. the inexhaustibly rich mystery that is God) which itself places a permanent question mark against the adequacy of any attempt to give it expression.[29] Whilst a realisation to this effect features as a traditional tenet of Christian theology, it must nevertheless be acknowledged that at the level of theological practice it can all too frequently become submerged by a somewhat less humble tone rather more at home with rigid certainties than it is with open questions. At its best, what I have sought to identify as the continuing value in a liberal disposition in theology should help to restore to the practice of postliberal Christian theology something of the ethic of continual conversion and renewal by which it, along with the rest of Christian living, should be distinguished.[30] Whilst all of this reintroduces a greater element of risk and vulnerability to Christian theology than some of a postliberal persuasion might feel comfortable with, I would suggest that sustaining this spirit of kenotic theological enquiry throughout should be the memory that the central Christian narratives identify the very ratio and creative truth of God with the embrace of just such vulnerability.[31]

[29] For a reading of the Thomistic *analogia entis* which brings it much more closely in line with what Barth was up to in advocating an *analogia fidei* than Barth himself would ever have imagined possible, see Nicholas Lash, 'Ideology, Metaphor and Analogy', in *Theology on the Way to Emmaus*, London: SCM. Press, 1986, pp. 95-119. Lying behind Lash's argument is the hugely influential analysis by David B. Burrell, *Aquinas: God and Action*, London: Routledge, 1979. More recently, see Eugene F. Rogers Jr., *Thomas Aquinas and Karl Barth: Sacred Doctrine and the Natural Knowledge of God*, Notre Dame: University of Notre Dame Press, 1995.

[30] On this, see Rahner, 'Opposition in the Church', in *Theological Investigations, XVII*, tr. Margaret Kohl, London: Darton, Longman and Todd, 1981, pp. 127-38, here p. 129: 'The first thing that must be said about our subject is that, fundamentally speaking, there can and must be opposition and criticism in the Church, as one of its inner elements.'

[31] Were I to be asked to identify a single philosopher-theologian whose work exemplifies just the kind of self-consciously situated, yet rigorously critical and dynamically expansive approach to the task of Christian theology that I have been advocating in this essay I would point to Donald MacKinnon. On this, see Paul D. Murray, 'Theology in the Borderlands: Donald MacKinnon and Contemporary Theology', in *Modern Theology* 14 (1998), pp. 355-76.

Conclusion

An Outsider's View

Chapter 14

The Problems of a Liberal Religion

A Sociologist's View

Steve Bruce

Introduction

Although they can contribute much to each other, sociology is not theology, and for that, both are probably grateful. I take my role in this collection to be the illumination of the empirical reality, the realm of the social scientist, on either side of liberal theology: the social circumstances that saw it become popular and its social consequences. I will first introduce a typology of types of religion, then deploy it to describe briefly the impact of modernisation on religion, and, in the final section, make some guess about the future.[1]

Naming of parts

I want to begin by using the well-known organisation typology of church, sect, denomination and cult to describe a process of social evolution. Roy Wallis clarified the distinctions between the four most commonly used terms for religious organisations—church and sect, cult and denomination—to offer a simple but useful analytical device. He believed that most of the important differences in how people organise their religious lives can be identified if we look at just two issues: (a) does the religion claim a unique grasp of salvational knowledge? and (b) is the religion seen by others as respectable or deviant?

[1] The argument presented here is elaborated in greater detail in Steve Bruce, *Religion in the Modern World: from Cathedrals to Cults*, Oxford: Oxford University Press, 1996.

		External Conception	
		Respectable	*Deviant*
Internal	*Uniquely Legitimate*	CHURCH	SECT
Conception	*Pluralistically Legitimate*	DENOMIN-ATION	CULT

Figure 1: The Wallis Typology of Ideological Organisations[2]

On the top half of the table we have two forms that share the feature of being *epistemologically authoritarian*. The church and the sect believe that they and they alone have access to the source of truth. They and they alone are right. For most of its history and in most places, the Roman Catholic Church has claimed that only it has the ear of God. Members of the Exclusive or 'Closed' Brethren make the same claim. But there is considerable difference in the popularity, acceptability and prestige of the Catholic Church and the Exclusive Brethren.

The two forms in the bottom half of the figure are *epistemologically individualistic*. The social scientist has to leave aside the claim made by all religions that the final source of revelation is God and consider how in practice the purportedly final source is accessed. What the denomination and cult have in common is that they take the individual to be the locus for the determination of truth. Closely associated with that belief is what Wallis called 'revelational indeterminacy'.[3] Both forms accept that the truth may be revealed in diverse ways and through diverse agents. No individual or collectivity possesses a monopoly of truth. The modern Methodists think that you might be better off being a Methodist than a Baptist, but they recognise the Baptists and many other organisations as being every bit as valid as themselves. Similarly, the vast majority of purveyors of cultic wisdom and esoteric practice do not expect the monogamous commitment of their followers. Indeed the relationship between purveyor and consumer is so loose that terms such as member, adherent and follower are usually inappropriate in the cultic milieu. Each product is seen by most who consume it as one of many guides on the single but very broad road to enlightenment.

[2] Roy Wallis, *The Road to Total Freedom*, London: Heinemann, 1976, p. 13.

[3] Roy Wallis, *Salvation and Protest: Studies of Social and Religious Movements*, London: Frances Pinter, 1979, p. 45.

Again what separates them is the top line: the extent to which they have succeeded in establishing themselves in their society. The Methodists are a respectable part of our social and cultural landscape; cults are not. Or not yet!

Modernisation

The point of introducing these distinctions is to offer a simple way of describing the major changes in the religious climate of the Western world. We can observe the possibility and popularity of the four forms of religion in different sorts of society.

The key to the shift between these four forms is modernisation. I want to be clear that by modernisation, I mean the *historically and geographically specific* package of social, political and economic changes that came with urbanisation and industrialisation in Western Europe, and the forms of consciousness associated with those changes. I am not making any universal claims or offering observations about societies that have more recently been affected by some of those changes. The extent to which the patterns described in the secularisation thesis will be repeated elsewhere depends on the extent to which new circumstances match the old. This is an important qualification. Those of us who advance the secularisation thesis are often accused of two related vices: promoting the 'Enlightenment project' and supposing that secularisation is inevitable. It is true that sociology has its origins in the Enlightenment and that August Comte saw the promotion of sociology and the decline of religion as intimately linked. However, the version of the secularisation thesis that I expound here, which draws on the work of Max Weber, Emile Durkheim, Talcott Parsons, Peter Berger, David Martin and Bryan Wilson, owes nothing to Comte and everything to the idea of *unintended consequences.* Far from supposing that the world is now as it is because people wished it so to be, I am a Burnsian. With the great Scottish poet Robert Burns, I suppose that 'the plans of mice and men gang aft aglay'. If most social changes are unintended (or ironic) they can hardly be part of any 'project'. Nor can they be universally applicable. Far from supposing that secularisation is inevitable, I concur entirely with Ernest Gellner's basic point that the history of Western

Europe owes much to a number of highly unlikely combinations of circumstances.[4]

Nor do I suppose that the decline of religion is even. Even in the development of any one society there are too many contingencies for major social changes to occur in an orderly and linear fashion. Although I will not dwell on them, I have elsewhere identified a number of countersecularising trends, which I have summarised under the general proposition that 'religion declines except where it finds important social roles other than mediating the natural and supernatural worlds'. These roles can be grouped under the headings of 'cultural transition' and 'cultural defence'. The former covers various ways in which shared religion can provide resources to aid populations in social transition such as that caused by migration or rapid industrialisation. It is frequently observed that migrant communities initially become more orthodox and more observant than they were in their native settings. As an example of the appeal of evangelical Protestantism to the emerging industrial working class we could consider the rise of Methodism in early nineteenth century Britain or the spread of Pentecostalism in Latin America in the late twentieth century.[5] By role in cultural defence, I have in mind the enhanced salience religion gains when it becomes strongly linked to ethnic or national identity in a context of conflict or competition (of which, more below). In addition to those complications, we must also recognise that religious organisations have their own histories that are not entirely described by treating them as carriers of wider social change. Or to put it less formally, people make a difference. It may well be that the Exclusive Brethren in the fishing villages of the north-east of Scotland would have declined anyway. Changes in the fishing economy and the increased contact between the villages and the wider society were already weakening those communities. But the demise was hastened by a split in the movement caused by the scandal of the leader, Big Jim Taylor, being accused of sexual exploitation of female followers.[6]

With those qualifications, I will begin my account. Modernisation makes the church form of religion impossible. The church requires

[4] Ernest Gellner, *Plough, Sword and Book: the Structure of Human History*, London: Paladin, 1991.

[5] For an account of the appeal of Pentecostalism that draws explicit parallels with Methodism, see David Martin, *Tongues of Fire: the Explosion of Protestantism in Latin America*, Oxford: Basil Blackwell, 1990.

[6] Norman Adams, *Goodbye, Beloved Brethren*, Aberdeen: Impulse Books, 1972.

either cultural homogeneity or an elite sufficiently powerful and ruthless to enforce conformity. Modernisation undermines homogeneity and constrains the ability of élites to impose cultural conformity.

Diversity may come in three ways. First, a society may expand to encompass ever larger numbers of religious, ethnic and linguistic groups. Secondly, inward migration may bring foreign peoples into a society. Thirdly, a society may fragment. It is this third source I wish to concentrate on here. As Durkheim notes in his distinction between mechanical and organic solidarity, the increased division of labour and the growth of economies creates ever greater social diversity and social distance.[7] The feudal estate and closed village become the modern town and the city. In the medieval town, people of very different 'stations' and 'estates' inhabited different floors of the same tenement, threw their excrement into the same street, and lived lives that were similar. The modern town brought distinct class patterns to housing. Here the working class huddled together, here the merchants, and here the very poor. Industrialisation increased social distance. Increasingly different social circumstances created increasingly different cultures and that expressed itself in religious diversity as different social groups reworked the dominant religious tradition in ways that made sense from their position in the world.

As an aside, let me add here that whether or not a country became Protestant or Catholic at the Reformation is vital. In the Protestant countries, social fragmentation found religious expression. In the monolithic religious culture of Catholicism, emerging classes were less able to develop their own religious variant and instead became outright anticlerical. Thus in France, Italy and Spain, modernisation produced communism. In Britain, Scandinavia and America, it produces a variety of revivalist movements.[8] I shall not dwell on these variations but will concentrate on the Protestant model.

In addition to social differentiation, modernisation brought *structural* differentiation. Social institutions became increasingly specialised and the church lost many of its functions to secular alternatives. In most industrialising economies, religious institutions lost public administration, education, social welfare and social control functions to agencies with those specific remits. Where a church did retain some activity

[7] Emile Durkheim, *The Division of Labor in Society*, New York: Free Press, 1964.

[8] David Martin, *A General Theory of Secularization*, Oxford: Basil Blackwell, 1978.

in these areas, it was increasingly viewed in the light of secular rather than religious principles.

If social and structural differentiation can be seen as a threat to communities from within, modernisation was usually accompanied by a further threat to communities from above: what Bryan Wilson has called 'societalisation'.[9] With the expansion of the economy, close-knit, integrated communities gradually lost power and presence to large-scale industrial and commercial enterprises, to modern states co-ordinated through massive impersonal bureaucracies, and to large towns and cities.

At the same time as organic communities fragmented, modernisation produced a basic *egalitarianism*. Economic development brought change and the expectation of further change. And it brought occupational mobility. People no longer did the job they always did because their family always did that job. Occupational mobility made it hard for people to internalise visions of themselves that supposed permanent inferiority. One cannot have people improving themselves and their class position while thinking of themselves as fixed in a station or a degree or a caste in an unchanging hierarchical world.

The separation of work and home, of the public and the private, further makes for equality. Serf and peasant were not job descriptions: they were enveloping social, legal and political statuses. One cannot be a serf during working hours and an autonomous individual for the evening and at weekends. A temporary work-role is not a full identity and though work-roles may be ranked in a hierarchy, they can no longer structure the whole worldview.

There is a point here about the relationship between ideas and social circumstances that I want to clarify. The Reformation had, of course, laid great stress on the notion of the individual but it had done so in a one-sided way. Individuals had *responsibilities* to God. But it was three hundred years before individual responsibilities became individual rights and it was the fragmentation of the social world that made that possible. The feudal lord could not recognise that his serf and his lieutenant were similar beings without threatening the entire feudal order. But once a single all-embracing hierarchy was replaced by a variety of task-specific hierarchies, it became possible to be a low status factory labourer during working hours and a relatively high status Methodist preacher in the evenings and at weekends. Then one has a

[9] Bryan Wilson, *Religion in Sociological Perspective*, Oxford: Oxford University Press, 1982, pp. 45-6.

situation in which the factory owner can dominate his workers as workers but recognise their common humanity when he sits with them in church.

Put it this way: once we start to see people as occupying not just one but a variety of social roles then it becomes possible to distinguish between the roles and the essential underlying person. We can continue to rank roles while accepting that all individuals are much-of-a-muchness. Though they no doubt encourage it, specific inequalities no longer require blanket attributions of unchangeable difference. The notion of fundamental rights becomes possible; gradually rights were extended from rich men to all men and then to rich women and to all women and now to children, and, in some countries to animals also.

Egalitarianism is an important part of the equation because it explains why western societies gave up the usual reaction to diversity: repression. The egalitarian impulse of modernisation meant that, at the political level, the costs of coercing religious conformity were no longer acceptable: the state was no longer willing to pay the price of social conflict. Instead it became neutral on the competing claims of various religious bodies. In some settings, the neutrality was explicit (as in the Constitution of the United States); in others, it was implicit (as in the fudge which left the established Churches of England and Scotland with notional advantages over their competitors but removed their real privileges).

So we see one route to toleration: it takes a long time but the church, stripped of its social functions and deprived of the support of the state, gradually re-defines itself as the denomination.

There is a second route. Initially the schisms from the dominant tradition were radical sects that sought to replace the corrupt establishment with a religion the purity of which would fully justify a harsh regime of imposition. But as it became obvious that they had not won, and thus were condemned to minority status, most of those radical sects were able to make a virtue of necessity by discovering the appeal of voluntarism. They moderated and gradually became denominations.[10]

Thus far in a massively simplified view of the history of religion in the West, we have seen the church form faced first with competition from the sect and then both churches and sects converging on the denomination. Where does the cult come into this account? First with the new religious movements of the 1960s and 1970s and then with the

[10] This process is described in detail in Steve Bruce, *A House Divided: Protestantism, Schism and Secularization*, London: Routledge, 1990, pp. 48-71.

'New Age' spirituality of the 1980s, we have seen a flowering of alternative religions. Some, such as Transcendental Meditation and Rajneeshism, are westernised versions of traditional eastern religions. Others, such as Scientology, Exegesis, est and Insight are spiritualised versions of lay psychotherapies. In terms of adherents, new religious movements and New Age spirituality are insignificant. However, the cultic form of religion is, I would argue, a symptom of modernity. Like the denomination, it is liberal and tolerant and relativistic. It is further emblematic in that it represents consumer-driven innovation. This point is often missed because our attention is naturally caught by the most threatening and exotic but what distinguishes most of the late twentieth century's innovations from those of previous eras is that they are self-consciously eclectic, undemanding and relativistic. Even those (such as Scientology) which are at heart sects have had to accept the consumerist orientation of their potential market.

Secularisation

I take it to be unarguably the case that the power, presence and popularity of organised religion have declined in modern industrial societies. Except, as in places like Northern Ireland, where religion remains a part of an identity that is involved in bitter ethnic and national rivalries, religious organisations have lost members and influence. Britain is fairly typical. From the Middle Ages until the end of the nineteenth century, more than half the adult population regularly attended church. Now it is less than ten per cent. New religious movements, which at best can measure their members in hundreds, come nowhere close to compensating for the losses to the main Christian churches. Those losses are in the millions.

One response is to argue that we exaggerate the piety of the past. There is certainly plenty of evidence that the people of the Middle Ages were not the well-educated, self-consciously committed believers of a twentieth-century evangelical sect. However, there can be no doubt that they inhabited a religious worldview and that their lives were permeated by a strong sense of the supernatural. How else do we explain the institution of swearing oaths on the Bible, the fact that midwives were taught a simple formula for baptising babies thought too sickly to survive until a priest could be called, or the vast sums that were spent buying religious offices? [11]

The other way of attacking the secularisation account is to argue that modern people are 'really' more religious than they appear. For some time, professional optimists have responded to data on church decline by claiming that they represent only a loss of faith in churches and not a loss of faith altogether. Opinion polls that showed that those who said they believed in God vastly outnumbered those who went to church are presented as evidence of enduring spirituality.[12] However, we now know that those numbers too show the same decline as church membership and attendance data.[13] In every modern industrial society, the last hundred years shows a decline in every index of religious belief or practice. This needs to be explained.

I do not take the view that religion has declined because modern people have become too sophisticated or mature to believe in the old superstitions. We need only remember the Third Reich to disabuse ourselves of the idea that cultural change is explained by good ideas naturally defeating bad ideas. Nor do I take the view that science has displaced religion. The fossil record may prove Genesis wrong but most of my neighbours do not know that and it certainly does not explain why they are irreligious. A better claim can be made for the influence of technology. David Martin put it neatly when he talked of our *increasingly effective mastery* over the world reducing the demand and occasions for religion.[14] When there was no better cures for worm in sheep, it made sense to sprinkle holy water on the flock.

[11] The point, of course, is that when Keith Thomas, who is almost invariably the authority cited by those who wish to revise our impression of the past, argues that the people of the Middle Ages were not terribly religious, he is using an extremely narrow sense of 'religion'. As the title of his book makes clear they had a very strong attachment to magic and a firm belief in the supernatural. For this debate see Keith Thomas, *Religion and the Decline of Magic*, Harmondsworth, Middlesex: Penguin, 1973; and Steve Bruce, 'The Pervasive Worldview: Religion in Pre-Modern Britain', in *British Journal of Sociology* 48 (1997), pp. 667-80.

[12] Grace Davie, *Religion in Britain Since 1945: Believing Without Belonging*, Oxford: Blackwell, 1994.

[13] Robin Gill, C. Kirk Hadaway, and Penny Long Marler, 'Is Religious Belief Declining in Britain?', in *Journal for the Scientific Study of Religion* 37 (1998), pp. 507-16.

[14] David Martin, *The Religious and the Secular*, Oxford: Basil Blackwell, 1969, p. 116.

Also vital has been the increased rationalisation of the world. I should warn here against a common misunderstanding. Those of us who follow Weber's work on rationality do not imply any moral claims. We simply mean that life has become increasingly structured along what we might call bureaucratic principles. Modern technology assumes a world that is orderly and predictable. All complex objects can be reduced to separate components that are infinitely replaceable. The radiator for a 1994 Saab will fit any 1994 Saab. All complex processes can be reduced to discrete actions which can be infinitely repeated with identical consequences. We need not be conscious of it, but such a style of production, which through bureaucracy has spilled over into the management of people, makes it very difficult to entertain any notion of the sacred. There is only the mundane and the routine.[15]

But the most important part of any explanation of secularisation is that which concentrates on the role of social relationships in maintaining the plausibility of religious beliefs. I start from the anthropological point that people can believe anything, provided they have sufficient social support. Hence I concentrate on the effect of diversity. My argument is that cultural diversity *in an essentially egalitarian and democratic context* (and this qualifying phrase should be assumed for every subsequent mention of diversity) weakens the structural and interactional supports for shared beliefs.

First, as already noted, diversity removes state and élite support for beliefs by, for example, downgrading the place of religion in schools and colleges and the operations of government. The creation of secular education systems and health care provision removes many opportunities for religious beliefs to be legitimated and promoted. The solution adopted by some Lutheran states is perhaps more damaging. By changing support for one religion to equal support for a number of competing religions, the state is very obviously signalling that we cannot know which religion is true.

Secondly, and this is the Durkheimian point, the end of cultural consensus means the end of all sorts of low-key affirmations of beliefs. In sixteenth-century England, every significant event in the life cycle of the individual and the community was celebrated in church and given a religious gloss. Because they were managed by the church, birth, marriage and death, and the passage of the agricultural seasons, all reaffirmed the essentially Christian worldview of the people. The church's

[15] Peter L. Berger, Brigitte Berger, and Hansfried Kellner, *The Homeless Mind*, Harmondsworth: Penguin, 1974.

techniques were used to heal the sick, clean the soil, and fatten cattle. Every significant act of testimony, every contract, and every promise was reinforced by oaths sworn on the Bible and before God. But beyond these special events, a huge amount of credibility was given to the religious worldview simply by it being casually expressed in everyday social interaction. People commented on the weather by saying 'God be praised' and on parting, they wished each other 'God Speed' and 'God be with you'.

Once a religious worldview ceases to be part of what phenomenologists call the *taken-for-granted life-world*, it is significantly weakened. I am not suggesting that the appearance of alternatives immediately stops people believing. My point is that which Peter Berger expressed very well when he said that it is still possible to believe but it is clear to us that we have chosen God rather than the other way round.[16] The element of choice is hard to disguise and that carries the implicit recognition that it is me, the sovereign individual, who is deciding.

Diversity also removes one of the great reinforcers of religion: the close tie between religion and ethnic identity. In Poland and Lithuania, Catholicism was strengthened by the part it played in national identity and political struggles for independence. In Latvia and Estonia where there was greater religious diversity, nationalism was weaker and religious affiliation was not greatly enhanced by the nationalist struggles. We can see the same point in comparing the four Lutheran Nordic countries. The 1993 figures for those who say they never go to church are 40% for Norway, 44% for Denmark and 49% for Sweden. For Finland, it is only 15%. Now part of that difference may be explained by later and slower economic growth. Although the four countries are now similar in industrialisation, urbanisation and prosperity, until the 1970s Finland lagged well behind the other three. But the bigger difference is that Finland has a much shorter and less secure history of political independence and national integrity. Only since the collapse of communism have Finns been safe from Russian imperialism and a large part of what Finns may reasonably view as their country remains in Russian hands. In those circumstances it is not surprising that Finns should be more committed than their Nordic neighbours to the Lutheranism which distinguishes them from their Slav neighbours.[17] Acting as guarantor of

[16] Peter L. Berger, *The Heretical Imperative*, London: Collins, 1980.

[17] These data and an extended discussion of the role of religion in ethnic identity can be found in Steve Bruce, *Choice and Religion: a Critique of Rational Choice Theory*, Oxford: Oxford University Press, 1999.

ethnic integrity gives religion an additional purpose and appeal. It cannot do this when the ethnic group or nation is not religiously homogenous.

Of course, not every realisation that there are alternatives makes us question our beliefs. There are all sorts of 'restorative strategies' that people can use to handle the challenge of alternatives. An obvious one is to question the character of those who carry the alternative. When Irish Catholics settled in Scotland in large numbers at the end of the nineteenth century, the native Presbyterians did not give up their religion. Instead they labelled the Irish as alcoholic illiterate beggars who were of no account. This is why the diversity that results from internal fragmentation is a greater threat than that which results from migration or state expansion. When it is your own people who start to disagree with you, it is less easy to deflect the cognitive challenge.

To summarise, everywhere we look in the western world (and that includes the USA) we see the declining influence and popularity of organised religion. We also see significant changes in the nature and position of religion: religion has become increasing compartmentalised. It has become increasingly privatised. It has become increasingly optional. It plays little or no part in the operation of the social system and even for believers it makes little difference. Even within the main religious organisations one finds low levels of commitment and ideological relativism.

What has any of this got to do with liberal theology? The answer is that it is both symptom and cause of two key causes of secularisation: individual autonomy and cultural diversity. I suspect that some Protestant theologians would disavow the responsibility, but it seems clear to me that the Reformation played a major part in the rise of the individual. I am not concerned here with individualism as an articulate phil-osophical position or as a political agenda. I am interested in an inadvertent link between the Reformation, the general sense that the self is autonomous, and a general egalitarianism. Of course, the reformed self was more defined by obligations than by rights. It took more than 200 years for societies to develop such a degree of differentiation that the egalitarian principle could be recognised outside the limited sphere of the spiritual. But the seeds were accidentally sown by the Reformers.

The most obvious structural characteristic of the Reformation was the fragmentation of Christendom. David Martin put it neatly when he wrote that Protestantism was in favour of the voluntary principle to a degree which made it sociologically impossible.[18] Allowing that each of us could discern God's will ensured fission and schism. That gave us the cultural diversity that encouraged the state to become religiously neutral and mutated the church and sect certainties into the relativism of the denomination and the cult.

Of course this is to simplify things, but there were two polar extremes available to the churches. They could have fought tooth and nail against change (embracing it only grudgingly and slowly and all the while denying that they were changing). This is what the Catholic Church and the Protestant sects did. Or they could become enthusiastic proponents of the new spirit, the new liberty and the new age: the response of most Protestant denominations.

Liberal theology was both an endorsement and an encouragement of social change. Liberal theologians might dress it up in fancy formulations but essentially they accepted a free-for-all which helped hasten the decline of religion. Very specific liberal projects, such as the re-writing of the faith to make it accord with the presuppositions of 'modern man', were a dismal failure. Of course correlation is not cause but I will shortly offer good reasons for supposing that the coincidence of the rise of liberal theology and the plunge of church membership is actually more than simply coincidence.

The future of church and sect

For reasons given above, the *church* form of religion will survive only where circumstances, usually some external threat to national integrity, put an unusually high premium on communal solidarity. Thus it lives on in parts of eastern Europe but we must expect that, if Croatia or Bosnia, for example, construct stable democracies and if their economies prosper, then the social fragmentation that makes the church impossible will continue apace. Consider Poland. Once the Roman Catholic Church was relieved of its role as guardian of the nation and came to be viewed as simply one interest group among others, its popularity began to decline markedly.

It is not much of an exaggeration to say that *sects*, in the last fifty years, have recruited primarily through biological reproduction. Hence the key to their survival lies in their ability to control their environment

[18] David Martin, *The Dilemmas of Contemporary Religion*, Oxford: Basil Blackwell, 1978, p. 9.

for social reproduction. In most countries this has been made more difficult by increased state interference. Although the modern state permits considerable freedom in the private sphere, it also shifts the dividing line between the public and the private so that increasingly public policy is imposed on what were once taken to be private matters. For example in the United States, the cosmopolitan centre has become increasingly unwilling to allow the southern states to go their own way and to continue with distinctive patterns of behaviour with regard to race relations, gender roles, and church-state relations.

Nonetheless, in the United States sectarians still have considerable freedom to construct a sub-society in which they enjoy a hegemony comparable to that of the Christian Church in the Middle Ages. To support their churches, they have autonomous educational institutions, mass media producers, social work agencies, and leisure outlets, all bound together in an all-encompassing evangelical world. This does not prevent them being seduced by the blandishments of modern affluence. Even communitarian sects such as the Amish, which have resisted the outside world for three centuries, now lose their young people to the prosperity and freedom of the secular world. Nonetheless, for all that it may be increasingly difficult for self-selecting groups of people to cut themselves off from the wider society and hence from the wider culture, sectarians can keep enough of their children to decline at a slower rate than the religious mainstream.

The future of denomination and cult

I would like to stress that I am not talking here about liberal theology as it is produced by theologians but liberal religion as it appears in the lives of members of denominations.

Denominations are in free-fall decline. In every modern industrial democratic society (and that includes the USA) Christianity is in decline and that decline bears hardest on the liberal and mainstream churches, those that are, sociologically speaking, denominations rather than sects.[19] I will illustrate this point with some Canadian data: in 1957 90 per cent of Canadians claimed a religious identity and 82 per cent of them actually belonged to a church. By 1991, the number ticking a religious identity box in the census had fallen to 87 per cent and less than a

[19] For the sake of brevity I will neglect the cult and merely assert that it has all the problems of the denominational form of religion.

third of those actually belonged to a church. The interesting feature becomes clear if we compare different strands of Protestantism. For the denominational type, the proportion of those claiming an identity who also claimed to belong to an actual congregation changed from 74 per cent in 1957 to 30 per cent in 1990 (the Anglicans) and 84 to 35 (United Church). For those who claimed a conservative Protestant identity, the change was from 86 per cent to 55 per cent. This presents a considerable decline but considerably less than that experienced by the liberals. Or consider church attendance: for all Canadians, weekly church attendance fell between 1957 and 1990 from 53 to 23 per cent. But that total masks an important difference. In 1957 40 per cent of those who said they belonged to the United Church went to church most weeks; in 1990 it was 15 per cent. The drop for the conservatives was only 3 per cent points: from 51 to 48 per cent.[20]

The same patterns could be repeated from every other industrial liberal democracy. Christianity in general is declining drastically and mainstream and liberal Protestant churches are going faster than their conservative counterparts. This, I believe, can be explained. Liberal Christianity has a number of organisationally deleterious features that, I believe, are derived in various ways from its epistemological foundation.

First, in epistemology as in so much else now, there is a very positive evaluation of the human self and a corresponding decline in the notion of God the all-powerful creator. Little bad happens to people, even bad people. The idea that most people are going to hell has completely disappeared. Indeed, hell itself has vanished from all but the smallest and most conservative Protestant sects. The modern Christian self may not yet be divine (as it is in the New Age) but it is a pretty splendid thing.

Modern Christians are reluctant to accept authority; they no longer do what their churches tell them to do. An obvious example is the contraceptive practice of liberal Catholics. Even regular mass-going Catholics have the same family size as non-Catholics of the same class. They are fond of their Pope but they feel free to decide which of the Church's teachings they will follow.

A more subtle example was provided for me by an acquaintance who took an Alpha course with a rural Church of Scotland group which was

[20] The sources for these data and more material making the same point can be found in Steve Bruce, *Choice and Religion: a Critique of Rational Choice Theory*, Oxford: Oxford University Press, 1999, ch. 6.

composed of seven new Christians who were willing to spend ten weeks learning what a fairly conservative group of Anglican arminian evangelicals think are the essentials of the faith. At the final discussion group, one man said that he had really enjoyed it and found it helped him to understand what he believed but he was still sure that everyone would be saved in the end!

A further feature that liberal Christianity shares with the New Age is its primary purpose. It used to be the case that we obeyed God from fear and rather hoped that, as a result of obeying him, we might enjoy a pleasant life. But if he chose to send us trials and tribulations instead, well that was just divine providence. That is, therapy was secondary to the glorification of God. Suffering has now gone from the liberal vision. The purpose of church-going is to make us happy and comfortable and give our consciences a little jolt so that we buy ethically-traded coffee.

So we have considerable evidence that liberal Protestantism has declined faster than the conservative variety and we have a description of liberal religion that traces its substantive features back to the core epistemological proposition that is related to authority. How are these things connected and what are the implications of those connections for the future?

I want to suggest that religion of the denomination type is precarious because it is built on a diffuse belief system. Before I begin, I want to make it clear that nothing I am about to say makes any judgements about 'true' or 'real' religion. This need not be a moral exercise. I am only making observations about the differing potential for social organisation of different sorts of belief system. It no more follows from this that liberalism is bad religion than it follows from similar observations about the difficulties of organising anarcho-syndicalism that anarchism is not 'real' politics.

Liberal religion is weak because epistemological individualism makes it hard to develop consensus; reduces individual commitment; makes it hard to preserve the belief system from mutation; and weakens the will to reproduce the belief system.

Getting people to agree is always difficult. Consensus is not the default position, even for people who inhabit similar social circumstances. It must be engineered. To put it starkly, *consensus requires coercion.* In the church and sect types of religion, coercion is possible because it is legitimated by the claim to have unique access to the will of God. As the denomination and the cult do not claim a monopoly of salvational knowledge, they are severely constrained in what they can do to maintain discipline. Indeed they often relish their freedom from such oppressive notions.

Of course liberals share much in common. However, the consensus is greater the more abstract or procedural the proposition. Thus there is near unanimity on the principle of individual autonomy. There is considerable agreement on a variety of inclusive social principles: racism and sexism are bad, egalitarianism is good, everyone should be treated with dignity, and those principles should be extended to non-humans. However, when we get to specifics we find little agreement, *precisely because the things on which liberals do agree encourage autonomy and diversity*. This is in clear contrast to sectarian Protestants who have very long lists of quite specific beliefs that they hold in common.

Individual autonomy, the freedom to choose, competes with the power of the believing community. To the extent that the former is stressed, the latter is necessarily weakened. Insofar as liberals are bound to each other at all, those bonds are weak because they are entirely voluntary and their voluntary nature is repeatedly asserted.

One obvious illustration of a lack of consensus in liberal religion is the lack of a strong ethical or behavioural code. Where there is no source of authority other than the actor, there are no constraints (or at least there are none that derive from core religious beliefs). While sectarian Protestants suppose that there is a distinctive Christian way of life (and argue about what it must entail), liberals often seem to rejoice in rather perversely asserting that some non-Christian group (for example, the poor or communists) are more Christian than the Christians.

Consensus, group boundaries, and personal commitment are closely inter-twined. Hence the power given to the individual in liberal religion has important social psychological consequences. It is unlikely that such a religion will attract the high levels of commitment found in other forms of religion. Sectarian Protestants often give a tenth or more of their income to religious activities. Liberal Protestants give very little. There are two reasons for the difference. The diffuse belief system does not clearly demarcate what it is one is supposed to be committed to or clearly identify what would count as an act of commitment. If there is as likely to be truth outside your church as within, then there is no pressing reason to attend or support its work. If helping the poor without trying to recruit them to your faith is as Christian as evangelism (and many liberals would argue that it is more so), then Christianity will be displaced by social work and reforming politics. For the active liberal, secular agencies and social movements may well seem a more attractive avenue than religious institutions for channelling energies because their more narrow focus and clearer goals may make them better equipped to achieve results.

This, of course, is the danger of building bridges to the secular world. The liberal Christian may wish to show that secular thought and action is 'really' Christian (as in 'Christ was really a Marxist, feminist, eco-warrior or whatever it is this year') in order to sacralise the secular but in an increasingly secular culture the diffuse religious belief system will lose out to the dogmatic or focused secular alternatives.

One of the consequences of having consumers determine the 'product' (to borrow the language of the economists) is that there will be insufficient momentum to oppose the demands of mundane everyday life. Because they do not sufficiently share distinctive values that challenge the dominant social mores, the denominational and cultic forms of religion are unlikely to have much of an impact. In the late eighteenth and nineteenth centuries, the Methodists, Quakers and Anglican evangelicals banded together to promote a impressive range of social reforms. It is no exaggeration to say they civilised industrial capitalism. I cannot imagine liberals being similarly driven to oppose social evil but then I cannot imagine liberals being driven.

Many of the explanations of the relative careers of liberal and conservative Protestantism have missed the mark because they have concentrated on why the latter might be more satisfying than the former. This would only be relevant if liberal decline and conservative growth were explained by the decisions of members to switch. It is not. By and large people who are still in a church in early adulthood stay there until they die or, if they shift, move to something very similar. Sectarians recruit primarily their own children. The great difference between liberal and conservative religion is not appeal to potential adult members but success in socialising the young.

Liberal religion has a problem transmitting itself to subsequent generations, first, because liberals do not think it very important and, secondly, because they cannot agree what to transmit. Sectarians devote enormous effort to raising their children in the faith because they believe that unbelievers will go to hell. But if nothing bad happens to unbelievers (or in an extreme unitarian-universalist formulation, the category of unbeliever disappears altogether) then the most pressing reason to want others to share one's beliefs has gone.

But there is a second point that may seem glaringly obvious when set down in print but is often overlooked: even if liberals were motivated to imitate sectarian evangelistic efforts, they would not be able to match sectarian performance because sustained effort to convert people requires agreement on who should be converted to what!

An important point for understanding the future of liberal religion is to appreciate the extent to which it is parasitic on a more conservative or orthodox past. Liberal Christianity appeals primarily to conservatives. For those people raised in a rigid and orthodox religious culture, liberalism is liberating. It allows them to retain vestiges of their previous beliefs without being constrained by them. The act of rebellion can itself be an enjoyable experience. But a movement which is defined by relaxing the specific requirements of a religious orthodoxy, by challenging its doctrines and by increasing the autonomy of the individual, has little appeal to those outside that culture. Those of us who never believed that the Bible is the revealed Word of God or that Christ's death was an atoning sacrifice are hardly likely to become liberal Christians because liberals have given up those beliefs. The open prison may be attractive to the high security prisoner but it will not attract the free.

The denominational form of religion has a past that gives it an enduring presence. Its history has nostalgic appeal and the funds gathered during a more religious era allow it to sustain itself despite low present levels of interest. The mainstream churches could not sustain their present levels of operation on current giving but depend greatly either on what was originally public taxation and was then commuted into a capital sum for investment or, in the case of organisations such as the Methodist Churches that were always voluntary, on money left by rich benefactors in previous eras. Both heritage and invested capital are wasting assets but they give the denomination deeper roots than the cult. The innovative type of liberal religion, the spirituality of the New Age, has little momentum because it lacks a history in our cultures. What it gains in spread, it loses in depth. It attracts little commitment and cannot build communities to sustain its belief systems. Plucked out of context, what were powerful traditions become colour supplement trivia: Feng Sui becomes just another interior décor style. The decline of Christianity has removed much of the stigma from cultic religion but the result has not been the rise of powerful new religions to fill the gaps left by the demise of the old. Rather it has been a small number of left-leaning university-educated middle-class people primarily employed in the arts and caring professions constructing their own idiosyncratic and low salience spiritualities from a global cafeteria.

Conclusion

I would like to end by considering the possibility of religious revival. Against people such as me, who see the future of the west as increasingly secular, there are scholars who use the language of post-modernism to speculate that the death of tradition ironically opens the way for people to discover and develop new traditions. This hope of bounce-back owes less to any evidence of vibrant new religious movements (of which there is none) and more to two relatively unexplored assumptions.

The first rests on the philosophical supposition that people are enduringly religious, that there is something about the human condition that will prevent us being satisfied with a secular world, that we will always ask ultimate questions and thus generate religious answers. As we will always be human, so we will always be religious in some sense. I have two answers. First, it may well be that the 'human condition' is less of a fixed biological entity and more of a social construction that has generated religious questions because previous cultures have been religious. It may be that people in secular cultures will not ask 'ultimate questions' in a way that encourages religious answers. But, and this is my second response, even if many people all ask themselves the same question, the individual autonomy that we routinely claim for ourselves will prevent them giving a collective answer.

The second assumption is that specific social and cultural changes can be engineered if there is sufficient will. Whenever I present the case that individual autonomy (by which I mean only the modern democratic insistence that no one has any right to tell others what they must believe) at least one person in the audience lists various deleterious consequences of individualism and asserts that the growing appreciation of those problems will cause people, eventually, to embrace some form of collectivism and that there will soon be a revival of community spirit. We certainly find a great fondness for talk of community. But when I try to imagine how that talk might translate into the majority of us becoming sufficiently alike as to be able to see the world in a way that is sufficiently consensual to form the basis for a shared religion, I again come up against the twin obstacles of cultural diversity and individual autonomy.[21] Even if we could all agree that the world would be a better place

[21] In saying this I am not asserting that modern societies are immune to authoritarian movements. What I am saying is that modern societies are less vulnerable to such movements because they are more internally diverse. Hence,

if we shared a set of common values, legitimated by divine authority, we would not be able to agree on what those values should be nor on the shape of the divinity which gave them power. Or to put it more brutally, those who want a return to ideological consensus always want that consensus to be based on their ideology! It is always the others who must change. But even if there were a self-abnegating spirit abroad, we could still not expect that to produce the shift from diversity to homogeneity required for a revival of shared beliefs because such changes are beyond human engineering. If my basic sociological approach is correct in supposing that major social changes are almost always unintended and ironic, then we have no grounds for supposing that just because people will something, it will occur. Indeed, we may say that the very fact that we can suppose our wishes enough to re-make the world identifies the greatest obstacle to such engineering: the centrality of the desires of the individual.

The fondness of our politicians and social workers for talking about community should not blind us to the fact, well observed by Tönnies, Weber and Durkheim a century ago, that modernisation has destroyed the organic community. A collection of individuals voluntarily associating is not a community. The sovereign consumer of late capitalism is too self-regarding, too knowing, to step back into a condition of sublimation in an organic whole. Even when we are consuming the religious ideas and rituals of what was, in some other society or some other time, a powerful tradition, we cannot forget that it is we who chose the tradition.

there are fewer common characteristics that can serve as a basis for mass mobilisation.

Index